Heather McNeice was born in Northern Ireland and moved to Australia in 2006. She is a practising lawyer based in Noosa and is married with three children. Heather has long been captivated by Bhutan. On her first trip there in 2010, she was inspired to support a girls' education program established by Bhutanese organisation RENEW. She continues her support for this program by returning to Bhutan every year to lead small-group fundraising treks. *Yak on Track* is her first book.

heathermcneice.com

PRAISE FOR *YAK ON TRACK*

'Heather McNeice's vivid prose brings alive the Bhutan I knew when I travelled there almost twenty years ago. Her observations and experiences are enthralling and her story is filled with gripping episodes and tremendous humour. The dazzling country of Bhutan, the Kingdom of the Thunder Dragon, gleams off the page; richly rewarding to read, *Yak on Track* made me yearn to travel back to that fabled land. A delight.'

Joanna Lumley

'Heather McNeice's magical book, *Yak on Track*, is a glorious throwback to the great age of intrepid travel. Beautifully written, sensitive and insightful, it's a work that's sure to become a classic.'

Tahir Shah, journalist, documentary maker, and author of *The Caliph's House*, *In Arabian Nights* and *Paris Syndrome*

'Heather has a rare ability to take the reader with her as she strides fearlessly into wild, forbidding landscapes. A gifted writer, she beautifully and respectfully shares this mythical, magical country.
An inspiring read.'

Dr Bunty Avieson, author of *Baby in a Backpack to Bhutan* and *Dragon's Voice: How modern media found Bhutan*

'Heather's warm, witty and sharply observant book rekindles the joy of gazing on the world from a mountain top or high altitude pass in the Himalaya. It will bring a glow to the heart of anyone who has travelled in those mighty mountains or who hopes to do so. It is a reminder of the pleasure of life that comes after a little deprivation but also of how, with the passage of time after the event, the most important memory is of the people.

Greg Mortimer OAM, member of first Australian
team to climb Mt Everest, and AHF director

'As a writer Heather has that wonderful gift of transporting you from your busy urban life to the wild and remote mountain trails of Bhutan. We won't all have the chance to camp with nomadic yak herders at high altitude or set our days by Bhutan Stretchable Time but by sharing her extraordinary story with us, Heather gives everyone the chance to experience it.'

Carolyn Hamer-Smith, CEO,
Australian Himalayan Foundation

'Heather is a natural storyteller. *Yak on Track* is a great yarn, part memoir, part travel guide, a really enjoyable read.'

Jono Lineen, curator and author of
Into the Heart of the Himalayas

Affirmpress
books that leave an impression

Published by Affirm Press in 2018
28 Thistlethwaite Street, South Melbourne, VIC 3205.
www.affirmpress.com.au
10 9 8 7 6 5 4 3 2 1

Text and copyright © Heather McNeice
All rights reserved. No part of this publication may be reproduced without prior permission of the publisher.

Title: Yak on Track / Heather McNeice, author.
ISBN: 9781925712483

 A catalogue record for this book is available from the National Library of Australia

Cover design by Christa Moffitt, Christabella Designs
Typeset in 12.5/16.5 Minion by J&M Typesetting
Proudly printed in Australia by Griffin Press

The paper this book is printed on is certified against the Forest Stewardship Council® Standards. Griffin Press holds FSC chain of custody certification SGS-COC-005088. FSC promotes environmentally responsible, socially beneficial and economically viable management of the world's forests.

All reasonable effort has been made to attribute copyright and credit. Any new information supplied will be included in subsequent editions.

HEATHER McNEICE
YAK ON TRACK

AN UNFORGETTABLE ADVENTURE IN THE LAST HIMALAYAN KINGDOM

Foreword

by Her Majesty Gyalyum Sangay Choden Wangchuck

The Lunana plateau is Bhutan's largest stretch of wilderness. Every year, a small group of hardy trekkers attempt to cross it. Some make it, but many do not. Those who do are rewarded with a spectacular experience among towering Himalayan peaks and a glimpse of the lifestyle of the semi-nomadic herders who call Lunana home.

Heather's account of her trek through Lunana captures the rugged beauty of our country, its traditions and people. Her many visits to Bhutan over a number of years contribute greatly to her understanding and respect for our unique culture and way of life.

With humour and determination, Heather shares her journey that involves both physical and emotional challenges, in an environment that is far removed from her life back home.

The backstory to the trek is Heather's unwavering support through the Australian Himalayan Foundation for RENEW, a non-governmental organisation that focuses on assisting survivors of domestic violence, as well as providing scholarships to allow students in need, from the remotest corners of the country, to go to school. RENEW relies mostly on its international friends and supporters, like Heather and her trekking companion, Krista, and the Australian Himalayan Foundation.

I first met Heather and Krista in Sydney, in 2014, and in Thimphu, in 2015. I enjoyed hearing stories of their adventures in Bhutan and their fundraising efforts on behalf of RENEW. It has been wonderful to see the ongoing support that both have given us over many years as well as their commitment to enriching the lives of some of Bhutan's most disadvantaged students.

Bhutan is changing rapidly and outside influences are impacting our tiny nation as never before. But some of our unique charms will endure, attracting international tourists to visit our country. Some, like Heather, have manifested their love of Bhutan by making a difference to the lives of its people, for which we are grateful. *Yak on Track* is her inspirational story.

Her Majesty Gyalyum Sangay Choden Wangchuck
Queen Mother of Bhutan
Founder and President of RENEW

To Graeme, Molly, Robbie and Catherine

With love

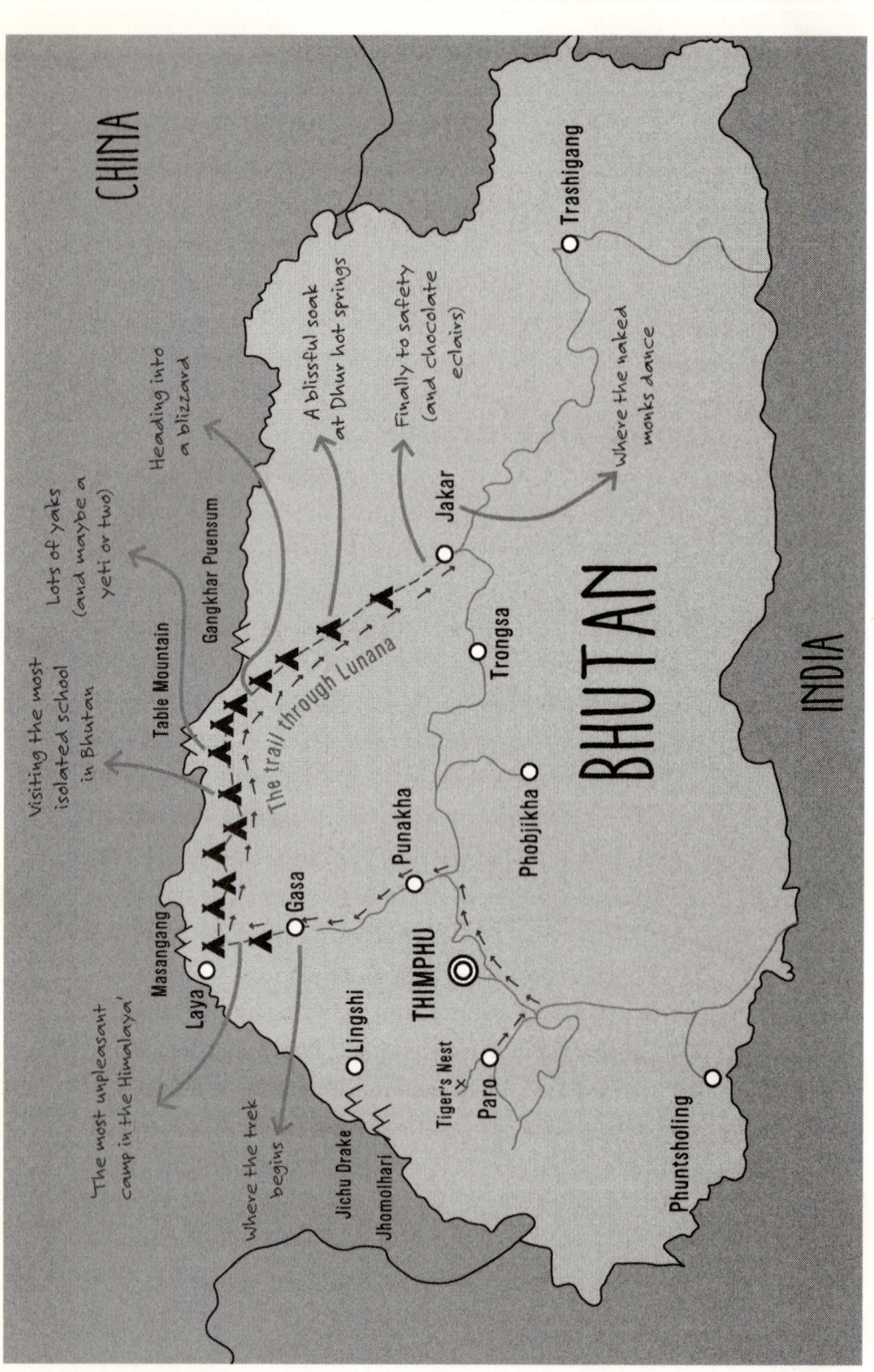

PROLOGUE

'That isn't the pass, is it, Norbu?'

In a cradle below us, an oval-shaped lake appeared jet-black, its waters reflecting the heavy, suffocating sky. On the other side of a wide snowfield another impossibly steep slope disappeared into the low cloud. At an altitude of almost 5000 metres, it was going to be a tough climb in thin, cold air and deepening snow.

'Yes, that is the Saga La.'

My heart sank. 'How are we ever going to get up there? Not to mention the horses.'

'You will be okay,' Norbu replied.

I felt ill.

We snaked around until we reached the slope immediately below the Saga La, the pass barely visible through the gloom. A sudden noise, like the crack of a whip followed by a boom, rang out. Up high, a block of snow lost its grip on the ancient rock. Hastened by gravity, it barrelled down the mountain, gathering momentum and sending up a plume of spindrift in its wake. The avalanche was far enough away that we were not in any immediate danger. Still, it was unnerving. I scanned the slopes anxiously and glanced at the others. Any concerns went unspoken.

More muffled rumbles signalled distant falls. I was emotionally and physically exhausted. Where were we? And where were we supposed to be? And how long before we got to where we were supposed to be?

Another stop behind the horses. I leaned hard into the slope to avoid sliding down the mountain. The snow was up to my knees and the horses were, quite literally, out of their depth. They were spread out in a long line but had come to a halt behind a jutting outcrop of rock that reduced the width of the ledge to a narrow strip. The horsemen were patiently trying to coax the terrified animals around it. Suddenly, one of the horses near the front skidded, his back legs scrabbling furiously to find solid ground. But the snow was too deep and too slippery and the horse had no grip. It slid a few metres down the slope, as several of the crew rushed to stop it tumbling further. They stood downhill from the trembling horse, hands on its rump and sides, heaving it slowly back up towards the ledge.

My stomach churned. I couldn't bear to see any of the horses injured.

More selfishly, I worried about the night ahead: if the horses couldn't get over this pass with all our gear, we had a major problem.

ARRIVAL

Approaching the only international airport in Bhutan, the Drukair plane suddenly dropped into a steep-sided valley, surrounded by towering mountains. Forested slopes, plunging ravines and a chequerboard of terraced fields fell away below us. Narrow trails twisted through dense vegetation, the age-old highways of this mountain kingdom.

The plane banked steeply.

'Look! We're level with the farmhouses!' Krista, my travelling buddy, exclaimed, pointing to a smattering of sturdy whitewashed homes, perched on incredible inclines. 'This landing is done on Visual Flight Rules.'

'What does that mean?' I asked.

'It means the landing can only be done in clear weather and the pilot relies on what he can see, rather than instruments. Except he can't see Paro runway until we come around this last ridge,' she added.

Krista had a pilot's licence and understood more than most why Paro airport had the dubious honour of being one of the most dangerous landings in the world. I was glad when we were safely on the ground.

Across the runway, the terminal building looked more like an ancient fortress than a functioning airport. Soaring mountains rose around us.

We arrived on a bright, sunny October morning. Twenty

minutes after landing, Krista and I were outside the airport, in search of our guide.

Leaving the international airport in Bhutan was a civilised experience. There was none of the chaotic traffic, blaring horns or jostling touts common to many Asian city airports. Instead, the Bhutanese tour guides, clutching signs announcing their guests' names, stood in an orderly line at the doorway. Behind them, a procession of neatly parked SUVs and minibuses awaited. Everything was calm and well ordered. Tshering Norbu didn't need a sign displaying his guests' names. He surged forward to greet us with a friendly hug, dispensing with the usual Bhutanese two-handed handshake.

'Great to see you both again!'

'And you, Norbu. And you're on time!' I joked.

The previous year we had been the only guests left standing, forlornly, at the airport, when Norbu had been late picking us up.

Norbu had been my guide every year, since my first visit to Bhutan in 2010 with my daughter, Molly. Then, he had introduced himself as Tshering. When I returned in 2011, he was still Tshering. But by 2012 he had decided there were too many Tsherings and, from then on, he would be Norbu. Now, in 2013, he was still Norbu, though his name badge said 'Tshering'. No change, he explained, he had simply lost his 'Norbu' badge.

The Bhutanese were very relaxed when it came to names. In much of the country there was no distinction between first and family names, even though most people had two names which could be used interchangeably, and, with a few exceptions, for both men and women. Babies were often taken to monasteries and presented to a senior monk, who would decide on a name from the limited options – apparently there were only about sixty names in use – and so many people ended up with the same name. To clear up any confusion, other identifying factors were brought to bear, such as 'Tshering Norbu from Paro who works as a guide' or 'Tshering

Norbu from Thimphu who owns the petrol station'. It must have made for an interesting telephone directory.

In the carpark, Norbu introduced us to Dorji, our driver for the next couple of days. Norbu and Dorji both looked immaculate in their *ghos*, the traditional Bhutanese attire for men. A little like a dressing-gown, it was made from plain, checked or striped wool or silk and had long, wide sleeves with starched cuffs in crisp white. Hitched up to knee-height by a belt, called a *kera*, it was complemented by knee-length socks and smart black shoes.

As Krista and I settled into the back of the car, we caught up on news of our families.

'How is Bum Molly?' Norbu asked.

'Bum Molly is really well,' I said, remembering how Molly had been less than delighted to see her name with the title 'Bum' on the front page of our itinerary. She had not been won over by the fact it was printed beautifully on local handcrafted paper, made from the bark of the daphne plant. Nor had Norbu's explanation, that the Bhutanese term for 'miss' is pronounced 'boom', helped her see the funny side.

How thrilled I'd felt to be in Bhutan for the first time. But that had been a relaxed seven-day trip, being driven around, staying in comfortable lodges, with the occasional short day walk to stretch our legs. Now, three years later, I was about to embark on a 240-kilometre trek, most of it at an altitude of between 4000 and 5000 metres. I had never spent an extended period at altitudes of over 4000 metres, our highest pass would be above 5300 metres and living at sea level didn't allow much scope for acclimatisation. A knot of anxiety tightened in my stomach. So much could go wrong. Was I totally out of my depth? Krista was super fit, six foot tall, and took one step for every two of mine. I wasn't sure if I would be able to keep up. With just the two of us, I didn't want to be lagging an hour behind her.

I had never been sporty as a child and I didn't really enjoy hiking until I spent six months in South America in my early twenties.

A few days after leaving London, I set off with Graeme, then my boyfriend, now my husband, from Mérida in Venezuela to hike in the Andes. I learned the importance of pre-trek training the hard way, when my legs seized up on the second morning.

To stifle my increasing anxiety, I focused on something less troubling.

'Norbu, how many varieties of rhododendron are there in Bhutan now?'

'I am no longer talking of rhododendrons,' he replied matter-of-factly.

Rhododendrons grew throughout Bhutan, and any self-respecting Bhutanese guide could speak knowledgeably about the many different species. Since I'd met Norbu, he had often referred to these national treasures, announcing grandly, 'Here in the Kingdom of Bhutan, we have X number of species of rhododendron.' Except X was a very fluid number, seeming to increase or decrease according to his whim. He was always a bit vague, too, when pressed on the finer details of Bhutan's rhododendron stock. After I'd teased him mercilessly about his sketchy botanical knowledge the previous year, he had declared that he would never again talk to guests about these native Himalayan flowers.

'Forty-eight?' I suggested. Just a few months earlier, I had emailed Norbu an article from *Kuensel*, Bhutan's daily newspaper, reporting that with the recent discovery of two new species, the official count was forty-eight. He hadn't replied to my email.

'Oh, come on, Norbu, you know we love hearing about your rhododendrons.'

He smiled, but refused to rise to the bait.

Still, it was enough of a distraction. By the time we pulled into Paro, all thoughts of collapsing from altitude exhaustion had been banished by the tally of Bhutan's flourishing species of flora.

THE SCHOOL THAT STARTED IT ALL

Bhutan had been on my bucket list for a while. But it always seemed too hard: three children, my work as a solicitor, moving continents. Life just got in the way. Plus, Bhutan was difficult to get to, relatively expensive, and you couldn't just turn up and do your own thing. All tourists had to be accompanied by a licensed Bhutanese guide and follow a pre-approved itinerary, which required a bit of advance planning. Finally, in 2009, the time had come. I organised a trip for early 2010. And, with no other willing travelling companion, I decided to take Molly, the eldest of my three children. She was eleven, and probably a little too young for hard-core hiking and lengthy talks on Buddhism, but I took her anyway. She has never been back. I have returned every year.

Molly and I travelled east from Paro over the Black Mountains, which form a natural boundary between western and central Bhutan. Our destination was the Phobjikha Valley: a beautiful, wide-bottomed glacial valley, overlooked by Gangtey Monastery. There, on a day hike through the valley, we chanced upon Phobjikha Primary School and I asked Norbu if we could pop in. I'd grown up with education, at home and at school. My dad had been a headmaster, and full-time teacher, at a four-teacher school in rural Northern Ireland. In a small school like his, there were no support staff. My mum was unofficial school secretary, helping in the evenings and weekends by typing up lessons and duplicating work sheets, in the days before photocopiers. I often joined in, winding the handle of the ancient duplicator machine, which clanked with each turn and spat out pages that were often blurred and never quite aligned. Although I chose law as a profession, schools were in my blood and I was keen to see education Bhutan-style.

Classes had just finished for the day. Excited schoolchildren, in traditional dress and bright-red rubber boots, spilled out of the low-set building to start their journey home on foot. There were no school buses in Phobjikha. Norbu told us that for many of these children home was a couple of hours' walk away.

A rustic, wooden stile brought us into the schoolyard, a dusty enclosure with a few patches of short, scrubby grass. The small, single-storey building, the colour of alabaster, stood out against the dark green of the forested hills behind it. It was embellished with auspicious symbols in russet and yellow, and a wooden verandah ran the length of the classrooms.

Primary-aged students were milling around, gossiping, playing chasey, throwing schoolbags. Like students everywhere. Three girls, aged about nine or ten, came charging over to us, whispering conspiratorially to each other, hands clasped over their mouths to suppress their giggles.

'*Kuzuzangpo la*,' I ventured.

'Hello' in Bhutanese had to be one of the most unwieldy greetings in the world and I was struggling with my pronunciation. My attempt made them giggle even more. A reluctant spokesperson was shoved forward.

'Good afternoon, madam. My name is Nima. What is your name?'

'My name is Heather. And this is Molly, my daughter. How old are you?'

'I am eleven years old, madam.'

'The same age as Molly. Could we see your classroom?' I asked.

More giggling.

'This way, madam.' Nima ushered us over to the school building, accompanied by her small entourage. I peered through the doorway into the classroom. The floor was rough wooden planks; paint peeled from the walls. A scratched blackboard at the front. Simple wooden desks and chairs. A set of lopsided shelves, only just clinging to the wall, displayed a small collection of curly-edged books. The contrast with Molly's school in Australia was stark.

Warming to her role as official escort, Nima proudly showed us around the school, as her friends drifted back to their game. A hand-written, framed sign hung above one classroom door: 'Gross National Happiness is for [sic] more important than Gross Domestic Product.' 'GNH', as it is referred to in Bhutan, was first mooted by the Fourth King, His Majesty Jigme Singye Wangchuck, in the 1970s as a measure of the nation's wellbeing. It has become the cornerstone of Bhutanese government policy, promoting sustainable development by balancing economic gain and spiritual beliefs.

On an outside wall, a well-worn blackboard kept students up to date with important news. That day there were two announcements: the Fifth King had attended the Paro *tsechu* (festival); and a four-year-old had been bitten by a rabid dog in Phuntsholing, on the southern border.

The afternoon was wearing on and students were starting to make their way home. It was time for us to go. I didn't realise it then, but a seed had been sown.

At the end of our trip I gave Norbu a goodbye hug and told him I would see him the following year – the parting words of travellers across the globe, who leave with heartfelt promises to return, never to be seen again. No doubt Norbu thought he'd seen the last of me. But my promise was not a flippant one. Inspired by my timid day hikes with Molly and the little school in Phobjikha, I embarked on what soon became an annual trekking trip to Bhutan, in support of a girls' education program.

THE ROAD LESS TRAVELLED

Krista is from Las Vegas but had been living in Noosa, in Queensland, my home since 2006. We were introduced not long after her arrival by a mutual friend, Susie, who invited her to join us on a training hike for that year's Bhutan trip. It was fitting that we should meet on a mountain, even if nearby Mount Coolum only reached the dizzying heights of 208 metres above sea level and hardly deserved to be called a mountain. But as we chatted during the climb, reaching the top together when the others were only half way up, I realised I'd found someone who shared my love of the outdoors and who, like me, didn't like to dawdle. We arranged to meet for another hike a few days later and, since then, we've had many adventures together, often involving trekking, mountains and margaritas.

Along with Susie and her brother, Krista had joined me on a week-long trek in 2012 to the base of Mount Jhomolhari, Bhutan's most sacred peak. We had made the trek a focus for raising funds for girls' education in Bhutan and, at the end of it, had decided we would return the following year. Now it was just the two of us, keen to push ourselves a bit harder. We would begin our journey in Paro town, then visit Tiger's Nest, Bhutan's most famous monastery, before a brief stop in Thimphu, Bhutan's capital, en route to its former capital of Punakha. Finally we would make our way to Gasa, where we would start the trek.

As a successful entrepreneur, Krista excels at seeing the 'big picture' whereas details are my forte. Krista had been happy to leave most of the logistics of the trip to me and I wasn't sure I'd shared with her a question posed by Bart Jordans in his book, *Bhutan: A Trekker's Guide*.

'Have I told you what Bart Jordans says about the trek?' I asked, flicking through the guidebook to find the summary. 'Here it is.'

'So why is the Lunana trek one of the most difficult in the world, with only a 50 per cent success rate? It comes down to a combination of factors: weather and snow conditions; having to cross several high passes; camping at high altitude; long days with very great distances to cover; the remoteness of the area; physical demands of altitude and duration; the need to start with a demanding section.'

I waited for her reaction.

'No, you hadn't told me,' Krista said, smiling. 'But if you had, I would still have come.'

It was a daunting description. Although tourist numbers in Bhutan were increasing every year, the majority followed a sedate cultural itinerary, on a well-worn path through the west of the country. Only a small percentage headed off into the mountains to trek. Of those, an even smaller number, probably no more than one hundred, found themselves in Lunana, looking up at the 7127 metre summit of Teri Kang. In the northern autumn of 2013, Krista and I were among those privileged few.

Until the last century, aside from a couple of European missionaries and some British military personnel, few Westerners had set foot inside Bhutan's borders. Visiting the tiny country in 1783, Captain Samuel Turner of the East India Company remarked that 'The Booteeas cannot possibly have a better security than in such a chain of inaccessible mountains and in the barrenness of their frontier.' More than two hundred years later, the geography remained unchanged: separated from India, to the south, by impenetrable jungle, and from China, to the north, by the soaring glaciated peaks of the world's highest mountain range, the Great Himalayas. The politics had, however, moved on.

Although just sixty years ago there was minimal foreign influence in Bhutan, that changed with the reign of the Third King, His Majesty Jigme Dorji Wangchuck. Often referred to as the 'Father of Modern Bhutan', he succeeded his father as king in 1952, at a time of great political upheaval in the region, and set about bringing his undeveloped nation into the twentieth century. It was no small feat. He abolished serfdom, set up the first National Assembly and introduced a nationwide education system; previously education had been available only to monks and the upper echelons of Bhutanese society. In close collaboration with India, he kickstarted development and road-building programs. By the early 1970s, a new monetary system had been introduced, replacing the age-old practice of bartering. At the same time, the reclusive country took its first tentative steps onto the world stage, joining the United Nations. Despite the Third King's untimely death, at forty-three, his reign marked a series of new beginnings.

The coronation of the Fourth King, in 1974, saw the first trickle of foreign visitors to Bhutan. From just a handful, who came by royal invitation, tourist numbers have increased dramatically. Yet many parts of Bhutan remain largely unexplored.

To its people, Bhutan was Druk Yul: Land of the Thunder Dragon. Like many other aspects of life in Bhutan, the name of the country itself was intrinsically linked with ancient Buddhist mythology. Legend had it that Tsangpa Gyare Yeshe Dorje, a revered twelfth-century Tibetan Buddhist master, set out with his disciples to build a monastery in western Tibet. There they saw nine roaring dragons (*druk*) rise from the ground and took this to be an auspicious sign. They called their branch of Buddhism 'Drukpa'. When the Drukpa sect of Buddhism became the state religion of Bhutan in the seventeenth century, the country adopted the name Druk Yul.

Buddhism has been practised for centuries by the majority of Bhutanese, in this last remaining Himalayan Buddhist kingdom.

Bhutan is the only country where the Tantric form of Mahayana Buddhism exists as the official religion. The Bhutanese celebrate their faith with quiet devotion as they go about their daily business. Most homes have a small altar room, where families begin and end the day in worship. The universal offering of water, presented in seven bowls, is made just before sunrise and again before sunset. The monasteries of Bhutan are home to vibrant communities of monks, who continue to play an active role in society. Temples take pride of place in every village. Religious monuments, paintings and prayer flags are scattered across the landscape, even in the most out-of-the-way places. More than just a religion, Buddhism is woven into the national psyche, permeating all aspects of everyday life. As we pulled out of the airport, the miniature prayer wheel on the dashboard turned hypnotically, each spin releasing the prayers printed on scrolls inside it.

PARO TOWN

Our first stop was Paro, a small, pretty town, just a few minutes' drive from the airport. The traditional buildings of the main street housed old-fashioned shops on the lower level. With wood panelling and carved wooden window frames, they reminded me of the half-timbered Tudor buildings of medieval England. Inside, food, household goods, hardware and clothes were piled up higgledy-piggledy. Discreet blue signs over the doorways announced the name of the proprietor and gave a vague indication of what was on offer: everything from 'garments' to 'meat' and the intriguing 'shop cum bar'. No billboards, no neon, no McDonald's, no Starbucks.

There was no hustle or bustle. Bhutanese guides and their foreign guests sauntered down the street. A couple of Western tourists, dressed head to toe in beige walking gear and matching wide-brimmed hats, looked as though they had stepped off the set of *Out of Africa*. Children chatted and laughed, pushing each other off the high pavement. Graceful ladies swept in and out of shops in floor-length *kiras*. The female equivalent of the *gho*, the *kira*, a rectangular piece of fabric, was woven from wool or silk, often with geometric patterns in bright colours. It was cinched at the waist with a tight belt and pinned at the shoulders with ornate brooches called *koma*. The outfit was finished off with a *wonju*, a brightly coloured silk blouse, and a short jacket called a *toego*.

At a wooden-shuttered window, a shopkeeper rested her chin in her hands, her elbows on the counter, watching the world go by. A monk, his crimson robes swirling around sandalled feet, brought together the old and the new: as he passed his prayer beads methodically through the fingers of one hand, he chatted into his mobile phone in the other. Above him, strings of shiny scarlet chillies hung in curtains from the upper storeys, drying in the sun. Curling strips of chewy yak meat, draped over a cord between two railings, spun in the breeze.

Nearby, an old lady sat hunched on a tattered piece of carpet, next to a straw basket full of little parcels of betel nut. Her red-stained teeth matched her lips. Chewing betel nut, known as *doma*, was a national pastime in Bhutan, as in many parts of Asia. It was one of the country's least attractive traditions. Betel nut, the fruit of the areca palm, was ground up and wrapped in a betel leaf with a dash of lime, then chewed until it disintegrated. It acted as a mild stimulant but was disastrous for dental hygiene, leaving teeth and lips stained scarlet. It was also understood to cause oral cancer. Undeterred by its unpleasant, potent smell, men and women alike chewed it continuously and then spat out the excess saliva, leaving the ground splattered in blood-red stains. This elderly purveyor of Bhutan's favourite stimulant was doing a roaring trade, with several young men stopping to buy her little sachets of betel nut, unfazed by her toothy display of the consequences.

We wandered along the main street, and then to the southern end of Paro town, where five identical *chortens*, easily the height of a three-storey building, stood in memory of the First King of Bhutan. *Chortens*, or stupas, are sacred Buddhist monuments made of whitewashed stone. The Bhutanese style is square-based and painted white, with a red band under the roof. Containing sacred relics or holy artefacts, they are often built to commemorate significant people or events, or to guard against evil spirits. They are found throughout Bhutan and tradition dictates that they only be passed in a clockwise direction.

Behind us, the seventeenth-century Rinpung Dzong, the setting for much of Bertolucci's film *Little Buddha,* rose majestically from the banks of the Paro river. *Dzongs* are colossal fortresses that preside over most of the principal valleys in Bhutan. Many were built in the seventeenth century, without plans or drawings. Their layout and design were overseen by senior Buddhist lamas and they stood as a testament to the vision and skill of those early engineers. They were constructed at strategic locations – at the head of a valley, on a mountaintop, at the confluence of two rivers – as strongholds to repel plundering invaders from Tibet, who thought nothing of a jaunt over the mountains to conquer their southern neighbours. These fortified buildings also provided a safe haven for entire villages in times of threat, the residents hiding themselves away in the depths of the *dzong* until danger passed.

Today, *dzongs* serve a dual purpose, functioning as both civic administrative centres and monasteries. With the monks' accommodation at one end and the local government offices at the other, they are separated by the *utse*, a central tower. *Dzongs* also continue to provide a fitting stage for the spectacular religious festivals that have been held for hundreds of years within their mighty walls. Like its counterparts in Thimphu and Punakha, Paro Dzong was a huge, magnificent building. Krista and I walked on, distracted by a game of archery being played nearby.

An arrow whirred past at head-height. I barely saw it. From the whooping and hollering a few seconds later, I assumed it hit the distant target.

Archery, or *dha*, was Bhutan's national sport and often drew large crowds of spectators. Today, there were only a few: a bunch of elderly men sitting opposite us, a row of bare, knobbly knees protruding from underneath their *ghos*.

The team in play stood on a mound of earth at one end of the ground, their opponents at the other, gathered dangerously close to the target: a small wooden board, just 30 centimetres across, with a bull's eye and concentric coloured rings. Wedged into the ground 145 metres away – more than twice the Olympic distance

– it seemed impossibly far. Yet the strike rate was impressive. A series of successful hits led to an eruption of cheering, followed by a traditional song and celebratory victory dance – well, more shuffle than dance. The archers formed a semicircle, stepping forwards and backwards in casual unison.

There was none of the quiet, gentlemanly respect that accompanied archery elsewhere in the world. Instead, when one team was shooting, the opposition did their best to distract them with persistent, loud heckling. Norbu explained that the opposing team traditionally poked fun and shouted rude, often lewd comments, to disturb the player's concentration. As the day wore on, and more alcohol was consumed, the banter became more raucous and was as entertaining for the audience as the archery itself. If only I could understand the language. Norbu translated from time to time but I suspected we were given a sanitised synopsis so as not to offend our delicate foreign sensibilities.

From the archery ground, Dorji drove us back through Paro town and along the road that followed the river, fringed by an avenue of graceful willow trees. The valley was green and lush, the result of the generous monsoon that the Bhutanese believed finished each year on Blessed Rainy Day, 23 September. Though maybe not every year.

High on a cliff above the valley, we caught a glimpse of Taktsang Monastery, perched on its mountain eyrie. We planned to visit it in the morning, before continuing our drive east to Gasa and the start of the trek. But first, it was time to catch up on some much-needed sleep.

TIGER'S NEST

They clung like limpets to the sheer rock wall. Eight hundred metres above the valley floor, the buildings of Taktsang Monastery looked like tiny doll's houses. Known as Tiger's Nest, or sometimes Tiger's Lair, Taktsang is the iconic image of Bhutan: whitewashed buildings, with red and gold roofs and gilt spires, squeezed onto tiny ledges on the side of a deep gorge, hemmed in by forests of blue pine.

Most religious sites in Bhutan are associated with myths and miracles, and Tiger's Nest is no exception. It was built in honour of Guru Rinpoche, a historical figure often referred to as the Second Buddha or Padmasambhava, who is credited with bringing Buddhism to Bhutan in the eighth century. Beyond that, the lines between fact and fiction blur. He is said to have been born as an eight-year-old from a lotus flower in Lake Dhanakosha, in what is now Pakistan, and had the ability to appear in eight different guises, which are often represented in temples built in his honour. According to Buddhist tradition, he turned his consort, Yeshe Tsogyal, into a tigress and flew on her back from Tibet, landing on a cliff face high above the Paro Valley. There, in his wrathful manifestation as Dorje Drolo, he subdued a local demon before meditating in a cave for three months. Tiger's Nest monastery, named after the flying tigress, was first built in 1692 around Guru Rinpoche's meditation cave, although it was devastated by fire more than once, most recently in 1998, when the main monastery and many sacred relics were destroyed. It was completely restored to its former glory and re-consecrated in 2005.

A hot contender for the title of most breathtaking monastery in the world, it remains one of Bhutan's most sacred sites.

From our lodge, it was a short drive to the carpark below Tiger's Nest and the end of the road. We looked up at the granite cliffs, where the monastery teetered high above us. From below, it seemed impossible that we might ever reach it. Without the help of a flying tigress, the only way to get to Tiger's Nest was by a steep climb on a twisting, rocky path.

We passed a ragtag collection of riding ponies, dozing under the trees. On the trail, we sympathised with those unlucky enough to be hired to carry unfit tourists, at least part-way, to the monastery. Several seemed to sag under the weight of their riders and were being dragged along by their keepers.

We weaved our way slowly uphill, through a thick forest of pine and cypress, the uneven trail doubling back on itself in continuous switchbacks. Although an important fixture on all but the most fleeting of tourist itineraries, Tiger's Nest was, first and foremost, a pilgrimage site. Pious pilgrims from across Bhutan, as well as further afield, slogged up the trail to worship at this sacred Buddhist monastery.

About a third of the way up, a single giant prayer wheel, mounted on a plinth in an ornately decorated wooden gazebo, creaked and groaned as an elderly Bhutanese man heaved it into life. Prayer wheels are an ancient tradition, found across the Buddhist world. A cylinder, usually made of beaten metal mounted on a shaft, is packed with thousands of mantras printed on parchment. They range in size from small hand-held versions, which can be spun with the gentle flick of a wrist, to those standing several metres tall – like this one, which needed a bit of effort to get it going. One clockwise turn of the wheel has the same effect as reciting all the mantras inside.

The large prayer wheel marked the end of the road for the horses. We watched them skip back down the track, relieved to be free of their loads, their morning's work done. Everyone had to walk from here.

Dark clouds hung around the golden rooftops of the monastery. Beneath it, a spectral mist trailed across the forests, sinking into the valley, leaving Tiger's Nest floating, ethereally. Rain was not far away. The path narrowed until it was an uneven staircase hewn from rock. From a distance, it looked as if it had been painted onto the walls of the gorge. We plodded behind an elderly man, who was whirling a hand-held prayer wheel and fingering prayer beads to accumulate extra merit in the endless quest for enlightenment.

A cairn marked a lookout point, at the same height as the main monastery buildings, though still separated from them by a gaping chasm. What an amazing feat of engineering that these buildings did not simply topple off the cliff face into the valley below. As we descended a flight of steps, I looked up to see small chapels, hermitages and monastic buildings wedged into crevices in the rock face, clinging to the precipice like the nests of cliff swallows. Even today, spending months, or even years, in solitary retreat, in tiny isolated huts, remains an important part of a senior monk's training. I paused for a moment to marvel at the lives of these devotees and to admire their dedication to their faith. Growing up in Northern Ireland had skewed my views on religion. There, dedication to faith in the 1970s and 80s resulted in the 'Troubles', a euphemism for decades of sectarian hatred and brutality, a civil war in all but name. Since then, I had shied away from the dogma of all religions, which seemed to be at the heart of some of the world's most vicious conflicts. But such violence was a world away from red-robed monks hiding in solitude in their Himalayan sanctuaries.

The air was damp and cold. Surface water trickled down the rock wall beside us, weaving a silvery path around cushions of dark green moss. Hundreds of prayer flags were strung between the trees and across the plunging gorge, flapping in the wind like bright coloured handkerchiefs pegged on washing lines. The steps resumed their never-ending, near-vertical climb. Perhaps this really was the path to Nirvana.

Finally, we arrived at the entrance to Tiger's Nest. Just inside the main complex, a party of Japanese visitors lined up in front of a sacred rock. With eyes closed and arms outstretched, they tried, in turn, to place a thumb in an indentation in the rock, believed to be the thumb print of Guru Rinpoche.

'Let's give this a try,' I suggested.

'You must say a prayer first and then make a wish,' Norbu instructed.

'Okay, here I go.' Krista closed her eyes and, stepping forward, touched her thumb impressively close to the target. I succeeded only in jabbing mine painfully into a bulge in the rock, nowhere near the holy thumb print. I couldn't help but smile. It was like a Buddhist game of pin the tail on the donkey.

Tiger's Nest was a labyrinth of temples, caves, nooks and crannies on different levels, brought together by stone passageways and steep, narrow staircases. In a small temple, a gleaming gilt door hid the entrance to the cave, known as the Dubkhang, in which Guru Rinpoche was believed to have meditated all those years ago. Pilgrims flocked here when the ornate door was opened for a special ceremony, just once a year.

The deep boom of a gong echoed through the buildings as we added our shoes to the stack of footwear piled up outside a temple. Inside, a row of statues sat along the back wall, their gilt faces looking down on us serenely. Each was swathed in rich brocade fabrics and hung with white *khatas*, the traditional ceremonial scarves of the Himalayas. Suspended from the ceiling, brocade hangings and banners with rainbow zigzags verging on the psychedelic added to the intensity of it all. Having grown up with a very austere approach to religious iconography, I found the startling colours, clashing patterns and striking images quite incredible. Adding to the visual assault, incense filled the air with a heady scent, its thin coils of smoke spiralling up towards the ceiling. A row of offering bowls, each filled with water, stood on a wooden altar, decked with silk flowers and illuminated by guttering butter lamps. Behind us, in a corner, a monk sat cross-legged, murmuring prayers. Norbu joined the other worshippers to perform the customary three prostrations in front of the altar, while Krista and I stood quietly at the back. The spirituality was almost palpable, and I felt as if I were intruding in this holy place.

By the time we started our hike back down from Tiger's Nest, the clouds had closed in and a steady drizzle made for a slippery descent. We skidded down the slope at breakneck speed, slipping on mud and soggy leaf mould all the way to the bottom.

Looking back up, Tiger's Nest was completely hidden from view, swallowed by the low cloud that now enveloped the slopes all around us. It seemed almost unreal.

'SHOOTING STONE, DRIVE CAREFULLY'

The next morning, our third day in Bhutan, Krista and I left Paro via the Lateral Road, en route to Thimphu, the capital. The Lateral Road cut roughly across the middle of the country, connecting east to west. Officially they drove on the left in Bhutan, but I wasn't sure anyone had ever told the Bhutanese. In the absence of a median strip, our driver, Dorji, drove confidently down the middle of the road. Thankfully, he was adept at executing a swerve to the left in the face of oncoming vehicles, most of which also hogged the centre of the road until the last possible minute. Perhaps it was all part of an unspoken game of chicken.

A drive along the main highway provided a snapshot of life in Bhutan's temperate valleys. Dense forests cloaked hillsides that rose almost vertically from the edge of the road. Gushing streams had carved dark channels into rocky cliffs, and winding footpaths snaked up absurdly steep inclines. The farmhouses, which had seemed so insignificant from the plane, were substantial two-storey buildings. They stood proudly on terraced slopes, their shingle roofs spread with fiery red chillies, drying in the autumn sunshine.

We passed impromptu roadside stalls, the vendors crouching under collapsing wooden shelters or on a sheet of plastic laid out on the grassy verge. Piles of fresh vegetables teetered next to bags of shiny red apples. Cubes of rock-hard yak cheese, threaded onto strings, hung from the front of stalls, like 1960s retro necklaces.

The road signs in Bhutan packed more of a punch than their

Australian counterparts, courtesy of the Border Roads Organisation of India, which is responsible for Bhutan's roads and associated signs. We passed an announcement of 'Shooting Stone, Drive Carefully', warning of imminent danger from the unstable, rubble-strewn embankment. Another read 'This is Highway, not Runway' which I hoped was a note of caution for motorists, rather than for errant Drukair pilots who might have overshot the airport runway.

About an hour after leaving Paro, we caught our first glimpse of the sprawl of Thimphu, Bhutan's only metropolitan centre. The city stretched out on either side of the Wang Chu River, surrounded by forests that swept down the valley sides. In the distance, the vast Tashichho Dzong, the seat of Bhutan's civil government, dominated the buildings around it. The expressway into the city was the only road in Bhutan that suggested a serious highway. Yet even on this modern road, Dorji had to swerve to avoid a cow ambling across the dual carriageway, apparently oblivious to the dangers of its grazing habits.

Thimphu lounged in a fertile green valley, 2350 metres above sea level. Most capital cities have a famous monument. Thimphu, in keeping with the country's devotion to Buddhism, has the Buddha Dordenma, a gigantic, gleaming statue of Shakyamuni.

Shakyamuni was the historical Buddha. Buddhists believe he was born in the fifth or sixth century BC as Siddhartha Gautama, a prince, in Lumbini in present-day Nepal. Predicted to be either a great spiritual leader or a great king, Siddhartha was confined to the palace by his father, who wanted to ensure his son became king. He lived a life of luxury and indulgence until, at the age of twenty-nine, curiosity got the better of him and he left the palace to explore what lay beyond it. He was soon confronted with sights he had never seen before: an old man, a sick man, a corpse and a holy man. Realising for the first time that there was no escape from life's suffering, Siddhartha turned his back on the comforts of the palace, becoming an ascetic. For six years, he pursued a life of self-denial, until his body became weak and he realised, through meditation, the wisdom of 'the Middle Way': a more balanced, less extreme way to live. This was the truth he had been searching for and Siddhartha gained enlightenment, becoming the Buddha, the Awakened One. He spent the rest of his life sharing his teachings, known as the 'dharma', meaning 'truth', which formed the basis of Buddhism.

The Buddha Dordenma was a recent addition to Thimphu's skyline. Cast in bronze, gilded in gold, it stood 51.5 metres tall on a hill to the south of the capital, watching over the Thimphu valley. It was one of the largest Buddha statues in the world. A colossal structure by any standards, it was expected to be a major Buddhist pilgrimage site. But the cost of the project was as colossal as the Buddha itself, reputedly more than US$100 million, much of it donated by a Singaporean businessman. I couldn't help thinking that this vast sum might have been better spent on improving the lives of the 750,000 citizens of this tiny nation, many of whom continued to live a subsistence lifestyle with limited access to medical facilities and education.

'I can't believe there are so many new buildings, Norbu,' I said, as we approached the city. 'Even since last year.'

'There are too many people in Thimphu now.' Norbu sighed. 'Everything is getting changed.'

Thimphu was home to a rapidly growing population of over 100,000, up from just 27,000 in 1990. In recent years, the building explosion had been staggering. Along the expressway, building after building was under construction, many four or five storeys tall, cloaked in scaffolding poles that looked as though they had, until recently, been growing in a bamboo plantation. Apartment buildings straggled up hillsides where, just a couple of years before, there had been none. This huge increase in urban housing, all along the valley, was fuelled by young people leaving the countryside to flock to the capital, on the promise of the urban dream. Sadly, that dream was not always realised. Thimphu was now facing high youth unemployment, misuse of drugs and an increasing crime rate:

social issues that, until recently, were almost unknown in Bhutan.

Despite recent development, Thimphu remained a capital city like no other. Although only established in 1961, during the reign of the Third King, it had the air of an ancient settlement, with many of its buildings constructed in traditional Bhutanese style: walls, tapering from a wide base, were painted white and adorned with carved wooden window frames and ornate facades. Even the petrol station was proudly Bhutanese, with pillars decorated with auspicious symbols and the shop encased in lavishly carved and painted wood. Thimpu was probably the only capital city in the world not to have a single set of traffic lights. Instead, traffic flow at the city's busiest intersection was left in the hands, literally, of a white-gloved policeman. He stood ramrod straight in an open-sided, richly decorated sentry box in the middle of the junction, directing traffic with graceful hand signals.

We passed the city's Centenary Farmers Market. Midweek it was deserted, but at the weekend it would be packed with locals stocking up on fresh produce. The previous year, Krista and I had wandered between piles of vegetables of every description, from the familiar velvety purple eggplants to the more unusual curly-topped fiddlehead ferns, pod-like crow's beak, bitter gourd – which looked a little like a prickly green sea cucumber – and banana flowers, large tear-shaped flowers the colour of monks' robes. The ubiquitous chilli was in plentiful supply, from smooth, shiny and fresh to wizened and dried, red, green, large, small, hot and mild. Upstairs, the overpowering stench of dried fish, imported from India, ensured I didn't linger long. So, too, the open-air butchery department. Great slabs of yak meat, some with a hoof and strip of black hair still attached, were suspended from hooks on a rack, blood dripping into a culvert in the floor. Slimy entrails and other unidentifiable animal parts were stacked in oozing heaps, the stuff of vegetarian nightmares. It had been a very different shopping experience from the sanitised supermarkets in Australia.

RENEW

Thimphu was a quirky city, with many fascinating attractions, but Krista and I were on a tight schedule, stopping in the capital only to meet with an organisation that was central to our trip.

The little school that Molly and I had visited in the Phobjikha Valley had made a lasting impression on me. The contrast with my children's school in Australia had been striking and it had prompted me to think about how I might support a school or students in Bhutan – and how to do so in a meaningful way. A friend suggested I contact the Australian Himalayan Foundation (AHF), a not-for-profit body in Australia that supports a range of award-winning education, health and environmental projects throughout the region. Through them, I found details of a recently launched program supporting girls' education in Bhutan. It was the perfect fit.

Before long, I had set a fundraising target of $5000 and committed to returning to Bhutan in 2011 to trek, with three friends, to the village of Laya. I had never been involved in fundraising before, in any shape or form, so I was slightly daunted. Where to start? I set up a GoFundraise page and badgered everyone I could think of to make a donation: an amount per kilometre of the trek. For 100 kilometres, most people generously gave $100, the average cost, at that time, for a girl to attend boarding school for a year. To my amazement, by the time I set off for Bhutan that October, I had raised over $11,000. Each year I have gone back, to visit remote schools and gather firsthand experience of the challenges of education in isolated communities, information that I could share back home.

Norbu dropped us in front of the ornate four-storey building that housed the Thimphu office of RENEW, the Bhutanese partner organisation of the AHF. Inside, Chimi Wangmo, then Executive Director of RENEW, and Pema Lhazom, the administrator of the scholarship program, were there to greet us. By contrast to Krista and me in our functional trekking clothes, both looked elegant in woven *kiras* and brightly coloured silk jackets.

Pema stepped forward with a familiar smile. 'Welcome back,' she said warmly, giving us a hug. 'We are so pleased to see you again.' We had met with Pema the previous year, along with another senior member of staff, Dr Meenakshi Rai, but this was our first meeting with the Executive Director.

Chimi shook both our hands. Until today we had only ever exchanged emails, and I was glad to finally get the chance to meet her in person.

We followed as Chimi led the way upstairs to her office, past a room full of young women weaving. Chimi stopped at the doorway.

'This is part of the vocational training we provide to women who have suffered domestic violence and who may have no means of supporting themselves financially,' she explained. 'We teach them to weave, so they can generate an income, and help them get back on their feet. We sell some of their finished products here at RENEW.'

RENEW, which stands for Respect, Educate, Nurture and Empower Women, was set up in 2004 by Her Majesty Ashi Sangay Choden Wangchuck to address domestic violence. In a country that promotes Gross National Happiness over Gross Domestic Product, domestic violence was swept under the carpet for many years. Victims of domestic violence had no voice, no recourse and nowhere to go. Through RENEW's tireless work to raise awareness of the issue and provide support to victims, they discovered that many disadvantaged girls in remote communities were not going to school. And so a scholarship program was established.

Despite a national road-building program over the last fifty years, many villages in Bhutan remained isolated in inaccessible valleys, where the only way to get anywhere was to walk. For children in these villages, the nearest school was often one or two hours' walk away. Having to walk for a couple of hours to school would be beyond the comprehension of most children in the Western world but in many areas of Bhutan, this was normal; there was no other option. And in some cases, distances were greater still, with some children living many hours, or even days, from their nearest school. These children could only attend school if they boarded. At an average cost, in 2013, of $100 per year (now closer to $200 per year), this sum was beyond the means of many Bhutanese families. And in the age-old preference of boys over girls, a family who could afford the boarding costs for one child would often send a son, rather than a daughter, to school. Many young girls living in isolated regions would grow up to be illiterate, with no real means of earning a living. In some cases, domestic violence was also a factor. Girls, in particular, became trapped in abusive homes, with their education falling by the wayside.

RENEW was working hard to address this issue. A network of community leaders and RENEW volunteers identified girls (and sometimes boys) in need and, where appropriate, and subject to available funding, they were accepted onto the scholarship program. Most of these children came from violent homes or lived in extreme poverty. Krista and I had visited several isolated schools and met with students who were funded by the AHF/RENEW scholarship program. It was very humbling.

As we sat in Chimi's office, surrounded by stacks of papers and files neatly organised on the shelves, I was conscious of the huge amount of work involved in keeping a non-profit organisation like RENEW afloat, especially in a developing country.

Krista must have been thinking the same thing: 'We really appreciate you taking the time to meet with us,' she said. 'You must so busy.'

'Not at all,' Chimi replied. 'We did have a very busy period working on the first domestic violence legislation in Bhutan, but I'm happy to say that the Domestic Violence Prevention Act is now law.'

'Congratulations, that's great progress,' I said.

'Oh yes, though of course there is still much work to be done. Some recent surveys show that many women in Bhutan think it is okay for their husband to beat them, even for trivial issues, such as burning the dinner. So one of the biggest challenges for RENEW is to raise awareness in the community that this violent behaviour is not acceptable. Still, although there is always much to do, we recognise how important it is to meet with our supporters. As you know, the need for the services we offer and the scholarships is always greater than the funds we have. We are so grateful for the money you are raising in Australia.'

Pema nodded in agreement. 'It is very hard to tell students that they can no longer continue their schooling, simply because we cannot afford it,' she added.

I was aware that there was currently no money to pay for students who did not do well enough in their Year 10 exam to continue in the state system to Years 11 and 12. These students, some of whom missed out by just one or two marks, had to move to the private sector if they wanted to complete their schooling. The cost of this was beyond RENEW's budget and so students who had been supported until Year 10 were forced to drop out.

'Yes, it is difficult, but we also have many successes to be proud of,' Chimi said. 'I would like to tell you about Sonam, one of our RENEW-sponsored students. Sonam was living in Chukka, one of the southern districts, with her brother and sister-in-law, but was being abused in their home so we accepted her onto the scholarship program. She became a boarding student at Bitekha School in the

Haa Valley. We have heard from her teachers that she is one of the highest-achieving students in the class and is determined to pursue her education and go on to university.'

'Another of our students at Bitekha School is Tandin. She was living with her grandparents in a small village in south eastern Bhutan, after her parents divorced and abandoned her. She was brought to RENEW after suffering severe violence, so we took her onto the scholarship program and she now has ambitions to continue to tertiary education and become a chef.'

'That's wonderful!' Krista and I agreed. Stories of students like Sonam and Tandin were the reason we tried so hard to raise money for this program. Opportunities were opening up for both these girls, and many others, that would not have been possible without the support of RENEW. Hearing about how well they were doing at school made our fundraising all the more worthwhile.

Chimi and Pema were excited to learn of our latest fundraising initiatives in Australia and of our trek through Lunana to raise awareness of, and funds for, the scholarship program. When I spoke to people at home about the benefits of the scholarship scheme for some of Bhutan's most disadvantaged children, particularly those affected by domestic violence, many were shocked that domestic violence existed at all. Maybe because it didn't fit the image of 'the last Shangri-La' or the fact Bhutan is such a devoutly Buddhist country. But it was a very pressing problem, like in Australia. The difference was that, in Bhutan, there was little support available for victims other than from RENEW.

I was full of admiration for the work being done by RENEW, and as we said our goodbyes to Chimi and Pema I felt more determined than ever to be in the 50 per cent of trekkers who made it through Lunana.

ROAD HOGS

Just when you thought you'd seen it all, something unexpected always happened in Bhutan.

'Look! It's a calf!' Krista exclaimed, as we drove out of Thimphu.

I followed her gaze and was taken aback to see a calf staring wide-eyed out the back window of the car in front of us. It seemed quite relaxed at being stuffed into the back seat of a family sedan. Only in Bhutan.

Leaving Thimphu behind, we began the climb up towards the Dochu La road pass and, from there, onwards to the Punakha Valley. We would spend one night in Punakha before driving to the small village of Gasa, the starting point of the trek.

Dorji's brow furrowed in concentration as he focused on squeezing past a never-ending stream of trucks on the winding road. Their enormous cargoes, piled higher than seemed possible, swayed alarmingly at every bend. As the road clawed around a series of tight switchbacks, with no obvious passing opportunities, we tailgated a brightly painted TATA truck crawling at a snail's pace. Its engine roared with a noise level inversely proportionate to the speed at which it was travelling. These heavily decorated monstrosities plied the roads of this region, engines screeching as they laboured up steep gradients. Meeting one of them, thundering down the middle of the road from the opposite direction, was enough to make the most seasoned Himalayan driver quake in their boots. This one belched out clouds of gritty black smoke, sending us scrabbling to shut the car windows before we were overcome by fumes. Dorji responded with enthusiasm to the 'horn please' instruction on the tail. Still it refused to budge. Then, without warning, it pulled out to overtake the two trucks in front. The fact that he was doing so on a blind corner seemed not to have registered with the driver. The four of us instinctively held our breath until the truck returned, without incident, to the correct lane. We eventually edged past the three-truck convoy, Dorji pushing the car to the very edge of the road. Everyone blasted their horns, whether as a friendly greeting or Bhutanese road rage, I couldn't tell.

Hongtsho, a small village on the road to the Dochu La, was a cluster of traditional-style homes mainly inhabited by Tibetan refugees. Dorji stopped the car next to a roadside police checkpoint. Access to large areas of Bhutan is restricted and tourists need permission to pass through. Bhutan's approach to tourism is very different from those of its Himalayan neighbours. Unlike northern India and Nepal, where droves of hippies and backpackers have been welcomed for fifty years, Bhutan has chosen to shun mass tourism. Opting instead for a high daily tariff and heavy regulation of visitors, the government has sought to minimise the impact of foreign travellers on the culture and environment of the country.

Outside the checkpoint, Norbu delved into the spacious front pouch formed by the folds of his *gho* (no need for pockets in Bhutan), from which he produced a bundle of papers. He flicked through them carefully to locate our road permit. As he did, I was amused, and slightly alarmed, to see a print-out of our trek route: a draft I had put together nine months previously, complete with several alternatives and queries. Krista and I were not joining a commercial group trek, preferring instead to organise our own trip so we could combine some trekking days and visit the two small schools on our route. As a lawyer, I liked to be organised. I had researched our route carefully and had been in touch with Norbu before we'd arrived, but there were still some unresolved issues. I had assumed, naively, that somebody, somewhere, would have given serious thought to my questions about where we would change horses for yaks and what days we could sensibly combine, to come up with a final itinerary. Instead I feared that this tentative draft *was* our final itinerary, which might not bode so well for the logistics of the trek. It was too late now, though, so I decided it was best not to ask. This was a lesson in letting go. Everything in Bhutan had a habit of working out for the best.

Krista and I went for a short walk with Norbu, and came to a modest, square *chorten*. Propped up against one wall was a slate, inscribed in elegant Tibetan script.

'What does it say?' I asked Norbu.

'*Om Mani Padme Hum*.'

The best known of all Buddhist mantras. I saw it many, many times on my travels in Bhutan, carved on *mani* walls, *chortens* and temples, or written on rocks on mountain trails.

'Are you sure?' I said.

'Yes,' he said, giving me a quizzical look.

I was thinking of an incident on a previous trip. 'Don't you remember the writing on the rock on the way to Gasa Hot Springs?'

'Ah, yes, when Gayley told you it was a prayer.'

In 2011, I had been walking with our driver, Gayley, to the hot springs at Gasa, when I asked him about the meaning of some Tibetan script painted on a rock. He had explained it was *Om Mani Padme Hum*. When we'd passed it on the way back, I made a comment to Norbu about the mantra. He paused, looking again at the colourful graffiti and smiled. It turned out it wasn't a prayer after all, but a warning about the importance of using a condom in the fight against AIDS.

Around the *chorten*, mounds of miniature clay *chortens* were tucked into gaps in the uneven brickwork. These tiny *chortens*, the size and shape of a swirly ice cream in a little tub, are called *tsa tsa*. Ordinary clay is transformed into a sacred offering with prayers said as the *tsa tsa* is cast and by placing a small scroll of mantras inside the base. They are often left in holy places, in memory of someone who has passed away or as a prayer for the wellbeing of a friend or relative.

Norbu guided us clockwise around the *chorten* and along the crooked path, weaving through a loitering herd of cows. They greeted us with a mournful moo. Krista mooed back.

'We always moo at cows in our family,' she explained.

Norbu looked over his shoulder. 'Cows say *baa*,' he corrected.

Krista and I argued the point, to no avail. Cows in Bhutan say *baa*; Norbu was adamant. Who knows where that left sheep.

DOCHU LA

Back in the car, the road from Hongtsho wound steeply up to the Dochu La, at 3100 metres. For some, the pass was the day's destination, a popular spot to take in the view. For us, it was a convenient stopping point on our road trip east. At the edge of the carpark, the information plaque promised a panorama of snow-covered summits across the horizon. The reality was disappointingly hazy, just a few indistinct peaks poking up through the cloud and no hint of Gangkhar Puensum, Bhutan's highest peak, which we hoped to see at close range in Lunana. With little in the way of a view to hold our attention, we wandered among the impressive display of 108 *chortens*, built around a larger *chorten* on the hillside. It was some compensation for the lack of sweeping vistas.

The Dochu La *chortens* were commissioned by Her Majesty Ashi Dorji Wangmo Wangchuck in 2004, in honour of her husband, the Fourth King. They commemorated lives lost in a conflict with insurgents in the border region between Bhutan and the Indian state of Assam. Like little whitewashed towers, with a shingle roof topped by a gilt spire, they were decorated with traditional Bhutanese wood carving and a delicate fretwork, painted in gold. About a metre and a half tall, the Dochu La *chortens* were arranged in three semicircles, with a larger stupa in the centre. Behind them the hillside was festooned with hundreds, if not thousands, of prayer flags, strung between trees in a tangle of colour. The traditional colours of blue, white, red, green and yellow represent the elements of sky, air, fire, water and earth, each imprinted with sacred prayers. Buddhists believe that these prayers and mantras are taken across the world for the benefit of all sentient beings: a spiritual message of peace, wisdom and compassion, carried by the breeze. Some of the flags here were bold and bright. Others were faded and ragged, worn to little more than mesh, their prayers long since scattered on the winds.

The road from the Dochu La, like many of Bhutan's roads, was blasted into the mountainside. No more than a narrow ledge, it was bounded on one side by a high curtain of rock and on the other by a vertiginous cliff, dropping hundreds of metres from the edge: crash barriers were not high on the list of Bhutanese road safety features. Even though it was the main trans-Bhutan thoroughfare, in places it was wide enough for only one vehicle to squeeze past debris deposited by recent landslides. Jumbles of loose soil and rocks spilled onto the roadside. As we crept around hairpin bends, vertical drops disappeared, in a haze of dark green pine forests, to the valley bottom far below. I tried not to look down. At times the wheels seemed suspended over a gaping void, resting on nothing but air. These roads were not for the faint-hearted. Just keeping them open – in the face of landslides, hastened by the monsoon rains of summer, and winter frost and snow – is a year-round battle in Bhutan.

On the roadside, a sheet of torn plastic, held up by a couple of branches, served as a makeshift shelter. Under it, a gang of stick-thin labourers sat on their haunches. Men and women, staring blankly. Nearby, three women, dressed in what had once been brightly coloured saris, smashed rocks on rocks. The smaller pebbles they produced would be used for road building. Babies were strapped to their backs in faded shawls; this was manual labour in the extreme. They had no machinery or modern technology, their only tools were a couple of shovels and a small pickaxe. No safety hats, no high-visibility jackets, no steel-capped boots. It was hard, back-breaking, dangerous work, carried out in a pall of grit and grime.

Another bend, another road gang, their dingy homes behind them at the side of the tarmac. These wooden shacks — without water, power or sanitation — a few feet from the path of thundering trucks, would not have looked out of place in the slums of Delhi or the favelas of Rio. I felt a pang of guilt as we swept past in our comfortable vehicle, fuelling the clouds of dust. The workers were from India or Nepal, labouring in one of the hardest, dirtiest jobs that most Bhutanese would consider to be beneath them. For the infant strapped to its mother's back all day, it was a miserable start to a life of hardship.

As we descended towards Punakha, the cool spruce and fir forests of the pass gradually gave way to oak and rhododendron and then to thickets of bamboo, orange and banana trees. On a stretch of empty road, a lone sweeper, an elderly, *kira*-clad woman, swept the gravel into the verge with her home-made brush: a simple collection of twigs, bound with twine. It seemed a thankless task.

PENISES OF BHUTAN

From the Lateral Road, we turned into a side valley, where a few homes and shops congregated around the crossroads. First impressions might have suggested some sort of sex-crazed enclave: gigantic penises, often several metres high, were painted on the walls of most buildings. Some homes displayed carved wooden versions, in a startling red, twirling from a string under the eaves. Souvenir shops had signs declaring 'Phallus Handicraft'. In the distance, the golden roofs of Chimi Lhakhang, the Temple of the Divine Madman, shone in the early afternoon sun.

The origins of this temple – and the phallic paintings on the houses – could be traced back to a crazy fifteenth-century Tibetan Buddhist master, Drukpa Kunley. Known affectionately as the Divine Madman, he remains one of Bhutan's best loved saints. His rather unorthodox teaching methods, which largely involved wine, women and song, are still celebrated today. He was often drunk, and used sex, salacious songs and poems to shock the conservative clergy of the day, challenging conventional preconceptions about Buddhism. His 'thunderbolt of wisdom' (his penis) left a lasting legacy in Bhutan: phalluses of all shapes and sizes appear, in both two and three dimensions, on buildings across the country, and cars are more likely to have a carved penis hanging from the mirror than furry dice. Unconnected with fertility rites, the painted penises of Bhutan were believed to be good luck charms to ward off evil spirits. The Divine Madman was especially celebrated here, at the temple built in his honour.

The temple stood on a hill near the small settlement of Sopsokha, surrounded by manicured rice terraces that cascaded in steps across the hillsides. It was warm here, 1600 metres lower than the pass, the air still. Heat rose from the open, sun-baked fields. Across the terraces, heads bobbed up and down, as farmers bent and straightened, busy with the harvest. No sound of machinery disturbed the peace. The harvest here was done by hand.

We walked behind a bald head that glistened in the brightness. It belonged to a round-bodied monk, picking his way carefully, in flowing robes, across the rice fields. A square *chorten* stood in splendid isolation, a prayer wheel set into each of its four walls. A simple place of worship in the middle of the rice field: incongruous anywhere else, but not in Bhutan. Even when toiling in the fields, the villagers could work on their karma with a nifty spin of a prayer wheel.

Closer to the temple, I watched a gangly teenage monk turning a prayer wheel that was bigger than him. He glanced up as we approached, but kept spinning the wheel, in tune with the rhythm. With each turn, a short stick fastened at the top clanged a bell. An aid to help the devout keep track of their rotations, each ring split the peaceful clonk and whirr of the spinning wheel. I imagined the thousands of gentle prayers from this holy wheel drifting over us as we made our way back to the car and along the river to the main Punakha Valley.

THE SHABDRUNG

It was a short drive from the Temple of the Divine Madman to the main Punakha valley, where the road meanders alongside the Mo Chu. As we rounded a bend, the formidable bulk of Punakha Dzong seemed to rise straight from the waters of the Mo Chu and the Pho Chu, the Mother and Father rivers. Tall, tapering, whitewashed walls soared skyward. Stretching 180 metres along the banks of the merging rivers, almost double the length of a rugby pitch, Punakha Dzong was a vast and stately structure.

Norbu pointed to the hill beyond the *dzong*. 'Can you see that hill? It looks like an elephant's trunk.'

According to legend, Guru Rinpoche foresaw that a man called Namgyal would come to a hill shaped like an elephant. There he would build a *dzong*. Even allowing for a bit of poetic licence, I struggled to see any resemblance to an elephant. Only Norbu was convinced.

This was the second *dzong* built in Bhutan by Shabdrung Ngawang Namgyal, one of the great characters in Bhutanese history. Not only was he the first leader to bring political unity to a fiercely divided nation, but he also left his mark on Bhutanese culture, laying down guidelines for national dress, architecture and religious festivals, which all remained integral parts of Bhutan's national identity.

Ngawang Namgyal was often referred to simply as the Shabdrung, which translates as 'at whose feet one submits'. He was born at Ralung, in Tibet, in 1594 and was an esteemed lama in his native country. Fleeing conflict and inspired by a vision of a raven, representing the protective deity of Bhutan, the Shabdrung made his way south, where he wasted no time in suppressing the warring chieftains of Bhutan's rival valleys. When he arrived in Bhutan in 1616, each valley, isolated from its neighbour by impassable mountain ranges, was ruled independently and there was no overall governing authority. The Shabdrung unified the country and introduced a dual system of government, appointing the Je Khenpo (Chief Abbot) to be in charge of spiritual matters and the Desi as ruler of secular affairs. This separation of church and state was reflected in the design and layout of many of the great *dzongs* built by the Shabdrung, which still functioned as both monasteries and centres of local government four hundred years later.

As well as reforming the government in Bhutan, the Shabdrung was a spirited and formidable leader when it came to protecting his adopted homeland from Tibetan invaders. He saw off several attacks from across Bhutan's northern border, before going into retreat in Punakha in 1651, where he died soon afterwards. Incredibly, the Shabdrung's demise was kept secret from the people for a staggering fifty-four years, in case it should spark a new power struggle. In an elaborate ruse, edicts were issued in his name and his lengthy disappearance from public view was passed off as a meditation retreat. His body was preserved in an inner chamber in Punakha Dzong, where it still lies, watched over by two senior lamas. Only the King and the Je Khenpo are allowed entry to the chamber.

Many of the *dzongs* in Bhutan have played an important role in the country's history, but perhaps none more so than Punakha Dzong, despite having been ravaged by floods, fires and an earthquake. It was the seat of government for 300 years, when Punakha was the capital of Bhutan, and has served as the coronation venue for each of the five kings of Bhutan. The current king was married in Punakha Dzong in 2011 and, as the winter residence of the Chief Abbot of Bhutan and the Central Monastic Body, comprising several hundred monks, it continues to play a significant role in the country's religious calendar. Today, Krista and I would keep going. We had both visited this magnificent *dzong* before.

FINAL PREPARATIONS

When we arrived at our lodge beyond Punakha Dzong, the evening light was just fading to a golden glow. The lodge, built around a former royal farmhouse, stood on the eastern side of the valley, in the shadow of a forested hillside. Norbu directed us across a pedestrian suspension bridge, the only access from the main road. It bounced with our every step, the spuming waters of the Mo Chu sparkling beneath us.

On the other side, a buggy was waiting to take us the final kilometre to the lodge. Verdant rice terraces nudged the edge of the farm track, and a scattering of farmhouses summoned their residents home, the day's work done. We passed a farmer crouched on his haunches by the side of the track. At the next corner another man, perhaps a neighbour, ambled along, a wooden hoe slung nonchalantly over his shoulder. The soft whisper of the breeze through tall grass was the only sound. The air smelled ripe and earthy, sweet and warm. It brought back childhood memories of September evenings in Northern Ireland, baling hay in the warm glow of the dying sun.

The tranquillity of the countryside carried through to the lodge. The original royal farmhouse was a beautifully preserved three-storey building, where timber and whitewashed stone blended in harmony. It stood in a pretty paved courtyard, bordered by a low wall and, beyond that, groves of citrus trees. All around cicadas whirred. From somewhere inside, the soft twang of a *dramyin*, a traditional Bhutanese stringed instrument similar to a guitar, drifted across the courtyard. In the warmth of this subtropical valley, it was hard to imagine we were in the heart of the Eastern Himalayas.

After dinner, Krista and I tackled the daunting task of organising our luggage for the trek that would begin the next morning. We emptied the contents of our bags onto the floor of our room, along with the additional 30 kilograms of pens, pencils and other stationery that we'd brought for the two schools in Lunana. With everything spread over all available space, there was a knock at the door. I hoped it wasn't housekeeping. They'd be lucky to find a path across the floor.

Krista opened the door. Norbu had arrived to discuss arrangements for the following day.

'May I come in?' he asked hesitantly.

'Of course,' Krista said. 'Excuse the mess.'

Norbu stepped gingerly inside. He looked from me to Krista to the apparent chaos of our room. There were piles of clothes to take on the trek, piles of clothes to be sent to Bumthang at the other end of the trek, hiking boots, snow boots, trekking poles, daypacks, boxes of pens and pencils, stationery and other items for the schools, a couple of hundred beanies we'd collected in Australia, sunglasses and reading glasses, medicines, snacks, cameras and solar panels scattered from one end of the room to the other.

'Is everything okay?' Norbu asked. 'Do you need help?'

'It's all under control,' I assured him.

Or at least it would be, soon. Despite the outward appearance of disarray, everything was arranged in such a way that we knew exactly what had to go where, what gifts were going to which school and what was staying behind. I could tell from his bemused expression that Norbu wasn't convinced we were on top of our packing, but he was too polite to say so.

'And you have the books, Norbu?' I asked.

The year before, on the Jhomolhari trek, Krista and I had been struck by the lack of books and other resources at the school in

Lingshi, a remote hamlet of two dozen homes, three days' walk from the nearest road. So this year we had decided to take reading books and stationery items as gifts for the only two schools in Lunana. Thanks to the headmaster of Matthew Flinders Anglican College, our children's primary school, and the generous support of its families, we raised $577 for this initiative. To save time in Thimphu, Norbu had kindly agreed to buy everything before we arrived and had even negotiated a discount.

'Don't worry, the books are already in the car,' he said, turning to leave.

'Before you go, I have something for you, Norbu.' I said, handing him the small gift I'd brought from Australia: a white T-shirt on which I'd had printed the cartoon image of a yak, with 'Pimp my Yak, Trekking Lunana 2013', written underneath. Bhutanese men often wear white T-shirts under their *ghos*, so I hoped Norbu liked it. I wasn't sure he'd get the meaning of 'Pimp my Yak', but that was an explanation for another day.

'Thank you,' he said with a slight bow. He barely looked at the T-shirt.

We agreed to set off at 7.30am for the two-and-a-half-hour drive to the village of Gasa, where we would start the trek.

'Are you sure you don't need help with the packing?' he asked again, casting another glance around the room.

'No, we're fine, we'll see you in the morning.'

'Okay *la*.'

The Bhutanese often tagged the word 'la' onto the end of a word or sentence in Dzongkha. It was a sign of respect for the person being addressed, as in '*kuzuzangpo la*' (hello) or '*kandinchey la*' (thank you), where it made perfect sense. 'Okay *la*' didn't have quite the same ring to it.

Norbu left us to our organised chaos.

Ten minutes later, without warning, the lights went off, plunging our room into blackness. Before we had time to scramble around for a torch, they came back on again, as suddenly as they had been cut. It was the incentive we needed: the possibility of packing in the dark spurred us into action and, before long, we'd managed to allocate everything to a bag. Whether it was the correct bag, time would tell. And so to bed, for our last sleep in a comfortable bed for the next sixteen days.

With a big day ahead of us, I hoped for a restful night. Unfortunately, it wasn't to be. At 2am, I awoke abruptly to the sound of a nocturnal intruder. The noise, magnified in the darkness, made my heart pound until it matched the clattering on the other side of the room. Remembering the torch next to the bed, I fumbled for the switch and anxiously shone the beam around. There on the table, happily munching its way through a cookie, was the interloper: not the crazed burglar of my frantic imaginings but a tiny dormouse, no more than an inch long, rattling the wooden lid of the cookie bowl.

Outside, it was raining heavily. I tossed and turned, eventually falling back to sleep, only to be startled awake again two hours later by the shrill ringing of the phone next to the bed. It was my husband, Graeme, calling to wish us good luck. I appreciated the sentiment, if not the timing. With the opportunity for a decent rest rapidly disappearing, I hoped, at least, that the morning would bring sunshine and a dry start to the trek.

A LONG AND WINDING ROAD

Dawn came all too soon. In the early-morning gloom, surfaces glistened with a heavy dew and a low mist hung in the valley. But the rain that had fallen throughout the night had eased. I felt hopeful that the weather might be kind to us.

After breakfast, we met Norbu in the courtyard, resplendent in a silk *gho*. He greeted us cheerily.

'Good morning, Aum Heather, Aum Krista.'

'Aum' is the Bhutanese word for Madam, used as a term of respect when addressing women in conversation. I hated being called Aum, especially by Norbu. We had become friends after many days trekking together, but it was a friendship overlaid by the expectations and obligations of the guide–guest relationship: sometimes I was Aum.

'Good morning, Norbu,' I responded, equally cheerily. 'We're going to Lunana!'

I was excited, but my angst had returned. I couldn't stop worrying about what might go wrong. What if I just couldn't make it? It occurred to me that Krista and I had never had a serious discussion about the possibility of one of us not completing the trek. In a larger group, one person dropping out would have little impact on the others. But with only two of us, was the other expected to abandon the trek too? Or keep going, alone? Neither option appealed. I wondered if now was a good time to raise it, but decided against it. Hopefully it wouldn't be relevant.

I pushed all thoughts of failure out of my mind and turned my attention to our guide, standing before us in full national costume.

'Norbu, aren't you wearing trekking gear?' I asked, concerned that he wasn't quite kitted out for the task in hand.

'Yes, but not yet,' he replied. 'Except for my Pimp my Yak T-shirt.' He smiled, pulling aside the collar of his *gho* to reveal the cartoon yak. 'I like it,' he said. 'What is "pimp"?'

I glanced at Krista and we both laughed. 'I'll tell you later,' I said. 'We should get going.'

'Aren't we having a *sungkey* ceremony?' Krista asked.

Norbu looked sheepish. 'I haven't organised one. The monks are not living nearby.'

'No *sungkey* ceremony!' Krista exclaimed, with mock outrage. 'You'd better hope we'll be okay without a blessing.'

In the past, Norbu had explained the importance of receiving this blessing before beginning a trek. A *sungkey* was a coloured string, or cord, that held religious significance in Buddhism. The cord was knotted and blessed by a monk, then tied around the neck or wrist. Buddhists believed that it provided protection and brought good luck; they wouldn't dream of starting an important journey without one.

Before setting off on the Jhomolhari trek the year before, the four of us had stood, heads bowed, in front of a monk while he chanted prayers, rang a bell, sprinkled holy water and scattered grains of rice, before presenting each of us with a *sungkey*. I happened to look up during the incantations only to see the esteemed lama vigorously twirling his index finger, which was wedged a long way up his nose. The monk's nasal mining didn't interrupt his prayers, but it did take away from the sanctity of the moment and I only just managed to suppress a giggle. In spite of this unpromising blessing, the *sungkeys* had done the trick and we enjoyed a successful trek in perfect weather. Norbu had put this down to our auspicious ceremony, unaware of the nose-picking interlude. The implications of setting-off without a blessing this time remained to be seen.

Norbu was not a mountain man. He was one of nine children from a farming family whose home village was in the lowlands of Eastern Bhutan. He graduated from the Institute of Language and Cultural Studies, going on to become a tour guide and, from there, to running his own travel agency. Most of his guests stuck to cultural tours rather than trekking, and this trek was almost entirely through a true wilderness area. I wondered how he felt about setting off into Lunana for the first time. If he was in any way nervous or concerned, he hid it well. I hoped I did too.

Dorji was waiting for us in a 4x4, already packed with holdalls and the boxes of books. Our bags were loaded into the back and we set off for the mountains.

The Punakha Valley is blessed with a subtropical climate and fertile soil. The road, which ran parallel to the river, was bordered by picture-postcard images of terraced rice fields, neat vegetable plots and citrus orchards. In early October, the fields teemed with villagers, eager to finish the harvest. They looked like tiny dolls in the distance, swinging sickles and stooping to bundle up their precious crop. They were almost indistinguishable from the life-size scarecrows planted in the fields to keep the cheeky birds at bay. Bundles of rice, pale yellow against the tan coloured earth, were stacked in neat rows. From afar they formed zigzagging geometric patterns, like a huge outdoor modern-art installation. As we wended our way upwards towards Gasa, a mosaic of green, bronze and gold fell away beneath us.

A sign announced the entrance to the Jigme Dorji National Park: 'Leave nothing but footprints, take nothing but memories.' I loved the simplicity of this popular maxim; it was especially fitting here, as we prepared to trek through Bhutan's most isolated region. For the first week of the trek our route would take us through this national park, the largest tract of protected forest in Bhutan. It was home to a vast array of plants and animals, including several elusive species such as the Himalayan black bear, red panda and blue sheep, as well as the endangered snow leopard and the Bengal tiger. I wondered if we would see any of them.

Once inside the national park, the road tapered until it was no more than a thin ribbon etched into the hillside. Soon we were bouncing over an unsealed, corrugated surface as we climbed more than 1000 metres from our lodge on the valley floor.

Clinging closely to the contours of the slope, the road corkscrewed upwards around tight, stomach-churning bends. By the time we were near the top, I felt as if I'd been flung around on a fairground ride. Krista didn't travel well on winding roads and was looking a bit green. We both needed a break and Krista needed a motion-sickness pill. Fortunately, I had one, but in my trekking bag.

'Can we stop for a moment, please, Norbu?' I asked. 'I have to get something out of my bag.'

We pulled in to the side of the road. As luck would have it, my trekking bag was buried at the back of the boot, under the rest of the luggage, and I felt embarrassed asking Norbu and Dorji to unload everything.

'Sorry,' I said, desperately trying to remember where I might have packed the tablets so I could find them easily.

'You do not need to be sorry. No problem,' Norbu assured me. Nothing was ever too much trouble for Norbu, although I felt sure he was secretly cursing me.

'This might take a few minutes,' I warned them, but I found the strip of tablets in seconds. Norbu looked vaguely impressed. No doubt he couldn't quite believe I knew where anything was in my luggage, after witnessing the chaos in our room the previous evening. Appearances could be deceptive.

Next to the road, a farmer and his wife tilled a field with a simple wooden plough, yoked to two cows. Farming here was mostly the product of hard physical labour, the speed and efficiency of modern machinery a distant dream. We watched for a moment before setting off again. Behind us, the Mo Chu coiled away in a series of classic S-shaped bends, curving through cultivated terraces in the Punakha Valley. Ahead, densely forested mountain slopes rose almost straight up, to the snowy peaks beyond Gasa. I couldn't wait to be in the mountains.

A BLESSING AT LAST

We jolted along the pot-holed dirt road from the village of Damji. On the other side of a spur, a grand semicircular fortress with three watchtowers seemed to hover in the clouds, like a mirage. This was Gasa Dzong, official name Tashi Thongmon Dzong, originally built in the seventeenth century by the Shabdrung.

Now at an elevation of 2770 metres, we emerged from the car into a fine drizzle that hung in the air like gossamer. Further down the valley, past the *dzong*, the snow-covered summit of Kang Bum danced in and out of view, as the mist parted for a moment only to close in again.

A policeman stationed outside the *dzong* was deep in conversation with an elderly lady. She waved us over, clasping our hands in turn, her rheumy eyes smiling kindly.

'Where are you going?' the policeman asked, in clear English.

'Lunana,' Krista replied.

'Ah, Lunana,' the old lady whispered, nodding her head and casting knowing glances at the policeman.

Neither of them had been to Lunana, the policeman said. They either were impressed by our trek or thought we were mad. It was hard to tell, but I worried it might be the latter.

'Why are you going to Lunana?' the policeman asked.

'We like to walk in the mountains,' I offered. This served only to compound their incomprehension: an inadequate explanation in a country where long walks through mountainous terrain were journeys of necessity, not pleasure. Even in the twenty-first century, many Bhutanese villages had no road access. For the people who lived there, walking was a way of life. Herding animals, attending to business in the nearest town, visiting a temple, going to school; all involved an unavoidable journey on foot, ranging from a couple of hours to several days. And the concept of measuring distance in hours or days of walking, rather than in kilometres, was an indication of how different the Bhutanese perspective on travel was from my own. The idea of setting off on a sixteen-day hike through Bhutan's most isolated and inhospitable plateau, for pleasure, was clearly anathema to the friendly policeman and his elderly companion. The policeman translated for the benefit of the old lady, who continued to smile knowingly, convinced that we had lost all reason.

'*Tashi Delek!*' They wished us good luck as we said goodbye. I hoped we wouldn't need it.

Moody dark clouds romped across an ashen sky but, for now, the rain had stopped and a bright sun played on the distant summits. Norbu appeared, unfolding his *kabney*, a fringed silk scarf worn diagonally across one shoulder and tied at the opposite hip. It was an essential part of the formal dress for men when entering a *dzong*; the colour indicating the wearer's social status. The King and the Chief Abbot were the highest rank and the only two citizens permitted to wear a saffron scarf. At the other end of the pecking order, ordinary citizens wore a white *kabney*. In between, various colours identified community leaders, judges, members of the government and the royal family. With Norbu formally attired, we made our way inside Gasa Dzong. Now I realised why he hadn't worn his trekking gear that morning.

The external walls of the *dzong* were at least a metre thick, their depth exposed by a glassless slot window that looked out across a sweep of mountains. Scrambling onto a ledge to peer through it, I imagined how, in days gone by, lookouts would have kept watch for Tibetan invaders, charging up the valley to launch an attack.

The grand, heavy door creaked open. We stepped into a hotchpotch of buildings and courtyards spread over three different levels and connected by uneven stone steps. Gasa was my favourite *dzong*. Smaller and more intimate than the great *dzongs* of Paro, Thimphu and Punakha, it had a haphazard, homely atmosphere. The first courtyard was paved with irregular-shaped slabs, clumps of green lichen creeping from between the gaps. Low walls were decked with jaunty sunflowers and rambling roses, their sweet scent filling the air, reminiscent of an English country garden in the height of summer. A row of potted pink and red geraniums and nodding yellow chrysanthemums formed a guard of honour on either side of a stairway. There was no sound. The *dzong* breathed a soothing stillness, the silence interrupted only by our footsteps on the flagstones, echoing around the high walls.

I was always overawed by a visit to a *dzong* in Bhutan, with shaven-headed monks living as they had done for generations, conjuring up an image of life in another era. As we climbed the steps to the second courtyard, a flock of young novices burst through a doorway, their gowns billowing like red sails in the wind as they fanned out across the quadrangle. A head poked through a curtain: a boy monk, no more than seven or eight years old. He had a round face and dark, almond-shaped eyes that stared at us curiously before he gathered up his robes and sprinted off to catch his peers.

We crossed the courtyard, abandoning our shoes outside the entrance to a temple. The thick soles of my woollen hiking socks were no match for the cold stone floor. With the interior illuminated only by a wedge of daylight from the doorway behind us, my eyes took a few seconds to adjust to the gloom. Gradually, elaborate wall paintings of images from Buddhist mythology came into focus. A small wooden table stood against the back wall. It was piled high with mounds of what looked like pastel-coloured modelling clay, that wouldn't have seemed out of place in the craft corner of a kindergarten. This was the coloured dough, made from flour and butter, that was used to fashion intricate sculptures called *tormas*. Placed as an offering on temple altars, they were often made in the shape of a flower, with hundreds of delicate petals arranged in concentric circles, off-white in the outer rings and more intense colours towards the centre. Even more elaborate *tormas* were skilfully sculpted into representations of Buddhist deities. The dough on this small table was still a long way from being altar-ready.

Krista and I stood quietly to the side while Norbu prayed, dropping to his knees on the floor in prostration. He did this three times, towards the altar, touching his clasped hands to the crown of his head, his throat and his heart, in one flowing movement. Each of these gestures symbolised respect for the enlightened mind, the enlightened speech and the enlightened body and was followed by kneeling to touch hands and forehead to the floor.

'I am saying a prayer for the safe trek,' Norbu whispered as he finished his worship. Maybe that would do, instead of a *sungkey* ceremony.

With head bowed, he approached the altar and folded an offering of a few ngultrums behind a small statue of Buddha. Krista and I did the same. This was the cue for the attendant monk to give us a blessing. From a burnished brass jug decorated with a peacock feather, he poured some saffron-infused water into Norbu's cupped hands, before repeating the ritual for Krista and me. We each drank a few drops, then spread the rest over the back of our heads. I hoped this blessing would stand us in good stead over the coming days.

A row of red cushions was arranged neatly on the floor. This was where the monks would sit, to pray and perform their ceremonies. The tools of their trade, a conch shell, brass bell and a *vajra*, were at hand. All held religious significance: the shell, representing the dharma, the Buddhist path; the bell, held in the left hand, symbolising wisdom and believed to drive away evil spirits; and the *vajra*, held in the right hand and shaped like a double-ended crown, representing spiritual power and capable of destroying ignorance.

Butter lamps burned among an assortment of offerings: cakes and biscuits, money, plastic flowers and small figurines of the Buddha and other deities. It was easy to see how these open flames could so easily start an inferno, sadly the fate of many of Bhutan's historic temples.

Norbu led us out of the temple and over to some rickety wooden steps, more ladder than staircase. A low rhythmic drum beat intensified as we climbed up. Accompanied by modulating, meditative chanting, it seemed to reverberate all around us. At the top of the steps, I could feel the deafening thud of the drums bouncing off the walls and vibrating through the floorboards. A doorway, slightly ajar, opened onto a dimly lit room. Rows of monks sat cross-legged on the floor, enveloped in robes the colour of claret. They were mostly teenagers or younger, reciting scriptures in low sonorous tones. Though they seemed to barely move their lips, the volume and tempo rose and fell in hypnotic waves. Yellowing texts in Tibetan script, fixed to rectangular wooden boards, lay on the floor in front of them. Many of the monks rocked back and forth, in time with the intonations. For the most part, their faces were hidden in the shadows until, one by one, they sneaked furtive glances at us. We were a distraction. It was time to leave.

Before we could make our way down, two young novices came bounding up the precarious ladder, as sure-footed as mountain goats.

'*Kuzuzangpo la*,' they said in unison.

'*Kuzuzangpo la*,' we responded.

'Can you ask how old they are, Norbu?' I asked.

One was twelve, the same age as my son, the other fourteen.

'How long have they been living in the monastery?'

The twelve-year-old had been there since he was seven, Norbu said. Buddhists considered it an honour to have a monk in their family and many boys were sent to join a monastery at a young age. But seven seemed so very young. I tried to imagine sending my son away, at such a tender age, to live in a cold, draughty monastery, following a strict timetable of meditation, study and chores. I wondered whether these boys came to live in the monastery through choice or necessity.

'Can you ask if they like living here, in the monastery?'

Apparently, they did. Whether this was their stock response to all inquisitive tourists or they were genuinely happy here was impossible to tell. They smiled broadly before disappearing in a blur of burgundy robes to join the chanting.

I could have spent the rest of the afternoon wandering through the *dzong*. But it was lunchtime and we had a trek to be getting on with. By the time we'd finished our picnic next to a quiet pond, Norbu had replaced his *gho* with more practical trekking gear and, of course, his new T-shirt. I wondered if it fitted him.

'Yes, yes,' he said, 'but it's a little bit tight on my bellies. But now I am going to Lunana. My bellies will be getting smaller.'

And on that note, we set off.

LUNANA: AND SO IT BEGINS

On the green across from Gasa Dzong a great mound of straw baskets and bulging hessian sacks, packed with what looked like trekking kit, lay on the ground. Half-a-dozen men loitered nearby, keeping a watchful eye on a swarm of hardy-looking mountain ponies. Norbu strode over to speak to them. Were they our crew and horses? Surely not all of them …

Trekking in Bhutan was organised differently from trekking in Nepal, its more popular Himalayan neighbour. There were no cosy teahouses in which to spend the night, no cafes along the trail for lunch and no Sherpas to carry gear. Instead, trekkers in Bhutan slept in tents, and camping gear, food and all other essential supplies for the trek were carried by packhorses or yaks. On most treks, including through Lunana, there was nowhere to resupply along the way.

The previous year, Norbu had introduced us to the crew before we set off but this time he pointed Krista and me in the direction of a muddy track and sent us on our way. It was a low-key start to the daunting sixteen days ahead.

From Gasa, we were heading north towards Laya, Bhutan's second highest village. In two days' time, our path would cut across the Snowman Trek route, which curved in a wide arc along Bhutan's northern border with China. Just south of Laya, we would turn eastwards, to trek through Lunana all the way to Bumthang, a region in central Bhutan.

Since my first trip to Bhutan with Molly, I had been intrigued by the Snowman Trek, a twenty-five-day odyssey starting outside Paro in the west of the country and finishing at the Nikka Chu (river) near Trongsa, or sometimes further east in the central region of Bumthang. This 350-kilometre hike along Bhutan's inhospitable northern border brought together a heady combination of distance, altitude, remoteness and extreme weather. Although it was often dubbed the toughest trek in the world, trekking in Bhutan, with packhorses to carry gear and guides who set up tents, cooked and even delivered tea to the tent door in the morning, added a touch of glamping to what was otherwise a demanding trek. The challenge lay in the unknown: the weather and the real risk of altitude sickness. With commitments at home, it was difficult for Krista and me to be away for over a month, the time needed to undertake the full Snowman Trek. But by starting at Gasa and walking north towards Laya, we could skip the first section – most of which we had already completed – trek through the most challenging section, Lunana, and take the longer exit route to finish near Jakar in Bumthang.

One of the most unpredictable aspects of the Snowman Trek was the weather. There were only two small windows, in spring and autumn, when it was possible to safely trek this route. Outside these times, it was generally too wet or too cold. Bhutan is battered by the summer monsoon, which brings over five metres of rainfall between June and September each year, more than any other country in the Himalayas. Trekking during this period, we could expect to spend our days in torrential downpours, knee-deep in mud, following trails overrun with blood-sucking leeches. From November, winter storms brought heavy snowfall and the risk of being stranded between high passes, with the whole region completely cut off for months at a time. Although trekking through Lunana was possible in spring, planning could be difficult, with uncertainty around when the passes would reopen after the winter snowfall. We had chosen to set off at the beginning of October, hoping for clear blue skies, warm sunshine and wide-open vistas of the Eastern Himalayas.

I had floated the idea of the Lunana trek with Norbu the year before. He had assured me that Krista and I could do it, no problem. In my enthusiasm, I had believed him – even though he had never done it himself and had very little idea of what it involved. Now that we were about to start, I was a little more focused on the reality.

We'd gathered from Norbu that the rain had continued later than usual this year, making the bumpy track of red clay slippery underfoot. Someone had forgotten to tell the rain gods that 23 September was Blessed Rainy Day and the official end of the monsoon. We were walking on a new farm road being painstakingly built through the mountains north towards Laya. Two years earlier, I had set off from Gasa on a picturesque trail behind the farmhouses, climbing up through an enchanting forest. The contrast with the start of the trek this time couldn't have been more stark: a muddy, furrowed track, trees felled and lying like broken matchsticks on the hillside, vegetation crushed and destroyed. It was one of the conundrums of Bhutan today: development versus preservation of a pristine natural environment.

The first road in Bhutan was built just over fifty years ago, in 1961. Before then, the only way to get anywhere was to walk, in rain or shine, through rugged mountainous terrain in the north, and uncharted, mosquito-infested jungle in the south. Villages such as Laya were almost completely cut off from the rest of the country and, consequently, had retained their unique culture, traditional dress and language. But life for isolated villagers was tough. Transportation was laborious and expensive. Everything from food to construction materials had to be carried in on the back of a horse or yak. Many children had limited access to education, and healthcare was basic. So, for the Layaps, sacrificing years of isolation in exchange for the benefits of a new road to Gasa was an easy choice. The road meant progress, a faster, simpler journey from their village to the services and facilities available in Gasa, Punakha and beyond, and an easing of the relentless struggle for survival. But it also meant destruction: of the ancient forests, through which the road was being built, and, more significantly, of a culture, unchanged for centuries. It wouldn't be long before the traditional Layap way of life was gone forever.

I was deflated by the creeping development, but I recognised too that I was influenced by romantic notions of simplicity and tradition: notions that conveniently glossed over the reality of life on the fringes of the modern world. Why should the people of these mountain communities be forced to walk several days to school or to seek medical help? Just so Western visitors could parachute in for a brief escape from the trials and tribulations of their comfortable, but hectic, lives? Development was inevitable. And, in the face of modernisation, Bhutan was trying hard to strike a balance between protecting its rich resources and meeting the needs of its people. In contrast to its neighbours, where large tracts of land were completely denuded of trees, resulting in soil erosion and all its associated problems, the Bhutanese government is committed to maintaining at least 60 per cent tree cover throughout the country. Currently the figure is over 70 per cent and Bhutan was recently declared the world's first carbon-neutral country. Fifty-one per cent of Bhutan has protected status as a national park, wildlife sanctuary or ecology corridor: a vast proportion, by any standards, and Bhutan has been internationally recognised as a biodiversity hotspot. It remains home to several of the world's endangered species, which have found a haven in its protected forests. That this level of protection for the natural environment has been maintained, at the expense of opportunities for economic development, is testament to the country's commitment to Gross National Happiness, which has environmental conservation as one of its four key pillars. The others are sustainable socio-economic development, preservation and promotion of culture, and good governance. Although scoffed at in some quarters, GNH has started to attract widespread international attention as the so-called developed world begins to question whether the constant striving to increase GDP may be the cause of, rather than the solution to, many first-world problems.

A fork in the farm road brought us to a stop. Left, or right?

The year before, at a similar fork in the trail, Krista and I had nearly headed off to Tibet, never to be seen again. This time, we decided to wait for Norbu. In the meantime, we provided a distraction for a gang of Indian road workers, who, like road workers everywhere, were having a tea break. When Norbu finally appeared, directing us on to the upper branch of the dirt road, he explained that he had been negotiating with the horsemen: there was an issue with the number of horses.

'Are there too many?' I asked.

'No, there are not enough. Their loads are too heavy. The horsemen will bring more horses from Laya when we get to the army camp.'

The throng on the green had been for us after all. And even they couldn't cope. Although we had arranged two extra horses to carry the books, Krista and I only had three bags between us and I wondered why we needed so many horses. I wasn't sure whether to be alarmed or impressed.

We skated and slid through the sticky clay of the fledgling road. A glistening waterfall across the valley sparkled in a single shaft of sunlight. It was flanked on both sides by ridge after dark forested ridge, sweeping down the valley like the ribs of a dinosaur skeleton.

Ahead, the rumble of heavy machinery grew louder, crashing and banging through the forest. A flash of yellow, just visible through the undergrowth, turned out to be an excavator, roaring back and forth, wrenching trees from the ground and ripping up vegetation. It sat precariously on a mound of red earth, scraping the hillside down to the bare rock. We stopped to wait: there wasn't enough room for all of us. When the driver saw us, he swung the arm of the digger off to one side and cut the engine. This was the signal for Norbu to usher us through. We clambered, one by one, up and over the mini-mountain of soil, squeezing between the cabin and the wall of rock where the road had been gouged out of the mountainside. On the other side of the excavator, a sheer cliff face fell away. There were no health and safety zealots on patrol, no warning signs, no one directing the driver to stop or pedestrians to wait. It was every man for himself. Once we were safely past, the engine burst into life again and the driver got back to tearing up the forest.

I contemplated all the benefits this new road would bring to the Layaps. Still, I was relieved when, after a couple of hours, the dirt road petered out and we were finally on a walking trail, the same trail that I had followed two years earlier. I felt myself relax, cocooned by the overhanging branches of the fir trees that had grown here, undisturbed, for generations. We were climbing steadily now but my delight at leaving the road behind more than made up for my apprehension over the steepness of the slope.

Before we saw them we could hear their bells tinkling, somewhere further along the trail. A string of horses came careering down the path towards us, driven along by three grinning horsemen. They shouted and whistled, ensuring that the small, stocky ponies, loaded with tightly packed sacks of grain, didn't slacken their pace. The lead horse was crowned with tassels of yak wool, dyed a vibrant red, like the plumes worn by Moulin Rouge show girls, and around their necks all wore a plaited yak-wool collar hung with small bells.

In 2011, I had asked one of the villagers in Laya to make me a bell collar just like these ones. We negotiated a price and a few hours later, the horse bells were delivered to our camp. Not long after, a procession of villagers arrived at the camp offering to sell saddles, halters, headdresses and all sorts of horse tack. Word had spread that the recently arrived trekkers were keen buyers of all things equine. They couldn't have known that the bell collar I'd commissioned was not destined to jangle around a horse's neck but to be displayed as a wall-hanging in my home. I sent them away disappointed.

'Stop on the uphill side,' Norbu yelled from behind us. This was the cardinal rule of trekking through these narrow mountain tracks: give way to pack animals and always stand on the uphill side of the trail. A spooked horse or yak might push you into the trees but you wouldn't be sent toppling over the downhill edge, to whatever lay beneath. So we pressed ourselves against the rocks on the uphill slope, to allow these sure-footed little ponies to pass. They slowed to give us an inquisitive look before trotting past, bells jangling. A few metres behind came the horsemen. Dressed in *ghos*, knee socks, trainers and baseball caps worn sideways, they merged the best of traditional Bhutanese and Western street fashions. We exchanged *Kuzuzangpo la*s as they passed.

We continued along a well-worn rocky trail that wound through densely packed rhododendrons and bamboo. It was a steady climb, up and up, to the Bari La pass, our high point for the day, at 3900 metres. By now, the sky was slate grey and heavy. Low cloud hid the mountain tops and rain was on the way. There wasn't much of a view at the pass, but we stopped anyway, sitting down under a jumble of prayer flags, strung across an outcrop next to the trail. I was glad of the short break. We were 2700 metres higher than where we had slept the previous night and 1100 metres higher than where we had started our walk from Gasa at lunchtime. We were defying all the guidance about altitude gain in a single day, our timetable dictated by the distance we wanted to cover in a limited number of days.

As we rested at the pass, two Indian soldiers came jogging down the trail. They stopped, greeted us in English and politely asked if they might join us. We swapped stories. They'd been stationed for several months at the army camp at Takchenkhar, where we would camp the following night. Like the policeman in Gasa, they seemed amused by the prospect of us going to Lunana. I wondered if everyone knew something we didn't.

We took our cue from the soldiers, who were keen to press on. Soon we were walking in light rain again, the forest, thick next to the trail, closing in around us. We walked into unseen spider webs, their fine threads trailing across exposed skin. In the dull afternoon light, gnarled trees stood like strange petrified statues on either side of the path. Above our heads, sinewy branches entwined like clasped fingers. A romantic bower, in bright sunshine, but today, in the drizzle and gathering shadows, the forest was a snarl of dripping greenery.

DÉJÀ VU

Our campsite for the night was at Chempsa, a simple clearing in the forest.

I had been telling Krista about my trek to Laya two years earlier, when we'd arrived at Chempsa late in the day, to find another trekking party camped on the only flat ground we'd seen all afternoon. There wasn't room for both groups so we'd been forced to keep going. An hour later, in the near darkness, we'd opted to spend the night on an unattractive muddy slope. Now, as Krista and I came over a rise, yellow domed tents stood out like beacons among the trees. I had a sinking feeling of déjà vu. Our tents were blue, and our horses still somewhere behind us.

The drizzle of the early afternoon had become persistent rain. After our hard climb, the prospect of trudging on for another hour in search of an alternative campsite, in the dark and through the mud, didn't fill me with enthusiasm. After weighing up the options with Norbu, we settled for a small clearing, just 100 metres beyond the other trekkers. The ground looked as if it had just been ploughed. It was muddy and waterlogged, squelching underfoot with every step. And it was far from flat. But it was probably the best we were going to get.

'Norbu, it's raining and our horses aren't here yet,' I complained.

The horses were often late on the first day of a trek. The horsemen took time to organise gear and perhaps both they and their horses needed a day or two to find a rhythm. But it was frustrating, hanging around in the rain.

'I think the horses are working to Bhutan Stretchable Time,' Norbu said.

Bhutan Standard Time, the official time zone abbreviated to BST, was often referred to, by the Bhutanese themselves, as Bhutan Stretchable Time and perfectly reflected the country's relaxed attitude to time-keeping. BST was just one of several acronyms used flippantly in Bhutan. The previous year Krista and I had been impressed by the number of Bhutanese men who'd told us they were working on their MBA and, in a couple of cases, a PhD. It was only later we discovered that this was the common term for 'Married But Available', progressing to 'Probably Heading for Divorce'.

I was cold, wet and tired, and another hour passed before the horses arrived. By then, the dwindling light had turned to a dreary darkness. The horsemen and crew set to work, turning our muddy clearing into a hive of activity, the feeble beams of light from their head-torches struggling to pierce the gloom. Kit bags and baskets were tossed onto plastic tarpaulins. Tents were unfurled. The kitchen tent was the first to go up, so the chef could make a start on dinner, now long overdue. Krista and I huddled in one corner. All around us, cane baskets full of provisions, pots and pans and other cooking utensils were stacked on top of each other, alongside bottles of gas, a heater, blankets and enough supplies to run a trek for twenty people, never mind two. Somehow, out of this muddle of boxes, bags and baskets, a functioning kitchen began to emerge.

Relieved of their loads, the horses tripped off in search of grazing. There wasn't much to be had, on our churned-up slope. There were so many horses, but only two of us. Did we really need twenty horses? Not to mention the multitude of bags, baskets and other luggage, and a crew of six – or was it seven, plus Norbu? It was hard to tell in the darkness. As well as Norbu, there was the chef, two or three camp assistants and three horsemen.

'Isn't that Tenzin, the Tibetan horseman from last year?' Krista whispered. Scanning the crew in near darkness, I couldn't be sure. The previous year, Tenzin had worn his hair long, scraped back in a ponytail. Not only had he accompanied us on the trek but he had also joined us for a night of Hindi karaoke in Thimphu (at which, of course, we all excelled). Was that him? Possibly. We'd have to wait for formal introductions to be sure.

The size of the crew, the large number of horses and all the kit reminded me of one of the early scenes in the William Ernest Bowman novel *The Ascent of Rum Doodle*. This parody of a British mountaineering expedition describes how a group of incompetents set out to summit Mount Rum Doodle, in the fictitious Himalayan country of Yogistan. At the outset, the narrator, Binder, explains that the team of seven mountaineers would need five porters to establish a camp near the summit of Rum Doodle. These five porters would need two further porters to carry supplies for the five, and another would carry the food for the two. Their food would be carried by a boy, who would carry his own food. With the equipment to be carried and camps to be established, in all 3000 porters and 375 boys would be needed. But 30,000 porters turn up for the expedition, because the only difference between the words for 'three' and 'thirty' in Yogistani is a 'kind of snort'. I wondered if there had been a kind of snort involved in our trek planning, which had resulted in too many crew, which in turn necessitated more crew to look after the original crew. There seemed no other logical explanation for just the two of us having such a large entourage.

Eventually, dinner was served. Krista and I ate at a small camping table in the dining tent. A battered old gas heater, the veteran of many trekking expeditions, would become our much-loved evening companion. It took the edge off the chill in the air for whoever was lucky enough to sit directly in front of its tiny flame. Dinner followed the same pattern each night: soup and a main course of rice, with meat or chicken curry and several different vegetables. And always accompanied by *ema datse*, the national dish of chillies served in a stringy yak cheese sauce. Dessert was hot fruit, announced tonight and every other night by Tenzin as 'butter fry', regardless of the fruit involved. We kicked off with bananas, pan-fried in butter and sprinkled with sugar. They were delicious.

The rain was relentless. It drummed against the walls of the dining tent and splashed in great muddy puddles on the ground outside. The tent roof sagged under the barrage. We had caught the end of the monsoon.

Exhausted after a long day, Krista and I retired to our tent soon after dinner. Outside, the horses snuffled and snorted. Let loose overnight to graze, but corralled by makeshift barricades of branches on either side of the campsite, they couldn't go far. They weaved their way in and out between the tents, catching their hind hooves on ropes, leaning against nylon walls. It was only a matter of time before the inevitable happened and our tent came crashing down. Cold wet nylon slapped me in the face and the two poles holding up the back of the tent lay on the ground.

'Norbu!' we both yelled in unison. We heard voices outside and, within a couple of minutes, the tent was back to where it should have been and I finally drifted off to sleep.

MUD, GLORIOUS MUD

The rain lashed the tent all through the night, slackening off only as dawn approached. I spent a restless night and was wide-awake again at 5.30am, nursing a dull headache. I reached over to unzip the door of the tent and look outside. A dismal, wet fog sat heavily over the camp, clinging to the dripping branches of the fir trees, their shadowy forms like ghostly silhouettes in the cloud. Visibility was less than 10 metres. The ground was saturated, our tent now pitched on soft, oozing mud. But it was the beginning of an adventure and even the atrocious conditions did not dampen my excitement.

'Good morning, Sunshine!' If I hadn't known Krista better, I'd have thought she was starting the day with a heavy dose of sarcasm.

A welcome mug of steaming ginger tea was delivered to our tent by a smiling camp assistant. Still ensconced in our sleeping bags, Krista and I were practised in the art of shuffling to the tent door, like caterpillars, to collect our tea.

Reluctant to step out into the dampness, I finally emerged from the tent and came face to face with the oldest of our horsemen. Callused hands dragged a fallen log across the quagmire, where he gallantly positioned it outside our tent. It was a precarious bridge to nowhere. As I nodded a silent thank you, I watched it sink into the liquid earth until only a suggestion of the trunk remained visible. Any weight and it would disappear completely.

Krista and I avoided the temporary bridge, opting instead for the relative stability of the mud, now splattered with mounds of horse dung. The blue nylon walls and roof of the dining tent hung limply, soaked through in the overnight downpour. Norbu was waiting for us.

'Good morning, Aum Heather, Aum Krista.'

'Please don't call me Aum,' I said. 'It sounds so formal. Or we will call you Ap Norbu.'

'Okay, Aum,' he replied. Old habits die hard.

It was time to meet our crew. Norbu assembled them all in the dining tent, where they stood awkwardly, like a receiving line at a wedding.

There was, as Krista had thought, the Tibetan horseman who had been part of our crew on the previous year's trek and had helped us consume several bottles of Druk 1100 Extra Strong beer on our night in Thimphu.

'I think you know Torchen already,' Norbu said.

'You mean Tenzin?'

'Torchen.'

'But last year he was called Tenzin,' Krista pointed out.

'No, Torchen,' said Norbu.

We had called Torchen 'Tenzin' for the duration of the Jhomolhari trek, and he had definitely been Tenzin, or had at least answered to Tenzin, but Norbu was adamant. We later discovered that his full name was Torchen Tenzin.

Continuing, Norbu introduced Sangay, an agile seventeen-year-old from Eastern Bhutan. Krista and I had already christened him Bandana Man. He wore a red bandana, tied jauntily across his forehead, and he leapt about like a man possessed, whooping and hollering to the other crew members. Norbu explained that Sangay was a qualified chef. On our trek he would assist the chef and help around the camp.

The third member of our retinue was Rinzin. He looked to be in his early twenties. He was dressed in a baggy, royal blue jogging suit emblazoned in white with 'Coco Number 9'. His outfit seemed more suited to a casual Sunday-afternoon urban stroll than a 240-kilometre, high-altitude trek. Rinzin was a city boy, from Thimphu. But he knew better than any of us what lay ahead: he had completed the Snowman Trek eight times and would be our trail guide through Lunana.

The chef, Leki, small and stocky with an engaging smile, appeared briefly, nodded shyly and disappeared back to the kitchen tent. Then there were the three horsemen, Agye, Norbu and Thinley, all from Laya. Agye, meaning grandfather, was a term of respect for an older man in Bhutan and was how we were to address the oldest of the three. We never learned his real name. His entire English vocabulary consisted of 'Very good, very good', given in response to almost any situation. Norbu and Thinley were younger. Norbu was tall and slim, with curly black hair and friendly dark eyes. Standing next to him, Thinley was shorter, no more than five feet tall. Unlike the rest of the crew, all of whom were kitted out in Western trekking clothes, Thinley wore a *gho* under his jacket, with short rubber boots. In a sheath that hung from their belts, all three horsemen carried a *patang*, a long-bladed knife – an essential tool for life in the mountains.

Introductions complete, the horsemen returned to organising fodder for their horses, although 'horses' was a bit of a misnomer. These sturdy beasts of burden with big floppy ears were mostly mules.

Norbu had remembered my aversion to eggs and milk so, for breakfast, I was served fried potatoes, pan-fried bread and dry cereal, while Krista feasted on porridge and omelette. There was nothing like a carbohydrate overload to start a trekking day. As we ate our breakfast, the horses were given theirs. Thinley uncoiled a length of rope that he tied, at ground level, between two trees. The horses were quickly rounded up and tethered, by one front leg, to the rope. They stood quietly, shoulder to shoulder in a long line, heads low, rainwater forming rivulets that coursed down their sides. They knew the drill and were content to wait patiently for their morning feed, distributed in individual nosebags ranging from baskets to hessian sacks and even half a soccer ball.

With breakfast over and daypacks ready, we were eager to get started.

'*Ju gey*,' Norbu shouted. 'Let's go.' The horsemen would load up the horses and catch us up.

I tightened my hood against the thick drizzle. Norbu and Rinzin led the way through a forest of graceful firs almost obscured by fog. The air was dank, heavy with the smell of rotting vegetation, and soon the drizzle had turned to heavy rain. We pressed on, the path gullied and uneven from the constant trampling of horses on this, the main thoroughfare between Laya and Gasa.

'Be careful, it's slippery!' Norbu warned.

We didn't need to be told. Deep, muddy puddles pocked the path. In some stretches, there was so much water on the track we were sloshing through a turmoil of bubbling streams. Away from the flowing water, we slipped and slid through a slick of mud, swearing like troopers. As my boots sank deeper into the sodden ground, I fought against the suction, revelling in each triumphant slurp as I hauled one foot out, then the other, with boot still attached. I taught Krista a new word: *glar*, a Northern Irish word meaning thick, dark, liquid mud. It described exactly the ground underfoot.

I had visions of ending up flat on my back in the muck. Some years before, at the start of the Annapurna circuit in Nepal, Graeme and I had set off on a short stretch of clean, paved path. It could have been the yellow brick road. Where the paving gave way to dirt, a dip several metres across had become a waterlogged sludge, with a generous sprinkling of cow dung floating across it. 'You wouldn't want to fall in that!' I'd quipped, stepping off to one side. But my last-minute evasive action hadn't been quite evasive enough. My boot skidded and I ended up face-down in the slimy pool of foul-smelling water. We had been walking for less than ten minutes and, already, I had to change every item of clothing. Now I prayed that I wouldn't repeat that rather inauspicious start to the trek.

Half an hour after leaving camp, our trousers were caked in mud to above our knees. My boots had been submerged so many times the waterproofing didn't stand a chance.

'This is ridiculous,' I said to Krista. 'Imagine if the next sixteen days are like this. It's exhausting just trying to stay upright.'

Krista looked up at the clouds. 'I knew we should have had a *sungkey* ceremony.'

'THE MOST UNPLEASANT CAMP IN THE HIMALAYA'

And still it rained. Droplets fell from the front of my hood and trickled down my face. Eventually, through the cloud, the outline of a rudimentary stone shelter took shape. This was Koina, an alternative overnight stop on the way to Laya. It had been beyond our reach the previous day, after our lunchtime start, although maybe that was no bad thing. 'Perhaps the most unpleasant camp in the Himalaya' is the unappealing description from a leading Bhutan guidebook. It sat in a sea of mud. We sploshed over to the wooden door, which stood slightly ajar. The hinges shrieked as Norbu pushed it open and we all ducked inside, dripping wet and grateful to find refuge from the driving rain. There were several of these guesthouses along the trail: simple stone structures, empty of furniture, which provide a place for locals and trekkers to bed down for the night. They were basic in the extreme.

It was cold and draughty inside, with an aggressive wind whistling through the glassless windows. A small, lean man with tousled black hair and a ruddy complexion emerged from a side room. Norbu introduced the caretaker. He was dressed in a well-worn *gho*, a baggy knitted jumper and rubber boots – essential footwear for his muddy yard. He welcomed us in, his palms pressed together in namaste, and immediately sprung into action. With practised expertise, he piled up firewood in the middle of the floor, doused it with a generous splash of kerosene and soon we had a roaring fire. Meanwhile, Rinzin poured ginger tea, from a thermos buried in his backpack, into a collection of tin mugs. It was delicious, brewed from fresh ginger root and sweetened with a dollop of Bumthang honey.

Norbu and Rinzin gossiped with the caretaker while Krista and I attempted to dry out. Twenty minutes later, although not quite dry, we were at least warmed by the tea and fire and ready to brave the rain again. We thanked the caretaker and stepped out into the mud. I wondered if we would find somewhere dry to eat lunch.

From Koina, the trail rose and fell over a series of spurs, sweeping high above the river, then dropping dramatically down to the foaming water. In places the current had gnawed away at the banks until the path was no more than half a metre wide. We walked in single file. Steep ascents followed hard on the heels of slippery descents. Tall, limestone cliffs bordered the trail, with overhanging rocks providing a convenient nocturnal shelter; a patch of blackened ground was evidence of a recent campfire. The guesthouses along these mountain paths were few and far between and a traveller would be grateful to come across this protected spot to spend the night.

By late morning the rain had subsided. The clouds lifted and a few feeble sunbeams shone through. Perhaps our lunch stop wouldn't be as wet as I'd feared.

Lunch on a trek in Bhutan was prepared each morning by the chef. The food was kept in round aluminium tins, stacked in a large thermos, like an Indian tiffin tin, and carried by one of the guides. Leki always made sure we had rice, and lots of it. Sometimes white rice, sometimes the distinctive red rice, the only variety that grew at altitude. As at dinner, it was accompanied by a selection of curried vegetables and meat or chicken dishes. We could never finish it, but Norbu was concerned we weren't eating enough. It was not unusual, he said, for the Bhutanese to eat a kilogram of rice in a day. No wonder he thought we didn't eat enough. Or that his bellies had grown.

The guides insisted, out of respect, that Krista and I eat before them, rather than with them. Ignoring our protests, they waited politely for us to finish. So once we had eaten, we left them to enjoy their lunch. As we set off, a large bundle of greenery, hiding a wiry old man in its midst, appeared from nowhere. We stood aside to let him pass, the old man barely visible beneath his leafy load.

A slatted wooden bridge spanned the river. At one end, sections of steel telegraph poles had been piled up, awaiting collection.

'Electricity is coming to Laya,' Norbu explained, as he and Rinzin came up alongside us.

One of the government's aims was to bring electricity to every village in Bhutan. Not a straightforward task, when many settlements were accessible only on foot. A little further on, a gang of Indian labourers struggled beneath the weight of the poles. Each section was several metres long, bound in the middle by lengths of rope fashioned into a rudimentary harness. Working in pairs, one man hoisted the load across his back and, balancing it carefully, pulled the harness across his chest. Guided by his partner, he staggered, bent double, a little way along the trail, before stopping to rest. These scrawny men were each lugging several times their own body weight. With no road access to Laya, transporting these awkward poles was a formidable task.

For most of the afternoon we enjoyed an easy walk on a wide flat trail, accompanied by the rush of the river. The clean scent of pine, fresh and pungent after the rain, filled my lungs. I walked on my own for a while, content to be alone. I enjoyed the gentle rhythm of the walk, my breathing keeping time with my steps. I let my mind wander until I was thinking of nothing at all, a luxury I often longed for back home, where stimulation and interruptions were never-ending and my legal work could dictate long days and late nights at short notice. Suddenly, a huge, black, cud-chewing yak blocked the way. It was enough to jolt me out of my daydream. While I waited for him to saunter off, I smiled to myself. There were always distractions; they were just different in Bhutan.

Our next encounter was less confronting: two teenage girls from the village of Laya. Originally from Tibet, the Layaps had retained their own language and traditional dress, which was quite different from that found in the rest of Bhutan. Women wore black yak-hair skirts, often decorated with a red vertical stripe, and matching black wool jackets, trimmed with brocade. A horizontally striped apron brightened up the sombre ensemble, as did their ornate jewellery, which included turquoise and jade beads and elaborate silver pendants. Layap women wore their hair long, with no fringe, in contrast to most mountain women in Bhutan, who sported page boy hairstyles with straight fringes. The Layaps' most distinctive item of clothing was a round conical hat made of woven bamboo, with a pointed wooden stick protruding about three inches from the top, and strings of small coloured beads hanging in a loop at the back. It was worn only by the women. One of the girls we met had added a more modern accessory – a badge with a photograph of the King and Queen, the same one that Norbu sometimes wore pinned to his *gho*.

The current King, His Majesty Jigme Khesar Namgyel Wangchuck, was affectionately known as K5. He was crowned as the Fifth King of Bhutan in November 2008, following the unexpected abdication of his father two years earlier. After successfully ruling for thirty-four years, the Fourth King decided that Bhutan should have a constitutional, rather than an absolute, monarchy. The monarchy was held in such high regard that many citizens were shocked and upset when the Fourth King proposed handing over power to a democratically elected government. But after touring the country to consult his subjects and prepare them for a new political era, he went ahead with his plan. Despite this dilution of the monarch's power, the current King, like his father, was hugely popular throughout the nation.

The Layap girls on the trail posed happily for a photograph before hurrying off, giggling. They were probably as fascinated by our strange attire as we were by theirs.

PRAYER FLAGS AND SOLDIERS

It was almost four o'clock when Krista, Norbu and I reached Takchenkhar, an outpost of the Royal Bhutan Army, an hour's walk south of Laya village. Our trekking permits would be checked here and we'd camp close by.

The army barracks were a cluster of squat stone buildings, with tin roofs glinting in the last rays of the sun. There was none of the high security you might expect at an army base anywhere else in the world: no lookout posts, no barbed-wire fence, no armed soldiers on guard. Not even a gate. Although close to the Chinese border, the camp seemed deserted. The only sound was the whip of prayer flags against the poles that towered over the low-set buildings. In Bhutan, where the Buddhist faith was a cornerstone of all aspects of life, there was nothing unusual in the juxtaposition of military might and gentle prayers, blowing in the wind from the fluttering flags.

On an open stretch of grass behind the camp, one of Bhutan's favourite traditional sports was underway: *khuru*, a form of outdoor darts. The target was painted on a small wooden board, similar to an archery target, angled into a mound of earth about 20 metres away from the players. The gigantic darts looked like bevelled sticks, with a metal-tipped cone at one end and flights at the other. As in archery games in Bhutan, a successful throw was celebrated by a team victory dance, executed sedately, the players standing in a circle and stepping backwards and forwards in unison, singing to celebrate their success. Krista and I watched the game while we waited for Norbu, who had disappeared with our permits. Behind the army camp, the jagged snow-covered peak of Masang Gang was just visible, a 7194-metre goliath marking the border between Bhutan and China.

The relaxed atmosphere of the army camp belied the sensitivity over the Bhutan–China border, a short distance away over the mountains. For centuries, China had laid intermittent claims to sovereignty over Tibet, Bhutan's northern neighbour. In 1950, the newly established Communist regime in China invaded Tibet and, over the next decade, embarked on a campaign of persecution of the Tibetan people and destruction of Tibet's rich cultural and religious heritage. Tibetan protests grew in strength, culminating in the uprising of 1959 and the flight of the Dalai Lama, the country's political and spiritual leader, and tens of thousands of Tibetans, into exile. Unsurprisingly, these events caused alarm in both India and Bhutan, with heightened tensions along Bhutan's border with what had been Tibet, and was now part of the People's Republic of China. Stretches of that border, close to India, remained in dispute, with dire consequences for the stability of the region should China decide to flex its military muscle against Bhutan. It was hard to imagine the gravity of these political issues as we watched the soldiers playing darts behind their barracks.

Norbu returned with our permits and we strolled over to the campsite, on a flat meadow not far from the darts field. We were soon joined by a friendly dog, with a thick, black coat and kind face, perhaps a resident of the army base, ready for a change of scene.

'She's just like the dog from last year,' Krista said, chasing her playfully.

'What was her name?' I wondered, remembering the dog that had accompanied us so faithfully on the Jhomolhari trek the year before.

'Bluebell, I think,' Krista replied.

'Yes Bluebell! Whose idea was that?' I mused. 'I think we need something a bit more Himalayan this time. What shall we call her?'

'How about Lunana, in honour of our destination?' Krista suggested.

'Lunana it is!'

While we were focused on our new companion, the crew were busy organising the camp. Among piles of luggage, semi-erected tents and grazing horses, Sangay was leaping around like a mischievous child. He seemed to have boundless energy, unloading baskets, putting up tents, jumping over kit bags, always with an infectious grin on his face. He did everything with a flourish and at breakneck speed, whether unzipping the tent door or leading the way on the trail. I had never met anyone with so much vigour and enthusiasm.

He also excelled when it came to lighting the gas heater which graced the dining tent in the evenings. Its shell was so dented it was only barely recognisable as a heater and it steadfastly refused to light for anyone else. Sangay used everything from a tent pole to a broken matchstick to persuade it to light. To everyone's amazement, he never failed. It had three panels, only one of which was ever lit. It wasn't clear if the other two didn't work or if the crew were rationing the bottled gas, which, like everything else, had to be carried up the mountain tracks on horseback. As our only source of heat in the evenings, we grew very attached to the flickering blue flame and worshipped it in the dining tent every evening.

This was where we passed the late afternoons before dinner: reading, updating our journals, checking the next day's route and playing cards. Often, the crew joined us when the camp chores were done. Tonight, we played a Bhutanese card game called Hazaray with Norbu and Torchen, watched closely by Rinzin and Sangay. The object of the game was to arrange thirteen cards into three hands of three and one of four. Each hand was played face up and a complicated set of rules dictated the winner of each round.

Miraculously, and with only a very loose grip on the hierarchy of various card combinations, first Krista and then I beat Norbu and Torchen comfortably, much to their amusement. As I reached over to pick up a pile of winning cards, my camping chair, unstable on the bumpy ground, began a slow-motion collapse, which almost sent me headfirst into the gas heater. Torchen and Norbu just managed to grab the chair in time to stop my down jacket going up in a puff of smoke. It was time to quit while I was ahead.

GATEWAY TO LUNANA

The next morning I was awake for what seemed like hours, listening to Leki and Sangay scrubbing pots, firing up the pressure cooker and gossiping with the crew. It was time to get up.

Our sleeping bags were mummy style: wide at the top, narrowing at the other end. The tapering was great for retaining heat but, with a fleece liner inside, getting in and out of it would have been a challenge for Houdini.

'How are you doing over there?' Krista asked as I tried to wriggle out of the various layers, only to end up in a twisted muddle.

'Ouch! I think I just tweaked my hamstring.'

'That could be awkward,' Krista laughed.

Starting day two of the trek with a limp was not ideal, especially when the limp was inflicted by a sleeping bag.

'Bed tea, madam,' came the announcement from outside our tent. It was such a funny expression.

I hobbled over to the door and unzipped the tent. Rinzin and Torchen were crouched outside with a thermos and two mugs. 'Ginger tea?'

'Yes, please,' we chorused.

'How are you today?' Krista asked.

'I am fine, madam,' Rinzin said. How are you?'

'Fantastic!'

Our exchange with our bed tea waiters was the same every morning, and was followed a short time later by the arrival of

Sangay with two stainless steel bowls of hot water: our 'washing water'.

Outside our tent, our new canine buddy Lunana sat expectantly, wagging her tail with enthusiasm when she saw us. These mountain dogs seemed to know that trekkers were a soft touch when it came to mealtime leftovers: they often appeared, out of nowhere, whenever we arrived.

We compared notes with Norbu on who had slept best (Norbu) and who had snored loudest (again, Norbu).

'Where are all the horses, Norbu?' I asked.

There were only about half-a-dozen of them, milling around.

'The horsemen have gone back to their homes in Laya last night,' Norbu explained. 'They have taken many of the horses with them. They are bringing more this morning.'

So they really did think we were light on horses. The extras, when they arrived, brought our horse train to an impressive total of twenty-three.

After breakfast, which we secretly shared with Lunana, Norbu sent Krista and me on ahead. He would catch us up, he said. The plan for the day was to retrace our steps back along the eastern side of the Mo Chu valley, until we reached the turn-off for the Lunana plateau. From there, we would trek east, through a side valley, to our next camp at Rodophu, at over 4200 metres.

It was an easy start to the day on a gently undulating path, and thankfully, the nip at the back of my thigh gradually lessened as we started walking. Lunana trotted happily alongside us. We were high above the Mo Chu, looking down on the turquoise water that thrashed between the near vertical walls of the gorge. After merging with the Pho Chu at Punakha Dzong, and undergoing several name changes, the river flowed through the Indian state of Assam before joining the mighty Brahmaputra and eventually emptying into the Bay of Bengal. But here in its upper reaches, the Mo Chu valley was narrow, close to the river's source: a vein of blue carving through the dark green pine forests that swept down to the water's edge. Gathering clouds hung insidiously over the tops of distant ridges, but overhead the sun shone. The scenery was idyllic.

We hadn't been walking for long when a strange footprint in the mud caught Krista's attention. Bigger than any usual animal track, it seemed to have a sixth toe.

'A yeti print!' I joked.

We had stopped to inspect it when Norbu arrived.

'We've found a yeti footprint,' Krista told him.

He looked at it carefully, sceptical perhaps, but not dismissive. 'It could be …' he said equivocally, kneeling down to study the outline in the dirt. He took some photos, which he would show to the rest of the crew later.

In many aspects of life in Bhutan, the lines between fantasy and reality, history and mythology, were blurred, and nowhere more so than in relation to the yeti, or *migoi*. Where else would you find a national park set up by the government specifically to protect the natural habitat of the yeti? The Sakteng Wildlife Sanctuary, or Migoi National Park, in Eastern Bhutan was just that. Also known as Bigfoot, or the Abominable Snowman, these fantastic apelike beasts, which walked on two legs and could apparently make themselves invisible, were believed to inhabit the remote forests of the north and east of the country. One of the first Westerners to claim to have seen a yeti in the Himalayas was William Hugh Knight, a British explorer who, at the start of the last century, described it as pale yellow, with large hands and splayed feet. Since then there have been numerous alleged sightings of these wildmen of the mountains, including by one of the world's greatest living mountaineers, Reinhold Messner, who claims to have seen a yeti in Tibet. For the most part, however, in the Western world, a lack of scientific evidence of the yeti's existence has consigned them to fairytales. The Bhutanese, on the other hand, had no doubt that yetis were flourishing in the mountains. Those who claimed to have seen them, and there were many, lived in fear of them. Such was the remoteness of some of Bhutan's forbidden forests that it was perhaps conceivable that an as yet unknown species of ape lurked in their midst. Anything seemed possible in Bhutan.

Not long after stopping to inspect the yeti print, we were standing in front of the turn-off to Lunana, one of the most isolated and untouched regions in the Himalayas. There was no sign, no obvious fork in the trail, just an immense tree and, behind it, an insignificant stony path that climbed up, away from the Mo Chu valley. It seemed improbable that anyone would stumble upon this turn-off, never mind know where it led, without a local guide to show them the way. There was no way of knowing that this trail would wind its way up through high mountains to the village of Thanza, the highest (at 4100 metres) and most remote settlement in Bhutan, and our destination in six days' time. Although I had walked past this point yesterday without even noticing that there was another path, today it felt significant, like a doorway to another world. Everything so far had been very familiar to me: Paro, Thimphu, Punakha, Gasa Dzong, the campsite at Chempsa, the trail up to the army camp. From here, I was heading off into the unknown. I thought of Lucy, stepping through the wardrobe door into the magical world of Narnia.

Lunana was Bhutan's most sparsely populated region. Administered as part of Gasa Dzongkhag (District), in 2013 the population of the whole district was 3082, a mere 535 households. Most people lived in and around the hamlet of Gasa, with large, empty, upland swathes, several days' walk from Gasa, inhabited only by semi-nomadic yak herders. Many of these people were believed to have come to Bhutan from Tibet, centuries ago, over the high Himalayan passes that provide the only access to Bhutan from the Tibetan plateau to the north. With no roads, the only option was to walk along trails trodden by lamas, herders, horses and yaks. And maybe the occasional deity. Life for the people of Lunana was hard, governed by the vagaries of the weather and especially winter snow, which cut them off from the rest of Bhutan for several months at a time. It was incredible that they were able to eke out an existence at all, in their remote mountain valleys.

Only a generation ago, subsistence living in Bhutan was the norm. However, with the steady development of a nationwide education program, older Bhutanese citizens have seen sweeping societal changes within their lifetimes. With the growth of an educated middle class came an urban/rural divide, as in nations across the globe, with urban dwellers considering themselves superior to their country cousins. Norbu told us that many of his countrymen looked down on the nomads of Lunana as long-johns-wearing yokels, whose subsistence way of life had remained unchanged for centuries.

I was excited to be heading towards the wild landscape of Lunana where, with luck, we would meet some of the nomads who roamed this high plateau. And so we left behind the roar of the Mo Chu, turning east on the secret trail which wound its way up the side valley, through ancient trees, with trailing branches garlanded in wispy chiffon-like moss, their trunks wrapped in a coat of lichen. As the path steepened, I was soon breathing heavily, all too aware of the increasing incline and decreasing oxygen.

HEADING HIGHER

We tramped on through the forest, treading carefully over roots that spread their tendrils, like knobbly fingers, across the rutted ground. Lunana followed closely behind us. On a steep hillside, we stopped to rest under a majestic tree, its long twisting boughs forming a wide canopy over the trail. A delicate web of Spanish moss dangled from every branch, trapping teardrops of dew that sparkled in the sunlight. In Ireland, fairies would live in a tree like this.

On the slopes above us, a herd of handsome yaks, snuffling through scant tufts of vegetation, caught our scent. They looked up briefly before returning to their grazing, the gentle tinkle of the bells around their necks at odds with their great, lumbering bulk. Behind them, an abandoned stone hut, crumbling in an open meadow, was all that was left of their keepers' summer residence.

'Be careful,' Norbu warned as he picked up a rock, to launch at any yak that might decide to charge.

That yaks were easily spooked was noted by Captain Samuel Turner, believed to be one of the earliest Europeans to have encountered them. Turner was despatched to Tibet from India, in 1792, by the East India Company, to meet with the reincarnation of the Panchen Lama, the second-highest ranking lama in Tibet. On seeing yaks for the first time, on his journey through Bhutan, he wrote: 'They have a downcast heavy look, and appear, what indeed they are, sullen and suspicious, discovering much impatience at the near approach of strangers.' Apparently not much had changed in the intervening 250 years and, having no desire to be on the receiving end of a stampede, I was happy to give the yaks a wide berth.

The trail shadowed the river, the Rhodo Chu, which, over thousands of years, had sliced a deep gorge through the mountains. Tough lichens, cushions of moss and tussocky grass formed a patchy carpet across the rocky slope. Trees were few and far between. Those that managed to survive were little more than a collection of bare, angular branches, radiating out from thin trunks, like contorted limbs. Far below, endless forests of pine spread all the way down the valley, a sea of green broken only by the thin silver thread of the Rhodo Chu. Dark shadows on the hillsides tracked the billowing clouds that floated across the sky. In the distance, a crush of mountains seemed to extend to the furthest horizon and beyond, in waves of grey and blue, until they merged with the sky itself.

We stopped to catch our breath. While Krista and I grazed on trail mix and Bhutanese sweet biscuits, the boys were well supplied with small blocks of yak cheese. 'I have given up *doma*,' Norbu announced proudly. 'I am having yak cheese instead.'

It had been five days since Norbu's last betel-nut fix. On the trek, it wouldn't be difficult for him to avoid temptation: *doma* was not a Bhutanese habit that Krista and I were about to adopt.

'On the trek it is easy. But, in Paro, all my friends chew *doma*.'

The test of his resolve would be when he returned home. In the meantime, he was sticking to the yak cheese.

'Would you like to try some *chugo*?' he asked.

'Okay,' I said hesitantly, 'thank you.'

Norbu pulled two cubes off a piece of knotted string and handed one each to Krista and me.

The cheese had been dried and smoked until it was as hard as a brick. It would keep like this for years. Biting into it was a no-no and would pretty much guarantee an emergency trip to the dentist. The Bhutanese sucked it for hours to soften it before it could be chewed. I put the cube of cheese into my mouth, but it was like sucking on a stone. Not for me, this Himalayan delicacy.

'Is anyone looking?' I asked Krista.

'All clear.'

I surreptitiously removed it, launching it off the side of the mountain.

'Would you like some more?' Norbu held out the string.

I declined politely. Krista did much better, managing to hold hers inside her cheek for the next hour. But it hadn't softened at all by then and, when we were out of sight of the others, it met the same fate as mine.

Before long, I felt another sneeze coming on. I had been sneezing my way through the morning, a mild allergy to something in the vegetation, perhaps. I sneezed once, then twice …

'Once more for good weather,' Norbu instructed.

I obliged.

The morning had yo-yoed between an overcast sky and spells of intermittent sun. By lunchtime, dark rain clouds threatened to envelop the valley and a squally wind was picking up. Norbu's theory of the lucky triple sneeze proved to be misguided. We managed to time our lunch stop to coincide with the first hint of rain.

As we bunkered down behind a wall of prickly bushes, cold droplets were soon dripping from branches that provided no more than the illusion of shelter. The rain quickly turned to sleet and, by the time we'd finished our curry and rice, my hands and face were smarting with cold. Once we'd eaten, Krista and I didn't hang around, leaving Norbu, Sangay and Rinzin to finish their lunch and carry on when they were ready. Lunana stayed behind with the guides, waiting for leftovers, little runnels of rainwater running off the end of her nose.

The freezing rain sent us scurrying down a slippery trail from our lunch stop. We were above the treeline now, the terrain desolate and barren, a stony scrubland with a covering of short, tough grass. According to the guidebook, we should have been surrounded by impressive glaciated peaks. We saw only banks of blowing cloud.

NOT QUITE THE RITZ

Our campsite for the night was at Rodophu. We descended to a flat marshy expanse of ground, crisscrossed by a maze of swollen streams. I was glad when Norbu, Rinzin and Sangay overtook us; it was easy to become disorientated in the swirling mist.

Soon, a little stone hut loomed through the cloud: the Rodophu shelter. Despite being marooned in a semi-flooded swamp, four walls and a roof would provide welcome relief from the drenching rain. I couldn't wait to be dry.

Lunana was the first to reach the doorway, where she sat and waited patiently outside. Someone had taught her very good manners. Even Norbu, who professed to dislike dogs, admitted she was well behaved.

The shelter was as unsophisticated as its Koina counterpart. Small shuttered windows rationed the daylight, and the walls and ceiling were blackened with soot. In the shadowy main room, a slightly-built man was tending to a blazing fire. He was well wrapped against the cold, in a practical tracksuit and padded jacket. Looking up as we arrived, he welcomed us with a wide smile, revealing several missing teeth. Those that were left were yellowing and decayed. He seemed pleased to have company, dragging out some scruffy mats as he waved us over to the fire. We didn't need to be asked twice. I wriggled out of my daypack, my shoulders glad to be free of the weight, and hung my jacket on a nail in the wall to drip dry.

Encouraged by the caretaker, who fussed over us like a mother hen, we edged the mats closer to the fire. The warm glow of the flames threw a circle of light across the centre of the room; beyond its reach, darkness took over. The caretaker chatted over his shoulder to Norbu, while water boiled in a well-tarnished pot that could easily have been a witch's cauldron. Soon we each had a welcome cup of tea; I cradled mine gratefully, feeling the warmth gradually bring my chilled fingers back to life.

As the caretaker added more logs to the fire, plumes of smoke swirled all around us. It didn't seem to bother the locals but I could barely keep my eyes open. I moved away, trying to avoid the clouds of gritty smoke that seemed to chase me around the room.

'Do you know why the smoke is following you?' Norbu asked. 'It blows on the trekker who has peed most on the trail!'

'That's not me,' I protested.

The others burst out laughing as I shuffled across to the other side of the fire. Lunana had edged her way indoors and now lay asleep, just inside the doorway. Like us, she was glad of the warmth from the fire. Norbu and Rinzin chatted with the caretaker in Dzongkha, sharing jokes and cubes of yak cheese. Norbu explained that they were discussing our early arrival at Rodophu. The caretaker thought we must have walked very quickly and Rinzin was complaining that the crew were having trouble keeping up. Apparently, most trekkers wouldn't expect to reach Rodophu until much later in the day, hence our absent horses.

With time on our hands, Krista took the opportunity to show me how her satellite phone worked. It was all very well having emergency equipment, but it wasn't much help if no one knew how to use it. I told her the story of how, a couple of years before becoming prime minister, Tony Abbott had been in a remote area in the Northern Territory and had become separated from his guide for several hours. Mr Abbott and his entourage had tried to raise the alarm, but were stumped by the lack of mobile phone coverage and the fact that no one could operate their emergency satellite phone. We hoped to be better prepared.

It was a couple of hours later that voices echoed across the marsh and a chorus of whistling heralded the arrival of the horses. The shelter was soon bustling with activity. The horsemen unloaded all our camping gear into the central room, slinging wicker baskets and canvas kit bags through the doorway onto an ever-growing pile of luggage. I noticed the baskets were numbered so, despite the apparent chaos, there was perhaps some sort of order to their routine. Sangay and Rinzin grabbed a tent bag and it wasn't long before our tent had been set up, much to my dismay, 20 metres away across the boggy meadow.

A kitchen was hastily established in a side room, where Leki set to work preparing snacks and dinner. Norbu, keen to shield us from the ruckus caused by the crew's late arrival, ushered us to our dining table, in a small dank room at the back of the hut. It smelled of mould and a cool dampness hung in the air. A wooden shutter rattled and banged with every gust of wind. I forced it open to let some light in, but with the light came the draught. It was too cold with the shutter open, too dark and stale with it shut, so Krista and I returned to the main room and the light and warmth of the fire.

Outside, the heavy rain and low cloud acted like a monochrome filter, reducing colour to shades of grey. Crouching by the fire, we watched a continuous column of yaks shuffling down a dogleg trail behind the shelter. This would be our route the following morning. Shortly afterwards, half-a-dozen rugged yakmen burst through the open door. Their cheeks were ruddy from the cold, their skin darkened by sun and wind, and their clothes wet and grimy from days of walking and sleeping rough. They greeted us with wide grins, clearly surprised to encounter two blondes on their way to Lunana. In these secluded valleys, where news was passed by word of mouth, the yak herders would be a valuable source of information about the state of the trail ahead. I was relieved when

Norbu reported that the higher passes in Lunana were still clear of significant snowfall. We didn't need to panic just yet.

Throughout the evening, men continued to seek refuge in the shelter, drifting in from who knows where. The rain came down in torrents. I was glad to be inside, sitting next to the heat of the fire, watching the flames and the strange shadows they cast on the soot-covered walls. The prospect of trudging back to our tent, across the bog, was far from appealing.

When dinner was ready, Norbu escorted us back to the dark little dining room, joining us, as he always did, for the soup course.

'My bellies are already getting smaller,' he said. 'I think I was eating too much at home.'

'Too much rice,' I suggested. 'Maybe if you have a smaller bowl, it will be easier to have smaller portions. And no second helpings. Or at least no third helpings.'

'Maybe you should go to the gym?' Krista suggested.

'I don't think so,' he replied. 'Gyms are coming up now in Bhutan but I don't think I need to go to the gym. I am going on the trek. And I am having to keep up with you two. You have walked very quickly again today but still the horses should not be so late,' Norbu apologised. 'They started late this morning because the horsemen went back to their homes in Laya last night. But I am not sure why they were so far behind. I am going to talk to the horsemen tonight, and tomorrow, I think they will be faster.'

We promised to try to slow down.

After dinner, we turned our attention to the school library books. There were sets of early readers, atlases, dictionaries, short stories and fairytales, mostly in English and a few in Dzongkha. One slim volume caught my eye, in the dim light from our solar lamp. I flicked through a slim Penguin book called *The Sensualist*, by Indian author Ruskin Bond. The title itself was a giveaway but the cover blurb confirmed my suspicions: '*The Sensualist* is the story of a man enslaved by his libido and spiralling towards self-destruction.

Gripping, erotic, even brutal, the book explores the demons that its protagonist must grapple with before he is able to come to terms with himself.'

I handed it to Krista. She opened it and read aloud the first line of the Author's Note: 'Let it be said at the outset that this book is not intended for the school classroom.'

'Norbu! Who chose this book?' I demanded, in feigned horror. 'It's really not appropriate for a primary school library. The author says so himself!'

Norbu was noncommittal about who had picked the text and didn't seem to understand what all the fuss was about. Krista put it carefully to one side and we agreed to conduct a careful review of the rest of the books. Thankfully, Mr Bond's treatise on unbridled male passion was the only anomaly among volumes of Enid Blyton, *The Brothers Grimm* and *The Atlas of World Geography*. Satisfied that the rest of the books were suitable primary school material, we spent a productive hour fixing stickers of the Matthew Flinders Anglican College school crest inside the front covers.

'My sneezing didn't bring us good weather today, Norbu,' I said. 'I hope it's not going to be raining for the next two weeks. What do you think?'

'We cannot know about it,' Norbu replied. 'We had to ask to an astrologer before we started.'

Not only had we not had a *sungkey* blessing, but now it turned out we should have sought guidance from an astrologer. Unlike in many Western cultures, where astrology had been reduced to trashy horoscopes in women's magazines, astrology in Bhutan was practised by highly respected scholars. The 500-year-old Pangri Zampa Monastery, near Thimphu, had been modernised and expanded in recent years and was now home to more than a hundred monks studying Buddhist astrology. Norbu explained that no right-thinking Bhutanese would dream of making an important decision without first consulting an astrologer: where to live, when to wed, when to start a long journey or set up a business. All important life events required this traditional blessing and guidance and, sometimes, a long wait. Even royalty dared not ignore an astrologer's counsel. After succeeding the throne, on the abdication of his father in December 2006, the Fifth King was forced to delay his coronation ceremony by almost two years until exactly 8.31am on 6 November 2008, deemed by the court astrologers to be the most auspicious time to herald a successful reign. I comforted myself with the knowledge that had we asked an astrologer when to begin our trek, we might have been forced to ignore his advice and go ahead anyway, to keep to our schedule. Surely this would have been worse than not asking at all?

I was a little sceptical of predictions based on astrological signs but, in 2010, I took the opportunity to consult a Bhutanese astrologer. Provided only with my date of birth, he pored over his charts, muttered to himself and then announced his conclusions. He declared me to be intelligent, loyal and someone who didn't depend on others. So far so good. My lucky colour was red, my unlucky colour was black (requiring a complete wardrobe overhaul), my lucky day was Thursday and my unlucky day was Wednesday. He predicted that I would be ill in my late forties but, thankfully, would recover and live until I was eighty-seven. It remains to be seen whether he was correct.

While astrology had retained a place in modern Bhutan, other social conventions were slowly being eroded by Western influences, mainly due to exposure to international media. Television and the internet only arrived in Bhutan in 1999 and, since then, both have had a huge impact. The Western world arrived in the homes of people who, previously, had little concept of life beyond their mountain kingdom. Bhutanese children were now as familiar with many aspects of Western popular culture as with their own established traditions. The previous year I had watched Norbu's young son, Dorji, playing Angry Birds on a mobile phone with the familiarity of any Western child.

Apparently, Dorji was also clamouring to have a birthday party, an alien concept when Norbu had been a child. In the past, a family might have gone for a picnic on someone's birthday, but even that was unusual. Now, children saw on television how birthdays were celebrated in the West, leading to demands for the thrill of balloons, cake, parties and gifts. Norbu lamented that some families had started sending cakes and other treats to school so their children's classmates could join in the birthday celebrations, and other families felt pressured to do the same. The bar had been raised in the birthday stakes and everyone wanted a slice of the action, as well as the cake.

The conversation moved on from births to deaths. Although frivolous birthday celebrations were a recent trend in Bhutan, the customs associated with death had long held great significance for the Bhutanese. Norbu explained that after a bereavement, prayers and elaborate rituals continued for forty-nine days, with the seventh, fourteenth, twenty-first and forty-ninth days being the most significant. Rebirth was the cornerstone of the Buddhist faith and death a beginning rather than an end, as the deceased started their journey to the next life. The rituals following death, in which family members, friends and monks all participated, not only helped loved ones through their time of bereavement, but were also believed to help the deceased in their journey to the next life and to obtain a favourable rebirth.

In the highlands of Bhutan cremation, rather than burial, was the norm. I had read a little about the ancient funeral practice of sky burial, where a corpse was taken to an auspicious place in the mountains and left to decompose naturally or be eaten by scavengers, often vultures and other birds of prey. Sky burial had originated on the high plateaux of Tibet and Mongolia; I asked Norbu whether this practice, so alien in the Western world, continued in Bhutan.

'Sometimes, we have the sky burial, but not so much any more,' he explained. 'I once came to a sky burial site above Paro. There was the body of a young child left there. As a father, it was very difficult for me to see that. I could not forget it.'

As Norbu described what he had seen – the child's body, with limbs contorted, not yet consumed by nature – I could understand how confronting this scene must have been for him and how the memory of it must have haunted him afterwards. Some years ago, I spent time with an archaeologist and an Aboriginal elder, exploring rock-art sites in a remote area of the Kimberley, in Western Australia. We came to a cave where, on a high ledge, the partial skeleton of a child lay, left there as part of a traditional Aboriginal burial practice. I had found it quite confronting and the image of it has stayed with me, many years later. Norbu had clearly been distressed by what he saw and I regretted asking about it.

We focused on sticking the last of the school crests in the books. By now, the floor of the shelter's main room was crammed with our crew and a dozen yak herders and other passers-by, who had appeared during the evening. All were bedded down for the night, lying on the floor under blankets, feet warming by the fire. Some were asleep already, others catching up on gossip, their faces silhouetted in the darkness by the dancing flames, the only source of light. They were characters from another era. Krista and I tiptoed past the slumbering shapes and out into the rain, to our forlorn little tent in the middle of the marsh. Lunana, who had been allowed just inside the door of the shelter, sensibly switched allegiance to the horsemen for the night and watched us disappear into the darkness.

MIST AT THE TSOMO LA

The weather made for a depressing start to the new day. Fog rolled in slow waves across the valley, engulfing everything in its path. Although we were surrounded by lofty summits, the mist was all-consuming and gave no inkling of the majesty that lay beneath it. Inside the tent, the moisture in the air seeped into everything. It was almost as wet inside as outside. My sleeping bag, my clothes, even the pages of my book, felt damp to the touch.

Lunana spotted us as soon as we emerged from the tent. She came bounding over to lick our hands and pranced around, as thrilled to see us as if she had been our companion for years, not days. Over in the shelter, the mist mingled with smoke from the fire and my eyes took a little while to adjust to the gloom. The whispering forms of the previous night were all awake, folding up blankets and packing wicker baskets to be loaded onto yaks. We ate a hearty breakfast and said our goodbyes. As we left, the yakmen formed a guard of honour outside the door of the shelter, waving us off with shouts of *'Tashi Delek'*.

It was 8.30am when Norbu, Torchen, Krista and I set off through the clouds, Lunana hot on our trail. The path climbed gently at first, then more steeply, through a wall of dwarf rhododendron. It was only day four of the trek but tonight was to be one of our highest camps, at 4940 metres. Although the previous year I had managed to climb to that altitude without any ill effects, we hadn't slept so high on the Jhomolhari trek and I worried that, after such a short time to acclimatise, a night at above 4900 metres might take its toll. Altitude sickness could strike as low as 2000 metres, although most people were unaffected below 2500 metres. Significantly, coping (or not coping) with altitude on one trip was no guarantee of how your body would react on another. Despite knowing that past experiences were irrelevant, I was conscious that I had not reacted well on previous trips, at much lower elevations than we would reach on this trek. In Colorado, I had fainted at the top of a ski slope, still attached to my skis, and on the Inca Trail, I had passed out within ten minutes of starting the hike, only to be brought abruptly back to consciousness by one of our group emptying the contents of his water bottle over my head, while I sprawled on the ground. I hoped I would not be repeating these incidents in Lunana.

When I'd organised this trip, I knew we were being ambitious with the itinerary and the timescale, but Krista and I had to juggle a long trek through Lunana with our home lives. So, from here on, we would be sleeping at or above 4000 metres – and for several nights, closer to 5000 metres. Only on the last two nights of the trek would we drop lower. Fingers crossed we would be okay until then.

There is a common misconception that the air at higher altitudes contains less oxygen. In fact, the percentage of oxygen and other gases in the air remain the same regardless of altitude; it is the atmospheric pressure that lessens with altitude gain. At 5000 metres, the lower barometric pressure means that the air molecules are more dispersed, so you have to breath in a lot more air to get the same amount of oxygen.

Norbu warned us to pace ourselves and to keep drinking lots of water. Dehydration was a common problem at higher elevations. A combination of breathing deeper and faster, coupled with sweating, meant our bodies would lose moisture rapidly.

For now, I felt well.

After a couple of hours of climbing, pockets of snow began to appear along the rocky slope. There was no warmth in the air. No noise. No sound of insect or bird in the bitter cold. A cluster of cairns sat atop a ridge: circular mounds of stones built by other travellers to mark a significant point on the route. Looking up, I'd let myself believe that these cairns might mark the pass. But, as I reached them, I saw the actual pass was still some way off, just visible through an ocean of mist. Krista had gone on ahead and Norbu and Torchen weren't far behind me. I stopped at the largest cairn to wait for them, intrigued by what looked like a vertical yellow marker protruding from a pile of rocks.

'What is that, Norbu?' I asked.

'We call it *chukar meto*,' he replied. 'It grows only at high-altitude.'

There were dozens of them, a series of pale yellow beacons sprinkled across the hillside. I later discovered that it was known as noble rhubarb, in English, although it looked nothing like rhubarb as I knew it, with wide green leaves and shiny deep red stalks. This rhubarb had creamy yellow, almost translucent leaves wrapped around a central stem. It stood upright, about half a metre tall, and was native to the Himalayan region, growing only above 4000 metres. It was thriving up here, near the Tsomo La, at 4900 metres.

One of the challenges of the Snowman Trek was the number of passes. Our route, over sixteen days, would take us over ten high passes, with today's pass, the Tsomo La, only the second. The approach to the pass was a scramble over slippery scree, covered in a smattering of snow, a mass of shifting, jagged stones that sank away beneath each footstep. It was exhausting.

We paused briefly at the Tsomo La. It was a bleak and godforsaken place, the desolation tangible. From here, we should have been able to see right across Lunana, with views back to Mount Jhomolhari and Jichu Drake. Twelve months earlier, in brilliant sunshine, Krista and I had hiked to the base of Mount Jhomolhari, which rose to over 7300 metres. We had walked in the shadow of Jichu Drake, Jhomolhari's more angular neighbour. Its serrated, snow-covered ridge had dominated the skyline for a day of our trek. Today, these stunning peaks were completely hidden from view.

A BRUSH WITH ALTITUDE SICKNESS

A bleached yak skull, with curved black horns attached, balanced on top of a pyramid of rocks. Coated in a layer of snow, with gaping eye sockets staring out across the plain, it was an eerie reminder of the fragility of life in this harsh landscape.

As we headed down from the pass, a cavalcade of yaks suddenly lurched from the cloud, barely visible until they were no more than a few metres away. We jumped out of their way. I looked back and they were gone, swallowed by the fog that had become the landscape itself. There was no evidence of development of any kind here: no electricity pylons, no phone lines, no permanent homes. Only the remnants of a yak herder's hut, used for a few months over summer, left to crumble during the long winter.

Visibility improved slightly as we descended out of the cloud. Tall mountains of grey-tinged shale rose up on all sides, slopes scarred by deep gullies, gouged into the rock by fast-flowing streams. Down below us a small glassy lake, the shape of a perfect teardrop, shimmered in the gloom, its surface masking the water's depth.

Bhutan was once known as *Lho phyogs sman ljongs*, 'Southern Land of Medicinal Plants', and, as we traced our way along meandering trails, across this high, treeless plateau, Sangay pointed out a plant, like a tall thistle, which he claimed had medicinal properties. The people of the highlands collected these plants, which were dried and ground into powder and were highly prized in traditional Tibetan medicine.

As the afternoon wore on, the obstinate mist that had enveloped us all day began to lift and a pale blue sky emerged, gradually, through the heavy cloud. I felt hopeful that the rain was finally clearing. It was four o'clock when we spotted our camp. The horses had overtaken us earlier in the day and it was a relief to see the blue of our tents, insignificant little specks, dwarfed by the looming bulk of Gangla Karchung. Sun and shadow danced across its craggy face in the ever-changing light.

From the summit, at 6301 metres, an icy glacier tumbled down, merging into the moraine behind our tents. On the other side, the pewter grey of a glacial lake was just visible. There was no plant life here, just rocky scree, making for a wild, rugged beauty. I was under no illusions about how cold it would be overnight.

In the dining tent Norbu seemed quiet and, unusually, retreated to his tent for a late-afternoon nap. It turned out to be a busy afternoon in the camp. The previous night, we had glimpsed the tents of another trekking party on the far side of the Rodophu meadow. As the trekkers from the group ambled past on the way to their camp, we chatted to a few. Then, from another group, a guide arrived out of breath, accompanied by one of his horsemen. They had left their guests with another guide and were searching for a stubborn horse that had wandered off with its load and was now well and truly lost. The guide was anxious to contact his office in Thimphu to let them know. With no mobile signal in this area, he was grateful to borrow our satellite phone. He and the horseman would spend the night in our camp and continue their search the following morning.

Norbu joined us for dinner, confessing that he didn't feel well. He had a headache and felt dizzy; he suspected because of the altitude. We were concerned, as was he. While I had worried that Krista or I might succumb to altitude sickness, it hadn't crossed my mind that Norbu, or any of the crew, might be affected. Without Norbu, the trek just wouldn't be the same. We gave him some Diamox and headache pills and sent him to bed, hoping that he would feel better in the morning.

Outside, the glacier glimmered. It was blisteringly cold.

THE DAWN OF A NEW DAY

The night passed in a fitful blur. A combination of snorting yaks, jangling horse bells, the altitude and sub-zero temperatures kept deep sleep at bay. Not yet fully awake, I was aware of the crew stirring in the dining tent, where they had bedded down for the night under piles of hairy horse blankets. I burrowed deeper into the warmth of my sleeping bag, delaying, for just a few moments, the inevitable onslaught of penetrating cold.

I crept out of the tent before our bed tea arrived. Outside, the frigid, brittle air stung the back of my throat. The ground was frozen hard, a glittering frost coating every surface like a dusting of icing sugar. There was no sign of the clouds that had lingered over the previous days. The camp was quiet, under the watchful gaze of Gangla Karchung.

Not far from the tents, I scrambled onto a smooth slab of polished granite, which sparkled with mica. Dawn was my favourite time of day in the mountains, when the tranquillity of the landscape had an intensity that was often lost in the distractions of the day. A pale moon still hung above and as daybreak arrived the empty sky was streaked with burnt orange and striking pink and every fluorescent colour in between. Rippling mountain ranges were layered in infinite folds, jostling for position in this postcard scene: rocky in the foreground, rising to snow-covered giants, before merging with the horizon in a purple-blue haze.

For millennia, these mountains have cast a spell over humankind.

Meaning 'abode of snow' in Sanskrit, the Himalayas stretch in a great crescent, from Nanga Parbat in Pakistan to Namcha Barwa in south-eastern Tibet. Since the early days of climbing, mountaineers and adventure junkies have flocked to these noble mountains, home to nine of the world's ten highest peaks. The headwaters of three of Asia's great rivers – the Ganges, the Brahmaputra and the Indus – each begins as a tiny stream in this vast jumble of gorges, mountains and glaciers. But it isn't just climbers, nature lovers and thrillseekers who are drawn by the lure of the Himalayas. For centuries, Buddhist and Hindu pilgrims have come to visit sacred temples and religious sites, tracing the origins of their faith back to this region.

The Himalayas seem to embody a deep spirituality and nowhere more so than in Bhutan. For those living here, it is the abode of the gods, a land of saints and sages, a safe haven for ghosts and spirits. Tantric masters hid sacred scriptures, called *terma*, in caves and under rocks, leaving them to be rediscovered in years to come by *tertons*, enlightened treasure-finders. Hermits hide themselves away in inaccessible caves to meditate in the serenity of the mountains. Tales of mystics with supernatural powers are commonplace, perhaps inventions of holy men of old, and believers seek out paradisiacal secret valleys, called *beyul*, where the spiritual and real worlds collide. Powerful unseen forces are revered, and both Buddhist and pre-Buddhist beliefs engender in the Bhutanese a deep respect for the natural world.

Watching the arc of the sun slowly appear from behind the horizon, I was enchanted: the otherworldliness of Bhutan seemed very real.

Perhaps there was something that brought mountains and spirituality together. Slemish Mountain is not far from my childhood home in Ballymena. An ancient volcanic plug, it stands a mere 150 metres above the Antrim Plateau and 437 metres above sea level. It is no more than a pimple on the landscape compared with the peaks that surrounded me in Lunana, but, just like many of Bhutan's sacred mountains, Slemish has deep religious significance: it is believed to be where Saint Patrick, Ireland's patron saint, found his faith. As I was remembering blustery summer afternoons as a child, scrambling up Slemish with my sister and parents in the footsteps of Saint Patrick, a loud whistle brought me back to reality. Agye appeared on the slope behind the camp, rounding up the horses that had been left to roam overnight. The aquamarine water of the glacial lake, which had been a lacklustre grey when we arrived the previous afternoon, now shone iridescent under an extraordinary blue sky. It was a promising start to the day.

Back in the tent, Krista was awake and our ginger tea and washing water had already been delivered.

'Guess what?' she asked as I unzipped the tent door.

'What? Is Norbu feeling better?'

'No, well, I don't know. But we get to wear clean walking pants today!'

'Yippee!'

With sixteen days of trekking and few, if any, opportunities to wash and dry gear, we had worked out our changes of clothes in advance: trousers had to last for four days. Neither of us had brought gaiters – an oversight in the conditions we'd had so far – so it was a treat to consign our muddy, wet walking trousers to a laundry bag and break out a clean pair. Such simple pleasures.

'I wonder how Norbu's doing? Have you seen him yet?' I asked.

'No, not yet. I hope he'll be okay.' Krista replied. We would soon find out.

Norbu appeared in the dining tent at breakfast.

'Good morning, Sunshine,' Krista said. 'How are you doing today?'

'Good morning, Aum. I am much better, thank you. The medicine you gave me is very good.'

I wasn't convinced that one dose of Diamox was responsible for Norbu feeling better, but I was glad that he did. He had just been talking to the guides from the other trekking party that we had seen at Rodophu.

'They told me there are more trekkers, a couple of days behind us. They are Russian,' Norbu said.

I had never met Russian trekkers before. I wondered if we would cross paths with them at some point.

'I was talking with the guides about your walking,' Norbu continued. 'They told me I shouldn't let you walk so fast or you will get sick. I told them only I am sick.' He paused, smiling. 'I was remembering the old man last year at Jangothang who thought you walked so fast.'

On our trek to Jhomolhari, Krista and I had met several local characters on the trail. As we rounded a corner, we almost bumped into two men, lounging on a grassy embankment by the side of the path. They desperately wanted to talk to us but they didn't speak English and our Dzongkha wasn't quite up to the mark. So we resorted to charades. They mimed something. We mimed back. We thought they might have been telling us we needed to take a bath (which we probably did). One of them rubbed his tummy. Was he hungry? I gave him some nuts. Then he patted his head and we thought he might be ill so I handed over a Panadol. That wasn't it either. I sat down. He sat down next to me. Was he lost? Were we? We decided we should keep walking. We set off, none the wiser about what they might have been trying to tell us. The more animated of the two started following closely behind. We began to wonder about his motives. Where was Norbu when we needed him? We quickened our pace. Our Bhutanese friend did the same. By this stage we were practically sprinting through the forest and for ten minutes he was right on our tail. Eventually we looked around to find he was no longer behind us and we breathed more easily. As we ate dinner that evening, who should turn up but our man from the trail. He spoke with Norbu, who thought the man was perhaps drunk. That explained a lot. He told

Norbu that Krista and I walked like 'running dogs'. We took it as a compliment. And now, on our trek through Lunana, we had a reputation to live up to.

Promising Norbu that we would slow down, we set off after breakfast on an open, sun-drenched trail.

'We will wait for you at the pass, Norbu,' I said.

'Okay la. Slowly, slowly!'

The clarity of the light, after the dullness of the previous days, was striking, and, exhilarated by the brightness and warmth of the sun, we settled into an easy rhythm.

The other trekking party had camped just behind us and it wasn't long before we'd caught up. I chatted with one of them.

'Do you think everyone who does the Snowman Trek is having a midlife crisis?' he asked.

I assured him that, as far as I was aware, I was not in the throes of a midlife crisis and I didn't think Krista was either. I wondered about the implications of his question for him and the rest of his party. When I told him I lived in Australia, he pointed out two other members of his group who had stopped just ahead and, per the Australian way, were liberally applying sunscreen.

I said hello to my fellow Aussies, Anne and David, who, it transpired, lived less than half an hour's drive from us, in the small town where our children went to school. David's children had attended the same school. Six degrees of separation was alive and well – even on top of a mountain in Lunana.

Although only nine o'clock, it was already hot in the high-altitude sun. We were in an exposed, dry basin, where the landscape was almost lunar. It was devoid of trees, of all vegetation; there was no surface water, no sign of life. The tough grasses had disappeared, ousted by grey scree. On the leeward slopes, the ground was partially hidden beneath streaks of gravelly snow. Lunana skipped on ahead. We followed at a steady pace, crossing a wide boulder-strewn plain, before a short but demanding ascent to the pass.

We had done the hard yards the day before, so the Karchung La wasn't much more than an hour's walk from our camp. But it was a tiring, breathless climb, scrambling over loose, sharp stones. Gasping in the crisp, thin air, I felt my heart pound and my calves scream as I plodded up the final incline. I stopped to admire two crystal clear lakes in a bowl to the right of the trail, glad of the chance for a brief rest. Nearly there.

Krista was already at the pass, which was marked by several cairns. I picked up a stone, as I always did, and added it to the pile of rocks. A vibrant string of prayer flags, like flamboyant party bunting, rippled against a blue sky. The altitude here was 5020 metres, the second-highest pass of the trek. I celebrated with a grateful shout of *'Lha gyalo'* ('May the Gods prevail'), the traditional acknowledgement in Bhutan on reaching a mountain pass. I felt ridiculously happy.

LUNANA AT LAST

'Wow!'

The high Lunana plateau unfurled in front of us, reaching to the very ends of the earth: a remote empty land of yaks and nomads. Ahead, our trail swept down from the pass in a wide arc, coiling away into the distance. It was eclipsed by the imposing peaks of Jekangphu Kang, Tsenda Kang and Teri Kang, giants of 7000 metres plus in a land of eternal snow. I wondered what secrets lay hidden in the folds of these mountains? What lives lived and lost in this wild landscape? What sacred treasures concealed by holy men in secluded valleys? Perhaps the Shabdrung himself had followed these deserted trails.

The Karchung La marks the division between the grazing lands of the Layaps and the Lunaps, the people of Lunana. From this point, it was still another three days' walk to Thanza. It felt like we had reached the point of no return. This was the real gateway to Lunana.

The view was truly breathtaking. Only the rustling of prayer flags, stirred by the breeze, broke the silence. Krista and I sat down to enjoy our 360-degree panorama. Back towards Narethang, the surface of the two turquoise green lakes glimmered like glass, reflecting streaks of high cirrus clouds and the bluest of skies. Behind them, a series of interleaving spurs, their bald domes a rich chocolate brown flecked with snow, gave way to a succession of serrated white pinnacles, like rows of Levantine minarets.

It wasn't long before Norbu crested a ridge below us, making his way slowly up to the pass, followed by Rinzin, Torchen and our faithful dog.

'Where have you guys been? We've been here for ages,' I shouted to them, as they zigzagged up the final incline to the pass.

'You were supposed to slow down,' Norbu shouted back.

'We did!' Krista responded.

We sat at the pass for a short time, all of us content just to be still. As we looked across at the infinite mountains, Norbu thanked us for bringing him here.

'I'm sure it's the other way around, Norbu,' I said, 'you have brought us here.'

'Until I met you two, I never really understood why guests wanted to go walking in the mountains,' he said. 'Now I do.'

The raw beauty of a scene as remote and spectacular as the one spread out before us was hard to describe. Photographs could not capture the vastness and splendour of such stunning topography. Only by being there could you hold that image in your heart. The view from the Karchung La was one that I would hold in mine.

The trail lurched steeply away from the pass. We launched ourselves, helter-skelter, down a confusion of stony scree, steep initially, then undulating along a pebbly moraine. Rocks large and small skidded underfoot. To our right, a string of glacial lakes, milky white this time, mirrored the snowy ridge above them. We followed a well-defined path, not carved for trekkers but worn into the hillsides by generations of Lunaps who had trodden these rustic mountain highways. In Lunana, these sinuous tracks remained the plateau's main access routes. Newly built farm roads, which were gradually replacing the network of footpaths across the country, had not yet reached Lunana. In all probability, it would not be long before they did. And then the thrill of this remote wilderness trek would disappear, lost forever in the inevitable march of progress.

With the worst of the day's exertions behind us, we stopped for tea and biscuits with Norbu, Torchen and Rinzin, all of us perched on car-sized boulders that littered the slope next to the trail. The weather was glorious and, away from the wind in the shelter of the moraine, we relaxed in warm sunshine. It was such a contrast to our miserable breaks in the rain over the last few days.

'Norbu, you have finally organised some sunshine for us,' Krista quipped.

'I am always trying to please my guest,' Norbu said. 'Did I tell you about my two guests from America? The ones who asked me if they could have a "garden meditation"?' he continued.

'No, tell us!'

'I told them that I would organise it straight away,' he began. 'The problem was I no idea what a garden meditation was. I called to my manager and we decided we must prepare a beautiful garden area for the guests, where they could to do their meditations. The staff made everything ready, in a quiet area in the grounds of the lodge. They swept the grass, brought pot plants, mats, chairs and snacks so we were all set for the garden meditation. Then I brought my guests.'

'They looked around and they said to me, "What is this, Norbu? Why have you brought us here? Where is the teacher?"

'I asked, "Teacher? Why you are needing a teacher?" After some time we worked it out,' he said. 'They did not want to meditate in the garden. They asked me for a *guided* meditation. But I thought they said *garden* meditation. So the staff had to come and take everything away again. We try very hard to please the guest but sometimes we make mistakes.'

As we sympathised with Norbu's wasted efforts, an impressive stream of horses trotted nimbly down the trail, escorted by the horsemen. Lunana gambolled along behind, her tail held high. I recognised some of the horses as ours. The rest belonged to the other trekkers who weren't far behind us. In total, there must have been close to sixty horses. They made quite a spectacle: following obediently nose to tail, carrying everything from our much-loved gas heater to an umbrella. One horse wore a wooden saddle but carried no load and I wondered if he was injured. Norbu explained that he was a young horse, a novice, learning the ropes of life on the trail. For now, he was excused from carrying any weight. His time would come.

We slotted in behind the horses. Showers of gravel rained out from under their hooves and they kicked up clouds of dust, forcing us to hold back. When we reached the end of the moraine, another awe-inspiring vista opened out, with the Tarina valley reaching away towards the magnificent sugarloaf of Teri Kang, sheathed in perpetual snow. At 7127 metres, it towered above the valley, dwarfing the summits on either side. Hanging glaciers twisted and turned down from the peak, flowing into glittering glacial lakes, the colour of lapis lazuli. For millennia, this landscape had been sculpted by glaciers and rivers and by the constant barrage of wind and rain, ice and snow. The results were stunning.

I thought of the lines of Welsh poet WH Davies: 'What is this life if, full of care, We have no time to stand and stare?' This was a place to stand and stare. It was a privilege to be here.

THE LONG WAY DOWN

I stood for a few moments, mesmerised by the view.

'That is the Tarina Valley,' Norbu told us, pointing into the distance. 'Our campsite for tonight is down there.'

'That's over 1000 metres below us, according to the guidebook,' Krista replied.

'Time to go down!'

It was a long, knee-jarring descent, which began with a precipitous track hugging a cambered ledge. To one side, a sheer drop. An elderly man, his face like a withered apple, suddenly appeared below us. He wore an ancient, dirt-stained *gho*, a pair of running shoes and a red knitted beanie, pulled down over his ears. His legs were bowed, like the sides of a horseshoe, yet he trotted up the slope behind his horses with an agility that belied his advancing years. There was no room for all of us on the slender path, so Krista and I retreated to a rocky outcrop, away from the drop. The horses edged their way past, one by one. The old man nodded a silent acknowledgement in our direction, without breaking his pace, apparently oblivious to the merciless angle of the slope.

Not far along the path, we stopped on a grassy platform for our picnic lunch. But Norbu was concerned.

'You should not sit here. This plant has a strong smell – it can make you ill,' he said.

Neither Krista nor I could smell anything out of the ordinary and didn't quite believe that we would be overcome by a noxious plant during our half-hour stop.

'Shall we risk it?' I asked.

'Yes, let's live dangerously,' she replied. 'It's worth it for the view.'

Behind us, a gushing waterfall spilled down the mountain, through thickets of rhododendron bushes spread across the slopes all around us. We looked straight across at a panorama of glaciers, glacial lakes and snow-covered summits. Lunana watched us like a hawk as we ate, waiting for any scraps that might come her way.

When we'd finished, we left the boys to their lunch while we set off down the trail. It would be a relief to sleep at a lower altitude tonight. I was looking forward to the temperature being a few degrees warmer and not having to gasp for air.

'See you at the bottom,' Norbu shouted after us. 'We will catch you up.'

'Okay la,' I shouted back.

Far beneath us, our horses looked no bigger than ants, the horsemen like the tiny matchstick men of a Lowry painting, weaving their way around the curves of the switchbacks. Krista and I zigzagged down the treeless hillside. Around sharp corners. Between low bushes and shrubs. On and on, down and down, for more than 1000 vertical metres. We stopped to shed a layer of clothing. Once more, to reapply sunscreen. I marvelled again at the old man's speed at the top of this never-ending series of tight switchbacks. I felt my toes jam repeatedly into the front of my boots and wondered whether my record of being blister-free in Bhutan would hold. Our conversation was a reflection of the moment: the steepness of the descent; how glad we were to be walking down, not up; how hot it was; what had happened to the crew, who were supposed to be catching us up. Finally, the trail levelled out as we approached the end of the descent: we had reached the valley that, just a few hours earlier, had seemed so far below us. A morass of streams came together and the ground was, once again, sticky underfoot.

'Ugh. Back to glar again.' Krista grumbled.

'So much for our clean trousers,' I replied.

Walking through mud was beginning to feel like second nature.

Norbu and the boys were nowhere to be seen, so we walked on without them. A few minutes later, a shrill whistle brought us to a stop. It was Norbu, with Rinzin and Torchen, breathing more heavily than normal as they hurried to catch us.

'You are so fast!' Norbu giggled.

Krista looked at the three of them, falling about laughing. 'What's so funny?' she asked.

'After our lunch, we took a short cut. We were going to surprise you. We were sitting there, chewing some yak cheese, waiting for you. We were wondering where you have been. Then, we are thinking you have gone already. We had to run so fast to catch you.'

'Well then you should have shared your shortcut!' I replied.

We were following the river, the trail overshadowed by cliffs that reared up into fluted crags, their upper reaches basking in the red glow of the afternoon sun. We walked through a river-nourished corridor of giant ferns, with mountain springs trickling out of walls of rock, bearded with bottle-green mosses and lichens. This was the Land That Time Forgot. If someone had told me dinosaurs still lived here, I would almost have believed them. In fact, the Tarina valley was a favoured grazing ground of another unusual creature: the takin, Bhutan's national animal. Legend had it that the takin was created by the Divine Madman. Having feasted on a cow and a goat, he was reputed to have taken the head of the goat, stuck it on the skeleton of the cow, and used his wizardry to bring it to life. And so the takin was born. With the rounded nose of a moose, the body of a bull, shaggy coat and short flat horns, it was one of the world's ugliest beasts. It was found only in the Eastern Himalayas.

'In summer, a herd of takins often graze here,' Norbu told us. 'But now, they have gone down to lower grazing for the winter.'

Takins were shy creatures and seeing them in the wild required perseverance and a touch of luck. An easier option was to visit the Takin Preserve, a small sanctuary on a hillside overlooking Thimphu. These Thimphu takins had lived in a mini zoo in the city until the 1980s, when His Majesty the Fourth King decreed that the zoo animals be given their freedom. Rather bizarrely, the takins were not rehomed but left to wander freely. They were soon cruising the streets of Thimphu with abandon, scavenging for food and causing traffic chaos. After a few weeks, they were brought to the hillside reserve, where they have remained, as a very well-fed tourist attraction.

We crossed several streams on sloping log bridges, Lunana dancing across without a sideways glance while I edged forward, anxious not to slip and end up with wet feet, or worse.

'Are we there yet?' Krista asked.

It had been a long day. We passed the other group's campsite but there was still no sign of ours. Then, as suddenly as we had been enveloped by the forest, we left it behind, emerging into a bright clearing. This was our home for the night, next to the babbling Tarina Chu. The horses, glad to be free of their loads, took it in turns to sink to the ground and roll awkwardly, as horses do, rubbing off the sweat and dirt of the day, before quenching their thirst in the river.

As dusk fell, I watched as Thinley expertly build a campfire, arranging a pile of dry leaves and bark with a pyramid of fallen branches over the top. Crouching down, his cheek close to the ground, he blew into the heart of the fire, encouraging the reluctant flames to take hold. It wasn't long before the branches were hissing and crackling, sending showers of sparks into the night sky. I hunkered close, letting the heat wash over me.

AROUND THE CAMPFIRE

On the other side of the fire, Agye sat cross-legged in the dirt, whittling a flat piece of log with his knife. His craggy face glowed in the orange light.

'Can you ask him what he's making, Norbu?'

'One of the horse saddles has broken. He is making a new one,' Norbu replied, without having to ask.

I could see the wood gradually taking on the shape of the saddles worn by the horses. Agye burnt holes through the wood with a metal rod, which he heated in the flames of the fire. Ropes salvaged from the broken saddle would then be threaded through the holes and used to secure the horse's load. This was subsistence life in the mountains, with a spirit of resourcefulness that had largely been lost from the highly developed world, where everything you could possibly want was available at the click of a mouse and, once broken, was discarded and replaced. In the wilds of Lunana, there was no local store to buy a replacement when something was damaged. These horsemen performed the role of farrier, vet and saddler, as well as tending to their charges on a day-to-day basis. Their horses were their livelihood and they looked after them well.

A fiery sunset dipped below the cliffs, turning the ochre through deep purple to black. The temperature fell with the dying light, but we had escaped the numbing cold and dampness of the higher elevations. My legs were gently tired and I felt relaxed, the efforts of the day behind me. I thought of campfires back home and tried to explain to Norbu about toasted marshmallows. Marshmallows hadn't yet made it to Bhutan and he didn't understand the joy of putting little pink balls of puffed sugar on the end of a stick and turning them in the embers. I promised to bring some for him to try the following year.

'Norbu, can you tell the horsemen about our visit to Laya in 2011?' I asked. 'I would like to ask them about the school.'

'Yes la, I will.'

I waited patiently for Norbu's speech in Dzongkha to finish. His translations always seemed to be much longer than the original English and I often wondered what embellishments he added for the benefit of his Bhutanese audience. While he spoke at length to the horsemen, I told Krista about my visit to the school in Laya.

In 2011, accompanied by the headmaster of Laya Community School, Phuentsho Drukpa, we had stepped inside a gloomy classroom. The students sat five or six to a wooden desk. As we came through the doorway, they immediately stood to attention, chanting in unison, 'Good morning, madam.' The teacher said something in Dzongkha to the Grade 1 children and in response the entire class performed a perfectly synchronised, collective nose wipe along the sleeves of their *ghos* and *kiras*. Tissues had not yet made it to Laya.

The struggles facing the children of Laya had really struck me. One boy, aged about six, had the taut shiny skin of burns scarring across his face and neck. The headmaster had explained that the little boy had been burned by a *bukhari*, the traditional wood-burning stove of the Himalayas. Often, young children were left at home to fend for themselves, while their parents worked in the fields or looked after their livestock. Although the *bukharis* were a great source of heat in high-altitude homes, they posed a serious hazard for small children who, left unsupervised, could sustain serious burns if they fell against them.

At another desk, I had been shocked to see a girl about the same age with black spots of frostbite around her nose and mouth, scars that would likely stay with her for the rest of her life, a permanent reminder of the harsh environment in which she lived.

Norbu had finished his speech to the horsemen about our visit to their village two years previously.

'Can you ask them if there are now heaters in the school, Norbu?'

There had been no functioning heaters in the school in 2011, despite the freezing temperatures in October, before the onset of winter proper. Moved by the plight of these students, my group had decided to contribute to the cost of buying *bukharis* for the classrooms, and I had always wondered if the heaters had made it to the small mountain school.

After much animated discussion, Norbu the horseman, whose children attended Laya school, confirmed that, yes, the heaters had been installed and the families at the school took it in turns to bring a log to heat the classrooms. I was delighted. It was a small world, especially in Bhutan.

'Do the horsemen know the girl who was sick?' I asked.

At the school, I had met one of two girls being sponsored by the RENEW scholarship program. The other girl, Karma, had been at home, sick, on the day of our visit but Phuentsho had insisted we visit her. We had followed the headmaster up the hill behind the school, to the simple stone house where she lived. There we found Karma, pale and drawn, lying on a pile of blankets. The others in our group had waited by the door while Norbu ushered me inside.

The home was bare: a rough mud floor, a few blankets piled in one corner, a couple of cooking pots and some boxes of dried food. And very little else. No electricity, no running water. A few possessions in the one basic room.

Crawling on the floor was a much younger girl, a toddler. Her short dark hair was matted, her only piece of clothing a filthy top. She seemed oblivious to our arrival.

Karma must have been taken by surprise to find the headmaster and several strangers turning up on her doorstep. She stood up shyly, her eyes downcast. I felt awkward, embarrassed to be intruding in her home when she was unwell, and suggested to Norbu that we should leave.

'It's fine,' he had insisted.

Norbu had spoken gently to Karma and she replied in a barely audible whisper. She had a fever and a headache, he said. Her mother was out with the yaks so she was home alone, looking after her younger sister. Norbu explained that her sister was three years old. She had been born disabled after their mother was beaten in a domestic violence incident during her pregnancy. The little girl was unable to walk and didn't speak. As I watched her haul herself around the room on her hands and knees, she wet herself. Urine ran down her mud-streaked legs and soaked into the floor. No one seemed to notice.

I found some headache tablets in my daypack to give to Karma but it was for her little sister that my heart ached. I wondered what life would hold for her. She had been dealt such a cruel hand: living in a mountain village two days' walk from the nearest road, and with limited health care facilities. It seemed very unlikely she would receive the medical support that she needed. It was a grim reminder of how tough life in these mountain villages could be.

'You were very sad,' Norbu said now.

'Yes, I was.' I replied. I had left their home in tears.

LIFE IN LAYA

One of the things I love about a trekking group of just two is the chance to interact, not only with the guides, but also the rest of the crew, in a way that rarely happens in a larger group. As we sat around the campfire in the Tarina valley, I enjoyed the opportunity to learn a little about the horsemen of Laya, who were equally curious about our lives in Australia.

Krista showed them photos on her iPad of our children's school, our homes, the beach, the ocean. They were mesmerised, both by the iPad itself, and the photos. None of the horsemen had ever seen the ocean. They all said they would like to but didn't think they ever would. It seemed such a foreign concept here among some of the world's highest peaks.

The horsemen's lives had been spent close to home. Agye had been to Tibet many years ago, walking across the mountains before taking a bus to Lhasa. But that was as far as it went, in terms of foreign travel. None of the three had been on an aeroplane. Talk of flying led to Norbu telling us about his recent, and only, aeroplane flight, when he had accompanied a guest from Bumthang back to Paro.

'I was very frightened,' he told us. 'I thought the plane would fall out of the sky.'

He had spent the entire flight in a clinch with the passenger next to him, panic-stricken at every change in engine noise.

'The horsemen would not like to go in an aeroplane,' Norbu said. 'They are preferring to walk.'

'What do they think of the new road being built from Gasa, towards Laya?' Krista asked.

A lengthy conversation in Dzongkha ensued.

'Ah, very good, very good,' Agye interjected, before lapsing back into Dzongkha.

'He says it will make their life easier when the road is finished,' Norbu explained. 'They are very happy that electricity is coming to their village.'

We learned that, with the advent of democracy, local political leaders were promising electricity and roads to previously isolated villages, hoping to win favour among their electorates. Electricity pylons, like the ones we had seen, were being installed and power would soon arrive in Laya. Life for the Layaps would change quickly.

After listening to a long speech from Agye, Norbu told us that the horsemen were intrigued by the fact that Krista and I were travelling in Bhutan alone, without our husbands. Agye wanted to know how we'd managed to get ourselves to Bhutan all the way from Australia, and was in awe of the ease with which we travelled. He explained, via Norbu, that the women of Laya didn't travel anywhere on their own and wouldn't feel comfortable visiting Punakha, the nearest big(ish) town. He said they wouldn't know what to say or how to behave if they were on their own. Krista and I were definitely not cut out for life in Laya.

The horsemen thought we were very brave. Since Bhutan was probably the safest country I'd ever visited, being brave hadn't crossed my mind.

'Are you not scared, being on your own?' Norbu translated.

I had been asked this question several times before leaving home: two females, with a male crew, in the middle of nowhere. Did we feel safe? The answer was yes, completely. Without exception, the crew were polite and helpful and treated us with respect. And, anyway, they couldn't keep up with us.

I felt both safe and relaxed here, free from the expectations of the material world, where I often felt judged on what clothes I wore, what car I drove, what school my children attended. Why did any of those things matter? Here, around the fire in Lunana with the horsemen, there was no misplaced sense of superiority; we were all as grubby and as smelly as each other. I was conscious of there being no agenda with these men. They were inquisitive about our lives, just as we were about theirs, each of us fascinated to learn how the other lived.

Sangay and Rinzin had finished their chores in the kitchen tent and came to join us. The conversation turned to matters of the heart.

'Do you have a girlfriend, Rinzin?' Krista asked.

Rinzin lived in a bachelor pad in Thimphu and we teased him about his love life. He smiled sweetly but refused to be drawn. We moved on to the topic of marriage. Agye told us that the Layaps mainly married among themselves. There had been some marriages between Layaps and Lunaps, he said, but the Layaps would not contemplate marriage with someone from Lingshi, for example, just three days' walk to the west, 'because we don't know where they've come from,' Agye explained. Similarly, people from the lowland towns and villages, such as Gasa or Punakha, were not suitable marriage material.

'Would you ever consider living in Laya?' Agye wanted to know.

I didn't quite know what to say; it was not a proposal to which I had given much thought. I found it hard to imagine countless days in a small mountain village like Laya. Yet the horsemen seemed to be at one with the world and I envied them the apparent simplicity of their lives. After a moment of consideration, Krista suggested that we'd both struggle to work in Laya without the internet. That seemed to satisfy them.

As the evening wore on, Agye brought a horse blanket over to the fire and laid it out on the ground. Curled up, and with the blanket pulled over him, he soon fell asleep. Lunana followed suit. The rest of us gradually fell silent, transfixed by the flames. A log collapsed, sending out a shower of glimmering sparks before fading into the inky darkness. Gradually the flames died back, leaving silvery ash and smouldering embers in their wake. It was the perfect, peaceful end to a fantastic day.

UPS AND DOWNS

We had met only a handful of people on the trail and the emptiness of Lunana was barely tempered by the few signs of human intrusion. The stony ruins of a yak herder's hut, a string of tattered prayer flags strung over a stream, a solitary cairn, teetering on a mountain pass: transient signs of the people who inhabited this plateau. This lack of human presence was a striking feature of our trek through Lunana and was in contrast to many Himalayan treks, where it wasn't uncommon to be stuck behind a queue of other trekkers for days on end: the trail to Everest Base Camp, which sees over 30,000 trekkers every year, was a case in point. Today, we would pass through the first permanent settlement on the trek, the village of Woche. We were now six days' walk from Gasa.

I awoke early. A tenuous darkness still lingered in the valley, the first rays of the sun only just creeping up from behind the ridge. A hoar frost had rendered the short blades of grass as rigid as the rocks scattered among them. The only sound was the river, pulsing over boulders on its journey downstream. I savoured the moment, the peace of the early morning and the calm, unhurried beauty of the sunrise. It would be another hour before the sun would reach our camp, to banish the chill shadows for another day. Until then, the cold called for several layers of warm clothes.

Krista and I set off after breakfast on our own again, accompanied by Lunana, who stuck close to our heels.

'The trail is next to the river,' Norbu had instructed us. 'We will catch you up. Then we climb up to Woche village.'

We followed a network of muddy paths that twisted through groves of trees and sunlit glades. Secluded but well-trodden, these trails were followed, season after season, by the Lunaps and their yaks as they moved from one pasture to another. Waterfalls over 100 metres high dropped down the sides of the cathedral gorge, like streaks of molten silver. Shiny black walls of granite glistened beneath the spray. We could have been walking through Tolkien's valley of Rivendell.

Krista and I relished being in this wilderness and we talked about the contrast between this trip and our previous lives. Krista grew up in Las Vegas, establishing successful businesses there and in the UK and Australia and travelling between them. I worked for many years in an international law firm in the City of London, juggling young children and the constant demands of corporate clients who would settle for nothing less than a twenty-four seven service. We had both left those frenetic times behind for a more relaxed lifestyle in Noosa but even there, work, study, children's activities and sporting commitments, school events, fundraising initiatives for the AHF, fitness and socialising left little down time. Our time in Lunana couldn't have been more different.

Norbu, Rinzin and Torchen caught up with us before we started the strenuous climb up to Woche village. An avenue of juniper trees closed in on both sides of the trail, forming a canopy above us. Dappled sunlight threw shadows over the uneven ground, creating flickering patterns of light and shade that made it tricky to judge where to step.

'This is ridiculous,' I said, as I took my sunglasses off and put them back on, yet again, in the ever-changing light.

'What does ridiculous mean?' Norbu asked. 'You say everything is ridiculous: the mud, the rain, the rice at lunch, the steepness of the slopes, the number of horses.'

It seemed an apt description for our experience of all of the above, but maybe we had been overusing it. It was time for a discussion on the etymology of 'ridiculous'.

As we talked about the English language and the use of words, we strayed on to some of the difficulties of English pronunciation. The Bhutanese, like many others, stumbled over the English 'th' sound. Norbu was no exception, pronouncing 'thirty' as 'tirty'. He could almost have passed for an Irishman. Almost. We went through a list of examples of the 'th' sound for him to practise but, for reasons unknown, he fixed on the word 'girth'. Perhaps it was being accompanied by all those horses. For the next week he'd wander the mountains of Lunana muttering 'girth' under his breath.

It was Norbu's turn to teach us some Dzongkha. We learned the word for 'mud', *dam* which was pronounced like dum. 'Dum, dum, dum' was the order of the day. He tried to teach us a couple of Dzongkha phrases, but with limited success.

'How are you?' '*Ga dey bey yoe?*' It didn't stick.

The response, which we finally mastered – '*Na mey, sa mey, ley zhom yoe*' – translated roughly as 'I'm feeling fantastic!' We practised it again and again.

Half an hour passed and Norbu posed the question, '*Ga dey bey yoe?*'

I'd already forgotten the response but then remembered '*Sa mey, na mey*', which sent everyone into fits of laughter.

'What's so funny?' I asked.

'This means "I'm having my ups and downs",' Norbu explained.

I'd got the 'sa' and 'na' the wrong way round, but, ironically, this alternative version perfectly described today's walk. Although there were, as always in Bhutan, more ups than downs.

Breathless from the steep climb, and thinking about our ad hoc English and Dzongkha lessons, we let the conversation lapse as we focused on getting to the top of the ridge. Lunana ran ahead, looking back occasionally to check that we were still following her.

Eventually, we emerged from the shade of the trees on the endless slope. To our left, the stubble of recently harvested fields, delineated by sagging stone walls, was the first sign of cultivation we'd seen since leaving Gasa. We had arrived at Woche.

We clambered over a gap in a wall and made our way towards a handful of houses. Woche village sprawled along a shelf, commanding a panoramic view over a sun-drenched valley. Across the valley, sweeping mountains were swathed in sage-green forest, while, behind the village, sheer cliffs rose heavenward. More hamlet than village, Woche consisted of fewer than a dozen dwellings, all south facing, built to take advantage of the sun on this high ridge. With their thick tapering walls of rammed earth and small, shuttered windows, the traditional Bhutanese mountain homes were designed to withstand bitter cold. They gave the impression of age-old permanence, their sloping walls reminiscent of the flanks of the mountains towering behind them. Houses aside, there was nothing here, apart from yaks and prayer flags and a few mangy dogs.

In Woche, as in most of the villages we would visit, the juxtaposition between the old and the new was there for all to see, on the roofs of the buildings. The traditional wooden shingles were held in place by smooth river boulders, like chalky ostrich eggs. Long ears of grain hung in bundles from the open space between the top floor and the roof, typically used for drying crops: a scene that I imagined had changed little in hundreds of years. Except that now, propped among the drying sheaves was a solar panel or two. Although the government was gradually bringing electricity into the mountains, it had not yet reached Woche and, in the meantime, solar was the only source of power.

Two little girls, aged about five and two, were draped over a wall outside one of the farmhouses. With sleek, jet-black hair and large doleful eyes, they met our gaze as we approached, before scampering off to hide behind their mother's *kira*. We waved to them but it was not enough to coax them out.

Norbu spoke to their mother. She invited us into their home.

In front of the house, shrivelled black mushrooms, like mature tadpoles, and fat bulbs of wild garlic were spread out on a tarpaulin, drying in the sun. Stepping over a high threshold, we found ourselves in a large, well-ordered room that had the faint smell of wood smoke. It was gloomy inside, the only source of light the open door behind us. The interior walls and floor were wood, the ceiling darkened by soot. There was no furniture, just a shiny *bukhari* standing in the centre of the room. Cardboard boxes, gleaming aluminium pots and pans, packets of dried food and bulging sacks of rice were piled high on the shelves. There were at least three dozen aluminium pans of all shapes and sizes and I wondered how one family could possibly need so many. Stacked along the side wall were piles of thick, neatly folded blankets that the family would roll out at night to sleep on and under. Ropes of plaited yak wool dangled from hooks on the ceiling next to twisting dark strips of drying yak meat. A photograph of the Fourth King, in a plain wooden frame, hung at an angle: the only decoration. The lifestyle of the people of these mountain villages was a simple one. Generations cooked, ate and slept together in one small room, where privacy and personal space were concepts from a different world.

An older lady appeared from behind a stack of rice sacks. She had been crouched next to the *bukhari*, warming her hands. Dressed in a dark checked *kira*, the pattern obscured by patches of grease, she stood up slowly, her slender frame casting a long shadow across the floor. Her skin, like that of most of the older residents in this region, was lined from years of exposure to the high-altitude sun. She greeted us with a slight bow, her hands pressed together at her chest in a gesture of prayer. '*Kuzuzangpo la,*' she murmured from across the room, before launching into a rapid exchange in Dzongkha with Norbu. She hobbled over to pull us into the room, clasping our hands in hers.

The mother of the two little girls stood quietly to one side, her younger daughter clinging to her skirt. The older girl played with an empty plastic drink bottle. She tossed it up in the air, watched it roll across the floor, then bolted after it, delighting in the rattle it made as it bounced across the wooden floorboards. I thought of my own daughters at the same age, and their overflowing toy boxes, and was struck by how the lottery of birth had such a profound impact on our lives.

Norbu interrupted my thoughts with the news that Ama (the Bhutanese word for grandmother and a term of respect for older women) had problems with her eyesight. She was very excited to hear that we had a supply of spectacles from Australia and watched eagerly as Norbu delved into his daypack. She tried on several pairs before finding some that helped with her vision. Although the likelihood of us having the perfect prescription for her was slim, the chances of her having her eyesight professionally tested, or prescription glasses made, were even slimmer. She was thrilled with her new Gandhi-style glasses and modelled them for us proudly, a beaming smile displaying her red-stained teeth.

I was frustrated by my inability to chat to this lady, to ask about her life. Our conversation consisted of a confusion of *kandinchey las* (thank yous) and *tashi deleks* (good lucks) with a couple of references to Thanza, Bhutan's highest and most remote settlement, if for no other reason than to establish our credentials. I thought it best not to risk my recently acquired Dzongkha for 'I'm feeling fantastic' in case I got it badly wrong.

Ama shuffled over to the back wall of the room, where she rummaged around on one of the shelves. From a plastic bag, she produced three strings of hard yak cheese which she pressed into our hands. The little cubes were covered in a smoky, grey grit. She insisted we take them: one each for Norbu, Krista and me. Although I knew I wouldn't eat mine, it would have been impolite to refuse and I was confident the crew would be delighted to help me out. We thanked her and wished her well.

By the time we emerged into the sunlight, word of our arrival in Woche had spread. A posse of young boys abandoned their game

I was so lucky to have Krista with me on this trek – not many people would willingly spend their hard-earned holidays walking through mud and snow for sixteen days. But it was an experience beyond anything either of us could have imagined.

Tshering Norbu, our guide, loved the T-shirt we had printed for him – although we never did explain the meaning of 'pimp'.

When the horsemen arrived with their herd at the start of the trek we were shocked – surely two of us wouldn't need twenty-three horses to carry our gear!

Our large group was soon joined by another four-legged friend: a stray dog we called Lunana, who saw straight away that we were soft touches. She always knew where to find the dining tent.

Teaching Norbu how to plank. It helped with his 'bellies'.

The school in Lingshi that Krista and I visited in 2012. On my first visit to Bhutan, a small rural school like this one inspired me to return each year, raising funds to educate some of Bhutan's most disadvantaged children.

The children in Thanza were more interested in Krista's phone than our adventures. While mobile phones are commonplace in much of Bhutan, they're still very much a rarity in these tiny mountain villages.

Handing out supplies at the school in Chozo Dzong. It's not easy to get desks and chairs to a school that's a seven-day hike from the nearest road.

This yak herder was in hysterics when I showed her this photograph, which wasn't the reaction I expected. Apparently her hat was on backwards.

After a long and happy life (hopefully) this yak's head serves as a handy hook and decoration. As for the dead mouse? Who knows …

People in the mountains were often happy to have their portraits taken, though we couldn't understand why so many stuck their tongues out. Inexplicably, Norbu said that 'it's a sign of shy'.

Left:
'Where's the bridge, Norbu?'
Our guide's response:
'We do not have.'

Below:
'Noble Rhubarb' must be one of the world's most striking plants. It only grows at altitudes above 4000 metres, and those we saw in Lunana looked more like trail markers than exotic flora.

What else were we going to do with all that snow?! With Norbu, Rinzin and Sangay.

The view along the Tarina Valley – it was a knee-jarring 1000-metre descent to the valley floor below.

Bhutan's most famous monastery, and a sight like no other: Tiger's Nest. As the story goes, a Buddhist saint arrived at this spot on the back of a flying tigress – we, on the other hand, had to walk.

Understandably we weren't permitted to take photos of the naked monks' dance, but there was no lack of spectacle to be found in Bumthang. Religious festivals in Bhutan are incredible riots of colour and activity.

Heading into danger – as the blizzard set in, and our team began to fall to altitude sickness and snow blindness, we had nowhere to go but onwards, simply hoping that that we would make it out the other side. Even then, the beauty of this harsh landscape was undeniable.

of archery to come sprinting over. They discarded their bamboo bows and arrows on the way and crowded around, staring, their faces breaking into welcoming smiles when we greeted them in Dzongkha. I asked Norbu why the children weren't at school.

'Their parents need them to help at home, with the animals and crops,' he replied.

Woche was several days' walk from Gasa, back the way we had come; Lhedi, the main village in Lunana, was still another day's walk in the other direction. School for these children would involve a demanding trek over high passes, and weeks spent away from their families. I wondered what the future would hold for them, without an education.

We waved goodbye to Woche and set off across a stretch of fallow ground. On the edge of the village, a row of tall poles, each with a dusty white flag flapping in the breeze, paid tribute to loved ones who had passed away. Grazing between the flags, a couple of grunting yaks gave us contemptuous stares. Following Norbu's example, I armed myself with a rock, in case of an unexpected charge. Lunana, who had hung back when we arrived in the village, perhaps fearful of the local dogs, came bounding up behind us, taking her place at the head of our little procession.

Norbu had told us, more than once, that the men in Bhutan did all the hard labour. When we passed a woman and young girl raking the soil, with not a man in sight, we questioned him again about this idea, which we were beginning to think was a figment of his imagination. All the field work in these isolated villages was done without the aid of modern machinery and, from what we had seen, often by women.

'Look, Norbu!' Krista said, pointing out four women, a little further on, threshing grain with a flail: two long skinny sticks, their ends bound to form a hinge. Swinging the handle, they swirled the top stick above their heads, bringing it down hard with a *thwack*, sending clouds of chaff into the air. They worked together in harmony, singing softly. Ignoring all the evidence to the contrary,

Norbu remained adamant that men were front and centre when it came to working the land. We agreed to disagree.

The trail leading out of Woche stayed high above the river. It was dry and unusually flat. In the clean, fresh air, the resinous scent of fir trees was unmistakeable. We found the perfect lunch spot: a flat, grassy clearing that looked back towards Woche and the snow-capped mountains beyond. The trees were a glorious riot of autumnal colours, the mossy ground soft, warmed by the sun, and the air perfectly still. It was hard to leave such a peaceful setting, so we stayed after we'd finished eating, relaxing and chatting with the guides. Our morning had had all the elements of the perfect Himalayan trek: sparkling waterfalls, a sunlit gorge, snow-topped mountains, friendly locals, warm sunshine and endless blue skies. It seemed almost too good to be true.

'Come on, Norbu, let's do a plank!' Krista suggested.

'Plank? What is a plank?' Norbu asked.

'On your elbows. Legs straight out behind you. It will be good for your bellies,' Krista instructed.

The three of us found a spot on the grass, doing our best to avoid the ever-present dried yak dung. And so began Norbu's daily plank routine.

Our horses trooped past; camp would be set up before our arrival.

'From here, it is almost all downhill,' Norbu assured us.

We had come to take such pronouncements from Norbu with a pinch of salt. His interpretation of 'almost all downhill' was often quite different from mine. But for once he was right. It was a gradual descent to our campsite next to the river. As we set off again on this, one of the shortest and easiest days of walking, Rinzin pointed out tomorrow's route on the other side of the valley: a high trail that climbed at an unappealing angle before disappearing in the direction of some impressive mountains. Tomorrow was going to be a different story.

MASS DEBATING MONKS

We followed a shingle path down to the banks of the Woche Chu. The river was a steely blue, the colour of the glacier that fed it, its turbulent water frothing over shiny black rocks. Over the bridge, a couple of hundred metres away, we found our campsite for the night, at the bottom of a rocky slope, covered in mosses and low alpine plants.

The crew hadn't quite finished setting up the tents so Krista and I told Norbu we'd wander back to the river.

'You must wash your legs,' he said.

'Okay,' Krista replied hesitantly.

'Does he think our legs are in dire need of washing?' I wondered, or was this the Bhutanese way of suggesting a paddle?

We found a stretch of sand next to the bridge and followed Norbu's instructions. Although the water looked inviting, we should have known better. A few seconds in the icy deluge was more than enough. Instead, we lounged on the sand, content to watch the crystal-clear water from a comfortable distance. A pair of dragonflies dive-bombed the surface, the afternoon sun bouncing off their iridescent wings.

After a relaxing hour on our little riverside beach, we made our way slowly back to the camp. I picked up a horseshoe, discarded on a patch of gravel. I would take it home as a lucky gift for Molly.

'Did you wash your legs?' Norbu asked.

'Our legs are quite clean, thank you,' Krista assured him.

In the dining tent, our afternoon snack awaited: ginger tea, cartons of sweetened mango juice, sugary biscuits and a big bowl of puffed rice. Called *zaw* in Dzongkha, crunchy roasted rice was often served to guests to stir into tea but was just as delicious on its own. We demolished the lot.

Before long, darkness fell: the deep, penetrating blackness of night in a remote valley, far from any artificial light. As well as setting up camp, the crew had been busy collecting firewood. Soon, another campfire blazed orange against the night sky. We gathered around it to eat dinner on our laps, swapping stories with the horsemen, watched closely by Lunana for leftovers. Tonight we had one of our favourite trekking treats, *momos,* or Tibetan dumplings, stuffed with meat and vegetables and served with a fiery chilli sauce – they were delicious.

Norbu made an innocent remark about our plans for Bumthang. Perhaps it was altitude-induced delirium, but I caught Krista's eye and we dissolved in peals of laughter. The crew looked at us quizzically.

A few days earlier, I'd been reading aloud to Krista from my Lonely Planet guide about places to visit in the Bumthang valley, where we would finish the trek. A description of the Namkhe Nyingpo monastery read: 'If you're here between 4.30pm and 6pm check out the mass debating in the courtyard, behind the main monastery …' While I read 'mass debating', Krista heard 'masturbating', and so began a running joke about the afternoon shenanigans in the monastery courtyard in Bumthang.

But how to explain this to a collection of Bhutanese horsemen and crew? After a lengthy but hilarious explanation, necessitated by gaps in Norbu's English vocabulary, he understood. In the process, he added a new and rather formal word to his growing English lexicon: 'masticate', which somehow came up in the course of this discussion. Whether Norbu translated for the horsemen, we would never know.

When it was time for bed, Krista and I bade the crew goodnight and retired to our tent, feeling relaxed and happy. What a difference the weather made. Not to mention a double entendre in the guidebook.

ROAST PHEASANT

Day seven of the trek. Today we were due to reach Lhedi, the main village and administrative centre of Lunana. But first, Agye had to shoe a horse. He emptied the contents of a shabby canvas bag onto the ground. A random collection of horseshoes clattered out, many of them bent and tarnished. From his pocket he produced a little twist of plastic, full of nails. Selecting one of the horseshoes, he hammered it into shape with a rock and nailed it onto the horse's hoof with the same rock. No tools. No fuss. Job done in less than five minutes.

Before we set off, I too had a job to do. A good friend in Australia, Michelle, had kindly sponsored the cost of the two extra horses needed to transport the school books. I wanted to take a photograph of one of the horses with her business name and logo, which I had printed and laminated before I left home.

The lead horse, in his fancy headgear, was the perfect candidate. I approached him slowly and managed to balance the card between his ears. But by the time I'd stepped back to take the photograph, the card had fallen and he was standing on it. I tried to move him forward but he refused to budge. I managed to retrieve the now scruffy card and wedge it under the strap of his head collar. He was having none of it. He shook his head crossly and sent the card between the hind legs of the horse next to him, where it would have to stay. The crew, who were eating breakfast inside the kitchen tent, looked on indulgently. They had probably decided the previous evening that Krista and I might be mad. Now they would have been in no doubt.

The day began with a steep ascent behind the campsite. We followed a winding yak trail that looped up through low prickly bushes while Lunana darted in and out between them. I felt tired this morning, stopping to catch my breath several times before we reached the summit. I found myself counting steps. One hundred steps, then rest. One hundred steps, then rest. Left, right. Left, right. The rhythm kept me going. I watched a solitary eagle, gliding on the thermals above our heads. I wished I too could move so effortlessly.

From the top of the ridge, we had an extravagant view for miles in every direction, our tents tiny blue dots far, far below. The climb continued towards that day's pass, the Kesha La. On our right, the cobalt blue waters of a slender lake rebounded the inverted image of the rocky slopes high above.

'This is Green Lake,' Norbu said.

I thought Turquoise Lake might have been a better name: the colour of the water was exactly that of the beads worn by the women in these high valleys as a sign of wealth and status.

I was excited to reach the pass, at 4666 metres. It was garlanded with strings of prayer flags flapping manically in the breeze. Krista and I were on our own again, enjoying the empty space. She had waited for me on the climb earlier in the morning, now I slowed down for her on the descent – an old knee injury was starting to niggle. We stopped to allow Norbu to catch up, but when Lunana arrived instead, we kept walking with her. The boys weren't far behind us.

A rocky trail interrupted by boulders spiralled down from the pass. As we skidded down, Norbu stopped abruptly, motioning for us to be quiet. A haughty Himalayan pheasant was roosting on a rock, perfectly framed in a grove of small bushes as it surveyed all who passed. Its luxurious brown and russet feathers provided perfect camouflage among the autumn colours of its perch.

'Maybe we will have pheasant for dinner tonight,' Norbu joked.

In reality, as Buddhists with a firmly held belief that all animal life was interdependent, killing any form of wildlife was off-limits for the majority of Bhutanese. Cementing this respect for all sentient beings was the conviction that, through an on-going cycle of reincarnation, you or I once were, or might become, that yak or monkey or pheasant. No one wanted to risk shooting a bird in case, by doing so, they exterminated their grandmother. No wonder the pheasant looked at ease.

Reincarnation was one of the central pillars of Buddhism: a belief that all sentient beings were caught in a continuous cycle of rebirth, called Samsara. Actions in past lives (karma) determined in which one of six realms rebirth would occur. Only by obtaining enlightenment could we reach Nirvana and be released from the suffering of Samsara.

I thought about this key tenet of the Buddhist faith a few months later as I read *Treasures of the Thunder Dragon: A Portrait of Bhutan*, by Her Majesty Ashi Dorji Wangmo Wangchuck. In it she tells the remarkable story of a little boy discovered in 1998 to be the reincarnation of Desi Tenzin Rabgye, an important ruler in Bhutan from 1680 to 1694. At a National Day celebration in Kanglung, in Eastern Bhutan, Her Majesty was intrigued by a little monk and brought him to the royal enclosure. Although only four years old, he approached the King and told him they had met before, when the King had been very old. He said that he had built Taktsang (Tiger's Nest) on the King's orders and now he wanted to return to Tango, where he had left his things. Speaking in Dzongkha rather than the native language of Eastern Bhutan, the little monk confirmed his parents' names as those of Desi Tenzin Rabgye's parents.

After being interviewed by a senior monk from the Central Monk Body, the little monk was taken to meet the Chief Abbot, where he observed all the intricate rituals associated with meeting

Bhutan's most senior lama, recalled his past life and displayed many other signs that he was, indeed, the reincarnation of Desi Tenzin Rabgye. He was taken to Tango monastery, outside Thimphu, where he took up residence and from then on was revered as the reincarnation of this important figure in the history of Bhutan.

IT'S A YAK'S LIFE

Spread out below us was the small village of Tega, spilling down the mountainside in a series of shelves. There were few pockets of human settlement in Lunana: this was one of them, and there wasn't much to it. Some stone farmhouses, surrounded by dry stone walls and clusters of poles displaying tall prayer flags.

A small *chorten* marked the entrance to the village.

'Wrong way!' Norbu chided as I wandered absent-mindedly towards the right side of it.

I corrected my faux pas. It was always clockwise; to walk anticlockwise was sacrilege. I hoped we wouldn't be stuck down by bad karma as a result.

The most striking feature of Tega was the view. Across the village and down the valley, Gangchen Singye, also known as Table Mountain, loomed large, a flat-topped massif covered in snow, dominating the Pho Chu valley.

Outside a farmhouse, a gaunt old lady, kneeling on the ground next to a small patch of barley, looked up as we approached, her eyes crinkling into the deep lines of her face. Her bony hands clasped a small sickle shaped like a perfect half-moon. She stood up stiffly and spoke to Norbu in a hoarse whisper. He told us that, although many of the villagers would soon be leaving Tega, she would spend the winter months here at her home.

Life was tough in these isolated villages, for all the residents but especially for the elderly. We were now seven days' hard walking from Gasa and at least the same distance from the nearest road in the other direction. In a few weeks' time, Tega, like the other small settlements in Lunana, would be completely cut off from the rest of the world when snow blocked the high passes. Villagers who spent the winter in Tega would be stranded in the mountains until the following April or May, when the snow melted and Lunana was once again accessible. For those who fell ill during the winter, there was little chance of any outside medical help.

As we wended our way between the farmhouses, we were greeted by the ferocious barking of a pack of flea-bitten dogs, which slunk from the shadows to check out the strangers in town. Dogs aside, it was strangely quiet in the village. There was hardly anyone around. We met one young woman who had just returned from rounding up her yaks. She told Norbu that she and her family, accompanied by two other families from the village, were preparing to set off the following day for their annual migration to lower altitude where they would spend the winter with their herd. The journey would take them five days and they wouldn't return to Tega until after the snows had gone. Theirs was a life dictated by the seasons, and followed by the semi-nomadic people of this high plateau for hundreds of years.

Yaks, awaiting their departure to lower grazing, peppered the fields on the outskirts of the village. They were the lynchpins of life in Lunana. The domestic yaks that roamed the plateau were believed to be descended from wild yaks caught in Northern Tibet, ten thousand years ago. With their thick coats and layer of fat, they were so well insulated against the cold that they couldn't survive the balmy temperatures below 2500 metres. Their grazing habits changed with the seasons and dictated where the herders and their families lived. In summer, they migrated to high pastures, returning to lower grazing before winter. A school education played second fiddle to these grazing habits, with children skipping classes for months at a time when their families followed the yaks to far off meadows. In the remote highlands of Lunana, where the nearest shop was several days' walk away, yaks were a source of meat, milk, butter and cheese. Their shaggy coats provided wool for weaving and their dung was used for fuel. All these supplies could be sold or bartered. As Buddhists, the Bhutanese were reluctant to slaughter their animals, but in the mountains, where food was scarce and protein in high demand, yaks who reached the end of their useful life might accidentally come to grief, falling down a steep slope or succumbing to some other 'yak-cident', en route to a hearty stew.

As well as providing sustenance and fuel, yaks were also widely used for ploughing and as pack animals, by both locals and visiting trekkers. They were hardy and sure-footed, could carry much heavier loads than horses and were better able to find a trail buried under snow. That made them the preferred beast of burden for long, high-altitude treks, despite their reputation for being cantankerous and their tendency to stray great distances overnight to graze.

As we made our way past the harrumphing yaks of Tega, the words (or some of them at least) of the funny little poem, 'The Yak' by Hilaire Belloc, popped into my head.

> As a friend to the children commend me the Yak.
> You will find it exactly the thing:
> It will carry and fetch, you can ride on its back,
> Or lead it about with a string.

And there it stayed for the rest of the day.

'SCHOOL AMONG GLACIERS'

We walked in single file, the path not wide enough for two abreast. For another hour, we tramped up the valley, until the trail opened out onto a flat grassy area, confined on one side by cliffs that tilted towards us, with great slabs of bare rock clinging tenuously to the upper slopes. Where the cliffs had given way, huge boulders littered the grass. A small stream flowed gently through the clearing and, on the other side, a sheer wall of rock fell vertically down to the river. Another perfect lunch spot. Lounging on a grassy carpet in warm sunshine, surrounded by dramatic scenery and with most of the day's walk done, I couldn't have been happier.

After lunch, we passed two tiny settlements of just a few houses each, overlooking the river. In front of one farmhouse, two little boys perched on a wall. They sat perfectly still, watching us with wide eyes, heads tilted, like a pair of roosting owls.

For the first time in several days, Rinzin took a call on his mobile phone. I guessed we must be close to Lhedi now, where, we'd been told, there was intermittent phone reception. He chatted excitedly, shouting 'Lunana, Lunana' repeatedly into the handset. Perhaps the person he was speaking to couldn't quite believe what he was hearing.

We skirted around a gushing waterfall. The distinct path we had followed earlier in the day had all but disappeared. We were walking along the valley bottom, where the trail was indistinguishable from the riverbed itself, a belt of smooth rocks, often wobbly and far from easy to walk on. Displaced boulders were evidence of the 1994 flood, when a glacial lake beyond Thanza, Lugge Tsho, burst through its moraine dam with devastating consequences. A raging torrent had swept heavy boulders, trees and other debris downstream. Tragically, at least twenty people lost their lives, and land and property suffered damage as far away as Punakha. Twenty years later, the river was a shallow flow, no more than a few metres wide, but clambering over the rocks alongside the channels I could imagine the violence of the flood, the destruction that it caused and the terror of anyone caught in its path.

A wet, muddy slope rose sharply from the riverbed to the village of Lhedi at 3850 metres and my breath was laboured and rasping by the time we'd slogged up to the top. As the district headquarters of Lunana, Lhedi was the most significant settlement on our trek route. Yet it was no more than a few dozen homes, built on a flat shelf above the river with a backdrop of tall granite cliffs. The houses were mostly two-storey, solidly built of local stone, some with a traditional shingle roof, some with aluminium. Scattered between the houses were huge slabs of rock, many not much smaller than the homes themselves.

Lhedi was bigger than Woche and Tega but, like them, had no shops, no market, not even a makeshift stall. There was, however, a basic health unit and a school, which, some years ago, featured in a Bhutanese documentary called *School Among Glaciers*. The Lunana Community School was a single-storey stone building, the once-white paint now flaky and peeling. It had been built in a U shape and its three sides partially enclosed a bare yard. The Bhutanese flag, a dragon imprinted on an orange and yellow background, flew proudly from a tall pole. School had finished for the day but we stopped to chat to a teacher who was locking up the classrooms. Norbu explained that our trekking company had been in touch with the local governor about our visit. The teacher wasn't sure whether the message had been passed on to the school but he promised to inform the headmaster that we were staying in the village. We thanked him and set off to find our campsite.

On a rocky outcrop above the school, a lone black yak stood motionless, silhouetted against the cliffs. It looked almost unreal, as if it had been stuffed and mounted on a rugged pedestal to keep watch over the village. A few minutes later, we found our tents, in front of the Basic Health Unit. It wasn't so long ago that Bhutanese health care was solely dependent on traditional remedies, dispensed by village healers. Today, a network of Basic Health Units operated across the country, providing limited Western-style health care, free to all Bhutanese. Traditional practices had not been completely relinquished, though; in fact, quite the opposite. The Institute of Traditional Medicine, in Thimphu, produced age-old remedies made from plants, animals, minerals and other natural products, dispensed medicine and trained doctors. It remained key to the country's health care system. Although there had been significant advances in the provision of medical treatment in recent years, in villages like Lhedi facilities were rudimentary and the health care workers qualified to provide only basic care. A serious injury or illness could be treated only if the patient could be transported to hospital. Until very recently, this had involved a difficult journey of several days on foot. The arrival of Bhutan's first helicopter means a medical evacuation by air is now more readily available, although, as always in the mountains, it is subject to the constraints of weather and terrain.

AN INVITATION TO BED TEA

The students of Lunana Community School, who lived in the village, were making their way home. Some carried their books and pencils under their arms, others had tucked them into the front folds of their *ghos*: there was no need for schoolbags. Spotting the new arrivals, a few of the children climbed onto a large boulder, from where they kept a careful watch on the goings-on of our camp. Several pairs of wide, dark eyes followed our every move.

Perhaps afraid that she was missing out on some excitement, an old lady emerged from a farmhouse to perch among the students. She was small and stooped, like many of the elderly mountain women we had met. In keeping with the traditional style of the highlands, she wore her greying hair short, falling in a perfect circle around her eyes. The sun-darkened skin on her face and neck was shrivelled and grooved, like corrugated cardboard. She looked ancient. When she smiled, most of her front teeth were missing, but her eyes were vibrant. And, despite the harshness of her life here, she looked elegant in her handwoven *kira*, pinned at the shoulders with large silver brooches and accessorised with heavy turquoise beads. I was intrigued by her yak hide boots, which curled up at the toes, like a genie's slippers. These were the traditional boots of Bhutan, rarely used now that cheap rubber imports were readily available. I had only seen the ornate felt versions, decorated with colourful embroidery, on officials at festivals or in tourist souvenir shops. These were the real deal. This lady, head to toe in traditional dress, could have stepped straight out of a bygone era. She spoke to us in rapid Dzongkha, apparently unaware that we had no idea what she was saying.

A couple of the students, brave enough to practise their English, took over.

'Excuse me, madam, what is your name?'
'Where do you come from?'
'What is your country?'
'What called your village?'
'Where is your husband?'
'How many children do you have?'
'What age your children?'
'Are you having boys or girls?'
'Do you like our village?'
'Where are you going?'

They were curious but shy. No one demanded pens, sweets or money: the common refrain of children along many Himalayan trekking trails. We answered their questions and asked some of our own. I was intrigued by their answers to 'What would you like to do when you grow up?': a doctor, a teacher, an engineer, a pilot. These children's parents were yak herders, mostly illiterate. Yet their career ambitions were on par with a typical Australian private-school student.

As the afternoon light faltered, our audience drifted away. The old lady left without a word, shuffling back to her home. A chill wind picked up, barrelling down the valley from the snows of Table Mountain. With the sides of the dining tent billowed furiously, as the gusts tugged wildly at the tent ropes, Sangay came to our rescue, securing the tent before it took flight. It was time to beat a hasty retreat. We ducked inside the dining tent, where a welcome mug of ginger tea was the perfect antidote to the shrieking gale.

A tall man in a smart *gho* arrived at the door of the tent. He introduced himself, in English, as Tenzin Thinley, the headmaster of the school. He had come to welcome us to Lhedi. We explained about the books and made arrangements to present them to the school the following morning.

'We don't get many visitors,' he told us. 'I am very pleased that you are visiting our school. I will see you in the morning.'

An hour later, two girls, aged about twelve or thirteen, delivered a handwritten note from the headmaster. It read as follows:

> *Ministry of Education*
> *Lunana Primary School*
> *Lunana-Gasa*
> *Bhutan*
> *Asia*
> *Invitation for the Morning Bed Tea – 2013*
> *On behalf of the Lunana Primary School, the undersigned would like to request the tourist families to kindly gather in front of your campus and humbly the students are liking to serve the morning tea at 06.30 AM. Hope the manager will consider the upon management request. Your cooperation shall be highly obliged.*
> *Thanking you.*

The letter was signed by Tenzin Thinley and bore the Lunana Primary School stamp.

An invitation to bed tea from the headmaster! How could we refuse, even if 6.30am was a bit earlier than we might have liked. We told the girls that we would be pleased to accept the headmaster's kind invitation. Their mission accomplished, they hovered at the tent door, unsure whether to stay or go. We encouraged them to stay and, with Norbu translating, asked them about their life in Lhedi. They were the school captains, they said, and were in their last year at the Lunana Community School. They both lived in Thanza, another day's walk up the valley, and boarded at the school here.

They didn't see their families for weeks at a time. They were hoping to continue their studies next year at a secondary boarding school in Damji, near Gasa, a week's walk from their homes in Thanza. One of them wanted to be a doctor, the other a teacher. They were clearly determined students and I hoped their parents would support them in their quest for an education, which so many children across the world took for granted.

SONGS FOR THE PRIME MINISTER

That evening, with help from Norbu and Torchen, we sorted through the rest of the books, pencils and crayons that we would give to the students the next morning, while reminiscing about our visit to the school in Lingshi, the year before

'It was very dark, but you two were determined to go,' Norbu remembered.

Krista and I had arrived at Lingshi School late in the evening, accompanied by Norbu and one of our horsemen. We had been forced to set out for the school as darkness fell due to Norbu's very late arrival into camp with one of our group.

As we'd approached Lingshi School, we were greeted by the gentle melody of children singing. The students were practising songs for the upcoming Prime Minister's visit. All through our trek, we had been two days ahead of the Prime Minister as he visited the isolated villages on the Jhomolhari route. We had seen several examples, along the way, of preparations for his visit, including the construction of a wooden platform in the middle of a deserted stretch of forest, where he would give a speech. It was an unlikely spot for electioneering, but then the concept of the prime minister of almost any other country I could think of setting off on a week-long hike through high mountains and sparsely populated forests seemed even more unlikely.

Peering into the stone building, I'd felt as though I'd stepped back in time. A single bare light bulb hung from the ceiling, its flickering glow barely making a dent in the shadows. There were no desks, chairs, or books. About fifty pairs of eyes, in a sea of grubby faces, had turned towards the open door. The children of Lingshi School sat cross-legged in rows on the rough wooden floor. A hush had fallen across the room as we stooped through the low doorway. We were the novelty attraction.

The headmistress, Madam Pema, arrived and, to our amazement, said that she had been expecting us. She had just returned to the school that day after walking, like us, from Paro. A forest ranger had told her that he had met us earlier and that we were planning to visit the school in Lingshi. The jungle telegraph was working well.

Madam Pema made us very welcome. She explained that most of the students were boarders at Lingshi School. The roof of the main school building had been blown off in a storm so, with no functioning classrooms, some classes had to be held in tents. Looking around at the children, seated quietly on the floor, I noticed that many of them had sockless feet, peeping through plastic sandals. Few wore warm coats or jackets. It was hard to imagine these children spending their school days in a tent, with daytime temperatures falling rapidly towards freezing.

One of the teachers had invited the children to sing for us. There were a few giggles and shy smiles before one little boy bravely stood up and gave a recital of 'Humpty Dumpty', in perfect English. Encouraged by this bold public performance, several of the children performed a variety of English nursery rhymes and a song in Dzongkha.

As we had set off back down the trail, the darkness was overwhelming. Our horseman and Norbu sang softly to themselves. Otherwise all was silent.

As Krista and I finished organising our gifts for Lunana Community School the following morning, I wondered if our visit could live up to the magic of our evening in Lingshi.

THE MOST ISOLATED SCHOOL IN BHUTAN

When we emerged from our tent in Lhedi at 6am the following day, anxious not to be late for our bed-tea appointment with the headmaster, darkness was still lurking. A pale orange glow was just beginning to sweep down the valley; it would be a while before it reached our tent. Despite the pre-dawn chill, village life in Lhedi was already well underway. The old lady who had visited us the previous afternoon shambled past, hauling a bucket of water. Just above our camp, a young woman squatted next to a humongous black yak, leaning against its expansive sides as she began the early morning milking. Three other yaks were corralled in the yard in front of her house. They stood meekly, their hind legs tethered to short sticks driven into the ground, waiting for their turn.

It was bitterly cold and strangely quiet. I was so used to background traffic hum in my everyday life that, even though it was a week since we'd seen a car, I had to remind myself that there were no vehicles in Lhedi, or in any of the other villages of Lunana. No vehicles and no roads. Instead, villagers wandered along stony paths between houses, disturbed only by the occasional wheezing yak or barking dog. It was staggering to think that Lhedi was the administrative hub of Lunana, that all officials arrived here on foot after a six-day trek through the mountains, carrying with them anything they might need. The lack of vehicles, or any form of mechanisation, gave Lhedi a stillness that can't be found in most human settlements today.

Shivering in the cold, Krista and I set off down to the school, in search of our promised tea. The school building was deserted and the classrooms locked.

'Do you think the headmaster has forgotten about us?' Krista wondered.

'We could have stayed in bed,' I said grumpily.

While we waited, we read the notices pinned to a board on an exterior wall. I marvelled at the newly introduced winter timetable, effective from 6 October, which was enough to strike fear into the hearts of any primary school children I knew. The day began with the 'rising bell' at 6.30am and finished at 8.30pm, with 'lights off'. In between, the children had 'morning study' from 7 to 8 am, followed by breakfast and cleaning before assembly at 8.45am. The main school day ran from 9am until 3pm with another period of cleaning, evening tea and sport. From 4 to 5.30pm the students were engaged in evening study. Dinner and more cleaning took place between 5.30 and 7pm after which there was yet more study from 7 to 8pm. It was a long day.

Where was the tea? After dragging ourselves out of our sleeping bags in the dark and freezing cold, we were ready for a hot drink. When no one appeared, we returned to the camp to discover that everyone was waiting for us. The two girls who had arrived with the invitation the previous evening were standing in the dining tent. They presented us with a packet of plain biscuits and a thermos of milky tea, made by the headmaster himself, they told us proudly. I didn't have the heart to tell them I don't drink milk.

At eight o'clock, we made our way back to the school, where Norbu had already displayed the books on a table in the schoolyard. About twenty children stood guard under the flagpole. As we approached, without any prompting they spontaneously performed a beautifully coordinated low bow, chanting in unison, 'Good morning, madam!'

Tenzin, the headmaster, greeted us, anxious to know if we had enjoyed the bed tea. He introduced us to the two other teachers at the school, both male. There should have been a fourth teacher, Tenzin explained, but he had been taken ill and had returned to his home village. There was no replacement so the others did their best and shared his classes between them.

Until midway through the last century, education in Bhutan had been confined to a few monastic schools and those wealthy families who could afford to send their children to boarding schools in India. As part of a series of measures to bring Bhutan into the modern world, the Third King kickstarted a national education program, which saw a rapid rise in the number of schools across the country. One of the initial challenges for the pioneers of the new school system was to decide on the teaching language, given the number of different languages spoken throughout Bhutan; the figure was often put at nineteen, an extraordinary number in such a small country. This proliferation of languages was attributed to the high mountains that formed natural barriers between neighbouring valleys, so that each isolated community developed their own distinct language. Many of these languages were unintelligible to anyone outside the immediate area and, in some cases, were spoken by no more than a few thousand people. Recognising the limited reach of these local languages, the government decided that the school curriculum would instead be delivered in English. Dzongkha, meaning 'language of the *dzong*', was proclaimed the national language in 1971 and taught in schools as a separate subject.

One of the two teachers at Lunana Community School spoke excellent English, although his delivery was formal and slightly stilted. It turned out he was the English teacher. His first question caught me off guard.

'Excuse me, madam, what is your marital status?'

It sounded like a question from a passport application form. I wasn't sure whether it was polite to enquire about his marital status also, but I did so anyway. He then asked me 'my good name' and told me that he had a wife and young child back in his home village.

His baby son had been only a few months old when he left to teach in Lunana and he had missed seeing him over the previous six months. Understandably, he was looking forward to the end of the school year and to returning to his family. This had to be the most extreme of the hardship postings in the Bhutanese school system. Just getting to Lhedi was an ordeal and, once here, there was nowhere to go until the end of the school year, when returning home would involve another arduous trek, assuming you made it out before snow blocked the passes. I had nothing but admiration for this dedicated little band of teachers, who had sacrificed their own family lives to bring an education to the children of Lunana.

'There are forty-four children enrolled in the school. However, today we only have twenty-six,' Tenzin told us.

He explained that many children drop out of school during the year. Their families were yak herders and, he believed, often did not see the value in their children attending school. If the parents moved away to graze their yaks, they took their children out of school and many did not return.

Tenzin told us that the school was due to close soon, before the passes were snowed in and the whole Lunana region completely cut off. The school might not reopen again until next April or May, he said, depending on when the snow melted. Although many Lunaps spent the winter in Punakha, the children did not attend school there, resulting in an extended break in their education, sometimes for as long as six months. By the time they returned, they had forgotten most of what they had learned the previous year. 'But what to do?' Tenzin asked.

The English teacher rang a brass bell. It was time for assembly and we were the guests of honour. The students lined up outside, facing the school building, with the teachers, Tenzin, Krista and me at the front. I felt a bit dowdy in my trekking gear, compared with the students, in their *ghos* and *kiras*. They stood formally in lines, hands clasped behind their backs, youngest at the front, and sang the national anthem before being led by a senior boy in a prayer, which everyone recited loudly after him. The whole scene was slightly surreal, with the backdrop of snow-capped mountains and yaks ambling casually past. No one paid any attention to them, except me.

Tenzin made a short speech in Dzongkha and the children chanted collective responses. I was invited to tell them a little about our trek. As I explained that we had travelled from Australia, the English teacher disappeared into a classroom and emerged with a world map, making the geography lesson a little easier. Pointing out our home in Queensland, I wondered whether these students had any concept of the vastness of Australia, how flat and hot it was compared with their mountainous kingdom. Krista spoke about the books we had brought and explained that they had been bought with money raised by our own children's school back home.

Speeches over, we had beanies, pencils and crayons to distribute. The children were thrilled and bowed politely as they accepted our small gifts with outstretched hands and a quietly whispered 'Thank you, madam'.

'Please, you must visit the classrooms,' Tenzin insisted.

The teachers escorted us proudly around the school.

The rooms were dark, with bare wooden floors and rough stone walls. The decor was spartan: no posters on the walls, just a traditional blackboard and a few wooden desks and chairs, the only indication that we were in a classroom. The children, about seven or eight in a class, were sitting quietly at their desks but all stood up together to sing 'Good morning, madam' as we entered each room.

The English teacher handed me a piece of chalk, suggesting I write my name on the blackboard. The students looked at me expectantly. I scratched out my name, the chalk screeching over the surface. I caught the eye of a boy in the front row. He looked away, casting his eyes down over his empty desk. Was he worried I might ask him to pronounce my name? It had the dreaded 'th' sound in the middle.

'My name is Heather,' I announced.

The teacher took charge, asking the class to repeat my name. Nothing. Were they stumped or just shy? I repeated 'Heather'. Wide grins stared back at me and a giggle spread across the room. The teacher pounced, addressing a girl in a beautiful green silk jacket. I was transported back to my own school days: I'd been painfully shy and hated being picked to answer questions. But the girl in the green jacket stood up, repeating my name almost perfectly before abruptly sitting down again.

'She is our top student,' the teacher announced. He proceeded to sing her praises as she jumped to her feet again, her gaze fixed firmly on the floor. I couldn't imagine any of my children's teachers singling out a student in front of a visitor in this way, but perhaps this was the expectation in Bhutan.

I wished we could have stayed longer at Lunana Community School but we had a long way to go and another school visit to make. The English teacher had told us it would take about five hours to reach Mendrelthang School, a sister school in the village of Chozo. From there, it was at least another hour to our camp at Thanza.

We posed with the teachers and students for an all-school photograph, before returning to our tents to pack up.

'*Ju gey!* Let's go!' Norbu shouted.

It was a beautiful, bright, sunny morning. The trail was dry, rambling through fir and juniper trees and, as the wind picked up, dust devils swirled across the stony ground. I revelled in the gentle gradient.

A little outside Lhedi we met an old man, his back bent almost double, limping along in the opposite direction. He flashed us a toothy grin while taking a drag on the last of his cigarette. It was unusual to see people smoking in Bhutan. In the only country in the world where it was illegal to sell cigarettes, anyone with a nicotine habit didn't generally flaunt it. Selling tobacco or tobacco products, along with smoking in many public places, was banned in 2005, although apparently the ban was not rigorously enforced. But since 2010 legislation had restricted the amount of tobacco and the number of cigarettes that could be imported legally into Bhutan. In March 2011, the new law was controversially enforced when a young monk, returning from India, was arrested for having in his possession $2.50 worth of tobacco, which he hadn't declared. He was sent to prison for three years, despite claiming that he had been unaware of the import restriction. I wondered whether the old man, out here in Lunana, knew about the tobacco restrictions. Even if he did, the chances of being caught by a zealous official at this remote spot were slim.

After our encounter with the elderly smoker, we crossed paths with a troupe of archers. They were from Chozo, they said, and were on their way to a tournament in Lhedi. They carried only their compound bows, slung casually over their shoulders, and quivers of arrows. The traditional bow in Bhutan was made from bamboo, but many Bhutanese now used the latest American-made compound bow. With a price tag of $500 and up, a compound bow had become as much status symbol as essential sporting equipment. We wished the archers *Tashi Delek* for their tournament and continued towards Chozo.

THE SCHOOL AT THE TOP OF THE LADDER

Once again, we were walking along the riverbed, boulder-hopping between the sluggish channels of the Pho Chu. Norbu, Krista and I walked together, relaxed in each other's company. There was no need for idle chitchat.

Four hours after leaving Lhedi, and an hour ahead of schedule, the small settlement of Chozo appeared in the distance. A rudimentary wooden bridge led to the right bank of the Pho Chu, veering off towards Thanza. Our horses, crew and Lunana took this route. Krista, Norbu, Rinzin and I kept left, to Chozo, threading our way between dozens of yaks. Some drank from the river, while others nibbled the sparse grass at the water's edge, completely oblivious to our intrusion in their serene mountain abode. We met a young girl with a basket on her back, collecting dried yak dung that would be burned in a fire. Up here, above the treeline, there weren't many sources of fuel.

Chozo was a huddle of simple stone houses set back from the river, at the base of a ridge. A web of twisting streams trickled through the village, coming together in a spidery, waterlogged jumble before flowing into the main river. We were back to soggy ground, jumping between rocks and tussocks of grass, trying to keep our feet dry.

I was saddened to see piles of rubbish – plastic wrappers, glass bottles and other food packaging – wedged against rocks or floating lazily in the streams. Discarded rubbish anywhere was offensive but in an otherwise pristine environment it jarred even more. Quick to lambaste the citizens of Chozo, I reminded myself of the practical difficulties of disposing of household rubbish in the back of beyond. Glass, plastic and aluminium did not just disintegrate. The nearest rubbish collection or recycling program was a week's trek away, over high mountains, and the only means of transport a horse or yak. Waste disposal in Chozo involved considerable time and expense.

Aside from the waste scattered across our path, Chozo's setting was spectacular. The pale blue glacial waters of the river flowed just below the village, bounded by banks of white silt. Behind the houses, rocky ramparts rose up to a brilliant white spine of crenelated peaks. And among the stone dwellings, a small, two-storey *dzong* was silhouetted against a perfect blue sky. This was the first *dzong* we had seen since Gasa, seven days earlier. It was the highest and least accessible in Bhutan.

Chozo was like a ghost town. The rhythmic beat of drums and the haunting, resonant sound of Tibetan horns echoed from a nearby home; if not for them, the village could have been deserted. Arriving at the *dzong* only served to heighten the sense of abandonment.

The centuries-old Chozo *dzong* was in need of urgent repair. The outer walls were riddled with cracks and the four-storey tower seemed to sag in the middle. It looked as if it might topple down at any moment. The crumbling walls appeared to have been painted recently, so maybe some repair work was underway. I wondered aloud if the monastery had been affected by earthquakes, but Norbu didn't know. Over the years, many of the *dzongs* in Bhutan have suffered structural damage from seismic shifts in the earth beneath them. The Himalayas are young, by world mountain standards. It was only 55 million years ago that the Indian and Eurasian tectonic plates collided, buckling along the line of impact to form what is now the highest and most dramatic mountain range on the planet. Those plates are still moving, resulting in frequent earthquakes across the region that have damaged many of Bhutan's historic buildings.

The heavy wooden door to the *dzong* was slightly ajar. Norbu pushed it open, the creak of the rusty hinges announcing our arrival to anyone inside. We stepped over the high threshold to find ourselves in a sunlit courtyard. Rough and uneven paving stones were interrupted by mosses and weeds, which broke through between the slabs. It was empty, silent. The stillness was broken by the whirring wings of a dove as it soared up from its nesting place high in the tower.

'The school is here,' Norbu announced.

'Here? How can the school be here?' I'd thought we were just visiting an ancient monastery.

Norbu pointed. A small painted wooden sign, above one of the first-floor doorways, announced 'Mendrelthang School'. I was taken aback. The school was housed in this rundown old building on the verge of collapse?

'We will take a look,' Norbu said. *'Ju gey.'*

Access to the upper floor was via a near vertical wooden ladder, the surface worn smooth by generations of hands and feet. Krista and I climbed up gingerly. At the top, we found the door to the schoolroom padlocked shut. There was no one around. The adjoining room had neither door nor floor: just a sudden drop through a gaping hole to the ground, several metres below. The walls were shrouded with dusty cobwebs that displayed a haul of long-deceased insects. It was hard to believe there was a school in the room next door.

Rinzin offered to try to track down the students, or someone who might know where they were. I hoped he would find them. It would be disappointing to have come all this way to visit the school only to find they'd gone home for the day, or maybe the year.

While Rinzin went off to investigate, Norbu, Krista and I lowered ourselves slowly down the ladder and found a place to eat our lunch. Clumps of weeds sprouted from the stony ground in front of the *dzong*, and a stack of empty Chinese whisky bottles was evidence of some previous shindig.

As we were finishing our picnic, Rinzin returned to report that he'd found the teacher and students: they'd been eating lunch and were on their way back. Five minutes later the animated chatter of the students heralded their arrival. Mainly boys, aged between about seven and twelve, they came hurtling around the corner, laughing and joking and falling over each other in their excitement. They scampered up the ladder at high speed, two steps at a time. On the upper floor, they leaned precariously over the low wooden balcony, a row of smiling faces grinning down at us.

The solitary teacher at Mendrelthang School arrived soon after his flock of rowdy students. He was aged in his late twenties, I guessed, dressed in a *gho*, the compulsory attire for all Bhutanese teachers. He introduced himself as Sangay and invited us to visit the school.

Carefully, we followed him back up the ladder. The heavy clunk of the bolt scraping against the solid wooden door echoed across the courtyard. A high doorstep and low lintel marked the entrance to the one small classroom. Inside, the room was panelled in dark wood. It was lit only from a single small window on the back wall. Dust motes danced across the centre of the room, in shafts of sunlight that slanted onto the wooden floor. Bright new posters of the alphabet, in English, were pinned to one wall but otherwise the room was bare. There was not a stick of furniture, no desks or chairs – not even for the teacher – no piles of books or school supplies. The students sat together on the floor. Sangay explained that the school had opened only recently. It was too expensive to have desks and chairs transported from Punakha or Gasa. Instead they would be made locally but he was unsure when this would be. We were well above the treeline in Chozo so there was no local supply of timber and the wood for the furniture, like everything else, would have to be brought to the village on a pack animal. Sangay lamented the expense of transportation and the difficulty of getting supplies for the school.

The school catered only for pre-primary and Grade 1, as a satellite school for the Lunana Community School in Lhedi. After completing Grade 1, the students would transfer, as boarders, to Lhedi. I noticed that the students were not aged four and five, as they would have been in Australia at this year level. In Bhutan, children were placed in these early classes at the age at which they started school. Away from the main towns, children started school at whatever age their parents decided to send them. So a Grade 1 class might have a six-year-old sitting next to a ten-year-old.

Echoing the comments of the teachers in Lhedi, Sangay explained that many of his students had dropped out during the year, as their parents followed their yaks to distant grazing. There were twenty-two children enrolled in the school but I counted only eleven on the day of our visit, just three of them girls.

While we chatted, Agye arrived with our box of gifts for the school. Much to the delight of Sangay and his little class, we set about distributing books, packets of colouring pencils, crayons and beanies. Sangay made a long speech in Dzongkha, which Norbu translated for us. He explained that the school had run out of pens and pencils and had a very limited supply of books. He was overwhelmed by our gifts, particularly given the high cost of bringing anything to this remote village, and thanked us from the bottom of his heart.

The children all put on their beanies, which had been generously donated by the outdoor shop Kathmandu in Australia, and posed for photographs. I felt humbled to see what a difference a small effort on our part could make to the children in these far-flung valleys. My heart sang as we said goodbye to the smiling children of Chozo.

'ALL FOREIGNERS WRITE BULLSHIT ABOUT BHUTAN'

We saw no one as we retraced our steps back through the village. It was eerily quiet.

'I never thought I would be speaking to so many principals,' Norbu said, breaking the silence. 'At first, I was nervous, but now I am getting experience. It makes me very proud, what you are doing in Bhutan.'

'Thank you, Norbu, we enjoy doing it,' I said, touched by his appreciation.

We crossed the bridge over the Pho Chu and began our walk along the opposite bank towards Thanza. Back across the valley, the white walls of Chozo Dzong dazzled in the bright sunlight. I wondered how old it was.

'There has been a *dzong* here for six hundred years,' Norbu said.

This seemed incredible, in this remote Himalayan valley, and I wasn't sure if Norbu was exaggerating. But, even if he was, most guidebooks described the age of Chozo Dzong in hundreds of years.

'Do you think the *dzong* is haunted, Norbu?' I asked.

'Why haunted?'

'I read a book recently about the Snowman Trek which said that Chozo Dzong was haunted by the ghosts of two brothers,' I explained.

'Who has written this book?' Norbu demanded.

'An American man, who has done the Snowman Trek. What do you think?'

Norbu's response was swift and pointed. 'All foreigners write bullshit about Bhutan!'

Clearly, Norbu could not be believed on everything.

Soon the valley opened out, becoming wide and flat. The *dzong* was a white speck in the distance behind us while, ahead, Table Mountain, which had been on the far horizon for the past few days, loomed tantalisingly close. We met two yak herders, encouraging their charges with whistles and flying pebbles along the trails back towards Chozo. They grinned and whispered as they passed us.

'What did they say, Norbu?' I asked.

'They are saying *"cha serps"*. It means "yellow hairs".'

I understood this to be a term used by the Bhutanese to refer to foreigners, rather than a comment on the dire state of our hair, by now unwashed for over a week. But perhaps the latter was more appropriate.

As we walked along, Norbu told us the folktale of Ap Wang Drugay. I had heard him tell it before but I was happy to listen to it again.

Ap Wang Drugay was a monk who infiltrated a nunnery disguised as a nun. Once inside, the temptation was too much for him and gradually a succession of nuns became pregnant. Perplexed as to how this could be happening, and suspecting that they were harbouring an imposter, the mother superior devised a test. The nuns were to jump over a fire, which required them to hitch up their robes, away from the flames. If there was a man in their midst, all would be revealed. To avoid detection, Ap Wang Drugay tied his manly parts back with a string that he fastened at his neck. Confident that there was nothing visible to suggest his true gender, he yanked up his nun's robes and took his turn at vaulting over the fire. But he had not bargained on the leaping flames singeing his carefully arranged string. All was indeed revealed and Ap Wang Drugay's elaborate ruse exposed.

Reflecting on the ingenuity of Ap Wang Drugay, I enjoyed the pleasant, flat walk from Chozo to Thanza, the midpoint of our trek and the highest (at over 4000 metres) and most remote settlement in Bhutan. The trail rambled across grassy meadows and passed a wide sandy beach bordering the river. Incongruous among the snowy mountains, it was said to be a legacy of a previous glacial lake outburst. And then, finally, a glimpse of Thanza, this distant outpost that had been our destination since we set out from Gasa. We slackened our pace, enjoying the easy walk. Herds of yaks speckled the slopes all around us: small black shapes in the distance, moving slowly as they grazed. A simple stone *chorten* marked the approach to Thanza and our campsite for the next two nights.

Our tents seemed to have multiplied. It turned out that another trekking group was also camping at Thanza that night.

'Are they the Russians?' I asked Norbu, as we walked into camp.

'What Russians?'

'Didn't you say at Narethang that there was a Russian party a day or two behind us?'

Norbu denied all knowledge of any Russians. After revisiting the previous conversation several times, we deduced that Norbu had not identified the other group as Russian. Rather, he'd said that they were *rushing*. The extra tents in Thanza belonged to the trekkers we had already met at Narethang, who were neither rushing, nor Russian. We later discovered from one of them that the third group, who were still a day or two behind us, were Canadian and had all been struck down by gastric problems. Perhaps that's why they were rushing.

On the far side of the campsite we spotted Lunana, striking up an acquaintance with the crew from the other group. We would have to compete for her affections in Thanza.

Exhausted, but thrilled to have made it to Thanza, Krista and I slumped into camping chairs outside our tent. Within five minutes we were ambushed by a swarm of high-spirited children, excited to inspect a couple of foreigners. The giggling, nudging gaggle closed in around us. Most just stared, although some were keen to practise their English.

'Look, this is the school at Lhedi this morning,' Krista said, playing a video recording she had made on her phone that morning of the students singing the national anthem at assembly.

The Thanza children were transfixed, crowding closer and pushing each other out of the way to get a better view of the screen. I suspected that some of them should have been at the school, rather than holed up in Thanza watching a video of it.

'Have you seen they're all wearing quilted jackets?' Krista remarked. 'I bet it's freezing here when the sun goes down.'

'It reminds me of a train journey Graeme and I did years ago from La Paz to Uyuni, in Bolivia,' I told her. 'We got on the train in La Paz in the sun, wearing shorts and T-shirts, and thought it was really odd that the locals were bundled up in overcoats and scarves, huddling under blankets. We soon discovered why – the windows were all broken and, when the sun disappeared, we were shivering in a howling gale, wishing we had a blanket.'

Like the Bolivians, the children of Thanza knew only too well how dramatically the temperature would drop: at this elevation, any hint of heat dissipated as soon as the sun sank behind the mountains. Krista and I soon scuttled off to our tent to find our down jackets.

For once, Lunana wasn't waiting outside the dining tent at dinnertime. Perhaps the other trekkers were more generous with their scraps.

Norbu came to join us.

'There's not much noise from the kitchen tent tonight,' Krista commented. 'Are they all asleep?'

'Some of them have gone to the village,' Norbu explained. 'Maybe for some night hunting …'

'Night hunting' was a term, widely used in Bhutan, for an old custom from the rural east involving boys sneaking into the homes of girls, under cover of darkness, for sex. It seemed to have been an accepted courtship ritual among farming communities, with willing girls leaving a window or door unlatched for their nocturnal visitor. Ideally, by the time the rest of the family awoke in the morning, the furtive suitor would have long since gone. Couples who were caught – through carelessness, bad luck or because they wanted to be caught – were often deemed to be married. While portrayed by some as a quaint rural tradition, today, night hunting was a sensitive subject, with critics citing stories of rape, unwanted pregnancies and sexual exploitation of women. With the growth in urbanisation, Western dating habits and changing social attitudes, night-hunting was rapidly becoming a thing of the past.

'No, no. I am joking,' Norbu said hastily, setting the record straight. 'They have gone to see if the villagers have any yak meat.'

We went to bed under a canopy of stars. With no light pollution, the wide band of the Milky Way arched overhead, clearly visible against the black sky empty of clouds. The darkness was all consuming. It felt as though I could reach out and touch it. If I hadn't seen the village across the river earlier in the afternoon, I would never have imagined that there were a couple of dozen households just 100 metres away. With none of the usual telltale signs of human habitation – no lights shining from windows, music playing, or noise of any kind – the village could well have been a figment of my imagination. It was almost as if Thanza didn't exist.

IN THE SHADOW OF TABLE MOUNTAIN

My sneezing from a few days earlier had stopped, but now I had a head cold. I was anxious that it not turn into something more serious. A blocked nose made sleeping difficult so, for the first time on the trek, I succumbed to drugs, hoping for a peaceful night's sleep. With a dose of Krista's potent cold and flu remedy, I slept the sleep of the dead and had to shake myself awake the next morning.

'How are you this morning?' Krista asked.

'I slept so well,' I replied. 'My nose is still blocked but I feel a lot better.'

'Ha! I've been awake for a bit and I thought you must be really sick – there was so much snorting and snoring going on,' she giggled, 'but then I realised it was a yak outside the tent.'

I was relieved but, listening to the grunting and wheezing from outside the tent, far from flattered. Surely my snoring couldn't have been that bad!

'Bed tea, madam,' announced Torchen and Rinzin cheerfully. It was time to get up and celebrate our second change of trousers on the trek.

The day dawned bright, but bitterly cold. There had been a hard frost overnight. On the walls of the tent, ice crystals had formed graceful patterns, like elegant sparkling ferns. As the sun rose, the snowy flank of Table Mountain crept from dark shadows through blushing pink to glistening white.

I had lost all sense of day or date. It just wasn't important. A loose grasp of time was not unusual on an extended wilderness adventure, and in Bhutan it seemed even more appropriate. For reasons unknown, the Bhutanese calendar was out of sync with the Gregorian calendar. Not only was the day of the week not what you'd expect, but months in Bhutan were given a number rather than a name, while years were described not in numerical form but as a combination of one of the twelve signs of the zodiac and one of the five elements of earth, fire, water, wood and wind. So, according to Norbu, it was the seventh day of the ninth lunar month in the Year of the Female Water Snake. That had more of a ring to it than 11 October 2013.

What mattered most was that it was the midpoint of our journey on foot, our only rest day on the trek and a chance to take it easy. I welcomed the lull in our usual routine, and enjoyed not having to pack everything up before we set off. Not so enjoyable was having time to inspect the physical effects of high-altitude trekking. The combination of searing cold, dry air and intense sun had wreaked havoc on skin and lips. My skin tone had gone from pale to ruddy. Krista's lips had blistered badly. We both had small but painful blisters on our fingers. My left eye was swollen, a sign of mild oedema caused by the altitude. Add to this the fact we hadn't washed our hair in over a week, and neither of us was looking our best. Not that anyone cared.

We enjoyed a leisurely breakfast, feasting on sausages and traditional pancakes made with buckwheat from central Bhutan, watched over by Lunana and a pack of fascinated children, who took turns to peek around the door flaps of the dining tent. We slipped Lunana a few sausages, hoping that Leki wouldn't notice that part of his breakfast had gone to the dog. Then it was time to explore.

The Lunana plateau was a primitive landscape, studded with dozens of glacial lakes. Captivating to look at, they posed a constant and significant danger. With the rapid melting of Himalayan glaciers, the volume of water held in these lakes had increased dramatically in recent years. This, in turn, led to a heightened risk of sudden and catastrophic flooding, the worst being the 1994 outburst from lake Lugge Tsho. Since then, the government had been battling to tame nature by artificially lowering the water level in some of the lakes most likely to burst. This morning, we planned to spend half a day hiking up the valley, in search of one of these unstable lakes, which had been diverted by engineers to minimise the flood risk.

'*Ju gey mosh*!' Norbu shouted. 'Let's go! We are going to follow Sangay to the glacial lake.'

'Has he been to the lake before?' Krista asked.

'He has been living in Thanza before, when his parents worked here,' Norbu explained.

So we followed Sangay's lead, if not his pace. We headed upstream, along the right bank of the river, crossing paths with a girl no older than nine or ten, who was herding a recalcitrant black yak back to Thanza. She kept him on the straight and narrow by lobbing small rocks when he veered off track. I thought of the comments from the teachers we had met the previous day, about students dropping out of school to follow their yaks.

'Do you think she should be at the school in Lhedi, Norbu? I wondered.

'Maybe, he replied, 'but I think her parents need her to help with the yaks.'

At intervals across the meadows were several rundown yak herders' huts, little more than rectangles of haphazardly piled rocks, most without a roof. Roofs were often just a tarpaulin, added when the shelter was in use and removed when the residents moved out. With winter fast approaching, the herders would soon be swapping these high-altitude meadows for lower grazing.

We loped on through pastures of rough grass and occasional tiny alpine flowers. They were all that could survive at this elevation: it was a tough environment for any form of plant life. A shallow lake captured the shimmering reflection of the rugged slopes rising from the valley floor. Crossing several small streams – sometimes on decaying wooden logs, sometimes jumping carefully from one stepping stone to another – we followed serpentine yak trails past tattered prayer flags, rippling in the breeze. There was something deeply calming about these little huddles of flags, over a stream, at the top of a pass, on a random mound of earth, often miles from anywhere, unleashing their prayers across the empty land. A haven of serenity in an already restful scene.

Ahead, Table Mountain stood in all her glory, a massive bulging bulwark of snow-covered granite that formed an impassable natural boundary between Bhutan and China. Back down the valley, it had looked as if, from here, we could touch the mountain itself. But now it seemed further away than ever. On the upper slopes, winds stirred up a snow plume that swirled from the summit. All morning, the mountain towered above us. We were accompanied only by our shadows, shrunken by the high overhead sun.

At the top of a gravelly moraine, we flopped down for a rest and to enjoy the remarkable scenery. Opposite, a barrier of ice and snow soared hundreds of metres high, falling away on the lower slopes to dark grey rocks, sculpted into precipitous cliffs. Below us, the blue-green waters of the river tumbled over piles of smooth, white boulders.

In Buddhist mythology, *beyul* were hidden valleys, blessed by Guru Rinpoche as places of peace, prosperity and spiritual enlightenment. Their locations were recorded on sacred scrolls and other *terma,* and they were said to be guarded by powerful protective deities. Perhaps this Arcadian valley led to one of Guru Rinpoche's secret *beyul*.

On the other side of the moraine, the aftermath of a rocky landslide barred our way. Boulders and scree had been washed down the valley side, into the river below, leaving a sheer drop of loose sand and gravel. Sangay danced across it without hesitation. Krista and I were a bit more cautious. It was hard to find a stable footing on the spill of rubble. One false move and the slope we stood on was likely to join the rest of the debris in the river, taking us with it. I was relieved when we arrived on firmer ground.

A low rumble echoed across the valley: an avalanche, somewhere nearby, the sound ricocheting around the mountains.

It wasn't long before we were confronted with another landslide. This time, even Sangay couldn't find a way across. Instead, we backtracked and then slid down a steep incline, to the corridor of boulders that ran alongside the river. Although flat, our route was now an eclectic muddle of unsteady rocks, worn smooth by the pounding water. They tilted precariously, as we jumped from one to the next.

'Are we there yet, Norbu?' I asked flippantly. We seemed to have walked quite a way, with no sign of the lake.

'We cannot find the bridge.'

Sangay had decided that we should have been on the opposite bank and sprinted on ahead, vaulting over boulders like a gazelle, in search of a way across. He and Norbu scaled the ridge behind us, on the lookout for a bridge, or the lake itself, while Krista and I relaxed by the river, enjoying the warmth of the sun. Lunana lay down next to us, nuzzling my hand with her wet nose, content to rest while the guides carried on.

'It's hard to believe how far we are from anywhere,' Krista said, voicing my thoughts, 'and how stunning it is here.'

Norbu and Sangay returned, forty-five minutes later, having found neither bridge nor lake.

'It has been some time now since Sangay has been here,' Norbu explained. 'The bridge may have been washed away.'

This was as far as we would go. If Shambhala, that fabled land of legends populated by enlightened beings, lay beyond, we would never know.

We retraced our steps. Sangay was very embarrassed that he had led us on a wild goose chase and scurried off to sit on his own behind a boulder when we stopped for tea and biscuits.

'Sangay, come and join us,' Krista urged. 'It doesn't matter about the lake.'

But he refused, staying resolutely behind his rock.

Krista and I strode on ahead, concerned about a much bigger issue than Sangay's hurt pride. It had been a week since we'd had a proper wash and we'd been fantasising, for several days, about the promise of a camp shower in Thanza. Despite its physical isolation, Thanza was, surprisingly, in touch with the outside world via a mobile phone tower installed as part of a flood warning system. With the luxury of mobile reception, Norbu called ahead, telling the crew to organise hot water for our shower, on our return to camp. Although there was something slightly ridiculous about this phone call, given the circumstances, we were not complaining.

Back at the camp, Torchen announced that our one and only shower of the trek was ready. Norbu teased us about our hair, unwashed for a week and full of dust.

'When we started, your hair was blowing in the wind. Yesterday, even in the strong wind in Lhedi, it does not move,' he said.

These long-distance treks were not for those keen to impress in the beauty stakes.

A camping shower, comprising a bag of warm water with a hose, had been set up in a shower tent but, with the bag hung so low, the top of the hose was level with my knees. If I raised the showerhead any higher, the tiny trickle of water stopped altogether. There was nothing for it but to tie myself in a knot on the plastic sheet on the ground. The long-awaited wash proved to be an unexpected exercise in contortionism. But at least I was clean.

A DAY IN THANZA

After our shower, Thanza beckoned. Krista and I followed Norbu, scrambling down to the river behind our tents. Rows of tattered grey-white flags, on tall wooden stakes, stood proudly like watchmen, guarding the entrance to the village. In the absence of a bridge, we stepped carefully from one slippery rock to another, before clambering up the muddy bank on the other side.

Thanza comprised several distinct settlements, each with ten to twenty houses, overshadowed by Table Mountain. Like the other villages of Lunana, there were no vehicles. Neither was there a main street, a central square or a market. There were no shops, nowhere to buy anything, without setting off on a strenuous trek across high mountain passes that were only open for seven or eight months of the year. The only alternative source of goods was smuggling from China, just over the mountains behind the village. Illegal, yes, but prevalent none the less, as evidenced by the Chinese food wrappers on the ground. But what Thanza lacked in civic resources, it made up for in rustic charm.

Spread across a few tracts of parched, stony ground was a collection of solidly built homes, adorned with paintings of fire-breathing dragons and other auspicious symbols. A warren of dry stone walls, that could have been plucked from a country lane in rural Ireland, wound between them. Most homes had bundles of pale yellow hay sticking out from beneath the eaves, like tufts of blond whiskers.

Piles of yak dung covered the ground. In the cold, clear air at 4000 metres, it dried quickly, leaving none of the pungent aromas associated with animal dung in more humid climates.

Along a rubbly path between the houses, we strolled behind a young mother, a baby strapped to her back. She sashayed along with the grace and poise of a catwalk model; I guessed she was still in her teens. Bundled up in a striped woven shawl, the infant slept peacefully, oblivious to the goings-on in the village. Such a contrast to the life of teenage girls in Australia. In Lunana, from an early age, children helped with household chores and livestock. Girls often married young. The whimsical and self-indulgent years enjoyed by the typical Western teenager were fantastical in Lunana, where survival from one winter to the next took priority.

On a patch of dirt, a middle-aged woman sat, her legs stretched out in front of her and a wooden back-strap loom balanced on her knees, held in place by a wide strap behind her hips. It looked very uncomfortable. On the ground next to the loom, batches of coloured wool, wound onto spindles, and several balls of black yak wool lay in the dirt. The weaver was gossiping with an older woman who stood beside her, expertly spinning wool from a coil around her wrist with a spindle that she flicked on her thigh. These women were spinning and weaving yarn in the same way as their ancestors would have, centuries ago. Fascinated, we stopped to watch. There was no noise other than the rhythmic clunk of the wooden sword on the loom, used to press the threads down to the end of the frame.

Behind the weaving, a mother and her two young daughters were pounding clothes in a basin of water. I waved to them. The younger of the little girls, about two or three years old, took one look at us and started to howl, before turning her back. Nearby, two scruffy children tossed sticks into a rusty tin, delighting in the clattering of a successful hit. Entertainment in Thanza was basic.

At one house, two women hauled bundles of grass from a stack in the yard to an ever-growing pile under the eaves. A head poked out from the gap below the roof, shouting instructions to the woman on the ground, who was lobbing the end of the rope up to her companion. With each failed attempt at catching the rope, the woman in the eaves cackled with laughter. And then, success. She finally grabbed the rope and, pulling hard, managed to heave a sheaf up to the top floor of the house. There were many more to go.

'Where are all the men?' I asked Norbu.

He smiled, but didn't answer.

Outside the next home, a yak calf, tethered to a short pole driven into the ground, stood placidly, with stoic acceptance of the curbs on its freedom. We stopped to talk to its owners, a delightful old couple who told us they had been married for fifty years. The woman was like a little sparrow, her tiny frame shrunken with age. She had short, grey-speckled hair, worn in the traditional pageboy style and, with her kindly eyes and gentle smile, she seemed to radiate contentment. She greeted us each in turn, cupping both her hands around ours in the customary Bhutanese handshake, with her head slightly bowed. Her hands felt rough and bore the scars of life with few domestic comforts, her nails dirty and broken. They were hands that had seen many years of hard manual labour. Her clothes smelled of wood smoke and earth and being outside.

Her husband, short and stocky, with heavy-lidded eyes and wispy hair on his chin, stood formally next to her. As Norbu chatted to this elderly couple, we learned that the wife was struggling with her eyesight and, like the old lady we'd met in Woche, was excited to hear that Norbu had a bag of glasses. She eagerly tried on several pairs, and was thrilled to find some that helped her to see better. She invited us into their home.

A black hairy yak head, complete with horns, was fixed to the wall next to the front door. The horns served as a useful pair of hooks, from which hung a walking stick, three balls of yak wool and, rather bizarrely, a dead mouse, its body dangling below one horn, suspended by a string tied to its back leg. As with the house we had visited in Woche, the home was empty of furniture and there was little evidence of the comforts of modern-day living. Piles of blankets, carefully folded, lined the walls and in one corner stood a small chest, with the lid open and a few possessions spilling out onto the floor. I wondered if they were the family treasures: some faded postcards, a comb, toothbrush and toothpaste, and a woven bag. An ancient radio stood on a shelf and a single bare light bulb hung from the ceiling, powered by the solar panels on the roof. There was no electricity in Thanza. We thanked this cheerful couple for inviting us into their home, which was typical of the semi-nomadic yak herders of the Lunana plateau.

Outside another farmhouse, a jumble of twigs, feathers and thread, woven into two circular cat's cradles, hung from a string. It looked a little like a Native American dreamcatcher. Norbu explained that it was a *dzoe*, a spirit catcher, to protect against any malevolent spirits. This was not a Buddhist talisman but a throwback to the age-old animist beliefs that pre-dated Buddhism and that still survived in parts of Bhutan.

As we strolled back to our camp, a sharp call from behind stopped us in our tracks. We turned to see an elderly lady who, despite her advancing years, was sprinting up the hillside after us, with the energy of a teenager.

'*Kuzuzangpo la*,' she shouted.

We stopped to wait for her and were rewarded with a gummy smile that lit up her weather-beaten face. She bore an uncanny resemblance to Nanny McPhee, her one-remaining front tooth protruding at a 45-degree angle. After a garbled exchange, Norbu explained that she was feeling unwell and wanted to know if we had any medicine. We did, but it was all in our tent. We told Norbu to tell her to come to the camp. I was surprised when she didn't come: her nearest access to medical help was at the basic health unit in Lhedi, a day's walk back down the valley. I wondered if perhaps she had made her way to the other trekking group camped nearby – there was no obvious reason for her not to seek out medication when it was on her doorstep.

Back at the campsite, half-a-dozen young ragamuffins tagged along behind a swaggering leader. Grinning in our direction, he was a cheeky Artful Dodger, setting up a target game for his band of grubby urchins. A large flat rock was placed several metres away and the boys took turns at throwing stones to try to hit it. Apart from us, the only other spectators were two old crones, sitting together on the ground. One of them peered out from beneath an impressive wool hat, like an over-sized, fluffy brown tea-cosy, typical of this valley. The other looked as old as time itself. Hiding behind her friend, she wore a knitted beanie, set at a jaunty angle high on her head, her snowy white hair peeking out from beneath it. I greeted them and, through a combination of sign language and my few Bhutanese words, asked if I might take their photograph. They replied with smiles and nods. The lady with the tea-cosy hat pulled her thick woven jacket tightly around her. As I took her photograph, she stuck out her tongue. Several of the older people I'd photographed did this; when I asked Norbu about it later, he replied, 'It's a sign of shy.' It made for some interesting photographs.

A little boy, possibly a grandson, played happily in the dirt near the two old ladies. With rosy cheeks and a round face, pierced by dimples on either side of a mischievous grin, he looked to be about four years old. He threw a stone and then ran over playfully to pick it up. Smiling, he threw it to me. I caught it and threw it back. He chuckled, excited to have a stone-throwing partner. Despite no common language, we spent a happy half-hour together, under the watchful eye of Grandma and her friend.

The stone-throwing game came to an end and the two old ladies and the little boy drifted back to the village. As the sun sank lower in the sky, an icy wind funnelled down from Table Mountain and cold shadows gradually crept down the valley. It was time to retreat to the relative warmth of the dining tent.

MAGIC MUSHROOMS

Over dinner, we talked to Norbu about the economy in Lunana. Although yak herding was the central focus of life for the Lunaps, Norbu explained that there was a relatively new, and booming, business in the highlands, across the Lunana plateau and as far as Laya: the harvesting and sale of cordyceps. This tiny and unusual fungus, which thrives in the high altitudes of the Himalayas, is a sought-after ingredient in traditional Chinese medicine. It is used for a wide variety of ailments and reputed to be both the Himalayan version of Viagra and a cure for cancer. The fungus grows on a ghost moth caterpillar that lives in the ground above 3000 metres. Once infected by the fungus, the caterpillar dies and acts as a host, with the fungus growing out of its head. Burrowed into the ground, only the tip of the fungus is visible to the naked eye, just barely. The cordyceps (known as *yartsa goenbub* to the locals) looks a bit like a small twig and to the uninitiated is almost impossible to spot among the scrubby alpine grasses. But crawling around on their hands and knees for days on end during the harvest months of June and July, in search of these elusive fungi, has brought rich rewards to those who collect them.

Cordyceps have been harvested and traded across the Himalayas for hundreds of years. However, in 2004, the Bhutanese government introduced a permit system, restricting harvesting to the people of the highland regions. With a limited number of harvesters, and a significant rise in the price paid by international buyers, these highly valued fungi have taken Lunana and Laya by storm. In 2012 the Bhutan Broadcasting Service reported that a kilogram of cordyceps had sold for over 1.2 million Ngultrum – approximately A$23,000 – an enormous amount of money by any standards, but a lifetime's earnings for the people of Bhutan's high villages.

Norbu told us that there were stories of mountain people having bags of cash stashed away in their homes, the proceeds of the burgeoning cordyceps trade. It's hard to tell how much of this is truth and how much exaggeration. Perhaps there was a hint of resentment from the Bhutanese who were not eligible for the cordyceps permits. In both Laya and Lunana, I saw little evidence of how any of this money had improved the day-to-day lives of the locals, who continued to live a subsistence lifestyle.

That evening, when Norbu joined us for soup, he announced excitedly that Leki had bought yak meat from the villagers: we would be having fried yak tonight. Although the Bhutanese generally enjoy eating meat, and Bhutan is widely reported as the highest per capita consumer of meat in South Asia, Buddhists traditionally do not slaughter animals. As a result, the meat eaten in Bhutan is imported, mainly from India. But sometimes, in the mountains, exceptions are made.

On a long trek, I generally stuck to vegetables. There was no means of refrigeration so I was cautious with meat that had to be kept fresh for days on end. But since Leki had gone to great lengths to get hold of fresh yak meat, I thought I would give it a try.

'How is it?' Krista, who ate meat throughout the trek, asked expectantly.

'It's as tough as old boots!' I replied.

'You're right, I don't think I can eat it,' she agreed. 'What shall we do with it? We can't send it all back.'

'Where's Lunana?

Perhaps sensing that some protein might be coming her way, Lunana was skulking around outside the dining tent and happily devoured the lot. When Sangay returned to serve us more, we sent him packing with a very definite '*Mi zhu*', Bhutanese for 'I've had enough, thank you'.

The pièce de résistance of our dinner turned out not to be sautéed yak but a delicious sponge cake, whipped up by Leki in a pressure cooker on his rest day.

'How was your dinner?' Norbu enquired, when he came to collect the remains of dessert.

'The cake was fantastic,' I assured him.

'And did you enjoy the yak?'

'Well ...' I hesitated, unsure if Norbu had spotted Lunana, guzzling down chunks of yak meat outside the tent. 'It was a little chewy ...'

'Then you must masticate for a long time.'

'Indeed!'

We spent our second bitterly cold evening in Thanza playing cards with the crew and trying to figure out our route for the next few days. From here, we would be leaving the wide Thanza valley, heading for Bumthang, via the Gophu La Pass. At 5345 metres, this would be the highest pass of our trek. Apart from the physical challenge of the second half of the trek, we also faced an additional and unexpected challenge. The trek notes I had brought with me, which we'd been studying carefully every evening, described a different exit route for the final section of the Snowman Trek, following the Nikka Chu to Sephu near Trongsa: the more common end point. Krista and I had decided to take a slightly longer route and finish near Jakar in Bumthang, a region further to the east, in central Bhutan. My trekking guidebook covered this route, but in reverse, beginning at Bumthang. And therein lay the problem. Not only did the description of the trek start at the end of our route and finish at our starting point, but each day's commentary was back to front, with ascents becoming descents and vice versa. In principle, it shouldn't have been difficult to read the notes in reverse: starting at the end of each day's entry, working backwards and swapping ups for downs. However, Krista and I soon discovered that it was almost beyond us; we managed to tie ourselves in knots over it. If it weren't for Norbu and Rinzin, we would probably have ended up back where we started.

Our original plan had been to say goodbye to the horsemen in Thanza and to change our horses to short-sighted, temperamental yaks. But the weather had been glorious for the previous week, with clear blue skies and not a hint of snowfall, and the horsemen were keen to stick with us until the end of the trek, earning another week's income. By the time they finished in Bumthang, they would be more than 200 kilometres from home – too far to walk back – so they would hire a truck to transport the horses by road to Gasa. From there, it was just a short jaunt back to Laya. Norbu was content to stick with what we knew and extolled the virtues of horses over yaks. Yaks were highly strung and easily unsettled. They often left trekkers waiting for hours in the morning while the herders rounded them up from their grazing. Norbu said he had also experienced them crashing around, damaging or breaking the contents of their loads. So it was decided. We would operate on the principle of 'better the devil you know' and press on with our three horsemen from Laya and their trusty steeds. It was a decision that would come back to haunt us.

I went to bed that night, feeling privileged to have had the chance to observe the goings-on of this remote village, that could have been taken from a Dickensian novel. Life here seemed tranquil and unhurried. Devoid of the trappings of the Western world and the pressures of our overscheduled lives, Thanza appeared to exude bucolic charm. But although it was easy to romanticise the lifestyle of these mountain people, I was struck by the austerity of life in Bhutan's highest settlement. On one level, the Lunaps appeared to be at one with their environment. On another, they were its prisoners. The climate in Lunana was severe, by any standards. I wondered how the people of Thanza passed the time during the long hard winters, when the village was completely cut off. Did they ever venture far from their high village, or was their world delineated by the mountains that surrounded them? There was very little evidence of modern gadgets or conveniences of any sort, apart from the solar panels wedged among the drying grasses on the roofs. No trees, at this elevation, meant keeping warm was a struggle: lighting a fire depended on collecting enough dried yak dung. And bathing, I imagined, was an irregular occurrence. There was no shortage of water but with the water temperatures barely above freezing, even in summer, taking a dip in the river was almost unthinkable. Children with dirt-smeared faces wore grimy, stained clothes. Being grubby was just an accepted aspect of life on this plateau, with skin and clothes blackened by the ever-present dust. Fresh food was extremely limited. The people of Lunana ate the same basic foodstuffs day in, day out. The nearest primary school was a day's walk away, and medical help for a serious illness required a helicopter evacuation. I was staggered that people lived up here at all.

FAREWELL LUNANA

The next morning, the walls of the tent were rimed with a glistening frost.

When we stepped outside, Lunana was fast asleep, curled up in a ball, head snuggled under her tail. A layer of ice crystals sparkled on her black fur. I marvelled at how a dog could survive the winters at these freezing high altitudes, with little in the way of reliable food or shelter. How different her life was to that of my pampered pooch back home, with her fluffy bed, pink lead and bag of chewy treats.

Overnight, our campsite had become yak central. Dozens of these shaggy-haired beasts had been brought down from their pastures, ready to act as pack animals for the other trekkers. The yaks were all tethered to short pegs in the ground, so they couldn't go far. Puffs of billowing breath condensed around them, in the cold morning air. They stood chewing their cud, snorting and grunting, beady eyes keeping a careful watch over us as we walked past. I was happy that we would be continuing with our horses.

It was with a sense of sadness that I said goodbye to Thanza, surely one of the most isolated and inaccessible settlements anywhere on earth. Turning away from the main Lunana valley, I was conscious that we had hit the halfway point. Although we still had another week to go, our destination now was Jakar and the end of our trek. We had walked east for a week, with the setting sun on our backs. Now we were turning south and already it felt as though we were homeward bound.

A taxing climb led straight up the slope behind the campsite. I tramped slowly between banks of low shrubs, my steps robotic, one after the other, over and over. Lunana, who usually ran on ahead, lingered a long way back. She seemed tired this morning. We called her name and, eventually, she followed us up the switchback to the top of the ridge. It was a slog, and my breathing was erratic, not yet resettled into its high-altitude rhythm. But, as always, walking in the mountains in the early morning was magical. The silence was deeper, the stillness more profound. Nothing stirred. There were no distractions. And the reward at the top of this unrelenting climb: a fantastic panorama. Left to Chozo and right to the gleaming snow and ice of Table Mountain. Below us, the village of Thanza was a set of toy-town houses, like a collection of tiny matchboxes, marooned at the base of towering mountains. It was like a scene from *Gulliver's Travels*.

A traverse along a side valley brought us close to the top of a beautiful waterfall. It cascaded over split-level platforms chiselled out of a wall of granite, sending up clouds of white spray as it tumbled down the cliff face. Another unexpected hidden gem, tucked away in the folds of the mountains, unseen except by the herders who passed this way and a handful of adventurous trekkers.

We had only met one other trekking party since leaving Gasa so it was a surprise to bump into three Westerners and their guide on this lonely trail. They were heading back to Thanza. One of them told us that he had pulmonary oedema, a serious and potentially life-threatening condition, caused by a build-up of fluid in the lungs that could lead to respiratory failure. It was one of several conditions that could develop from failure to acclimatise to high altitude. This man had sensibly decided that to keep going, over the 5000-metre-plus passes leading out of Lunana, was a sure-fire way to risk a serious deterioration in his health. Instead, he was retracing his steps to Thanza, in the hope of being evacuated by helicopter from there. We wished him well.

In 2013, Bhutan didn't own a helicopter. This trekker would have had to secure a helicopter through the Indian army. Given the unpredictable weather at such high altitudes and the operational commitments of the Indian military, the timescale for a helicopter evacuation was usually measured in days rather than hours. In most cases, it was the option of last resort.

Talking to this man, who had lived and worked in Bhutan for seventeen years, was a sobering reminder of the risks of altitude sickness. Although we'd been in the mountains for ten days, there was no guarantee that we would escape this arbitrary affliction. The highest elevations on the trek were yet to come and the risk remained. We thought of these trekkers several times over the coming days and wondered whether they were evacuated before the weather changed.

Lunana, who had been trailing behind us all morning, waited while we chatted and then, without so much as a backward glance, turned around and followed the three trekkers back towards Thanza. We called her name but she didn't look round. She dropped us as quickly as she had picked us up. Perhaps by calling her Lunana we had sealed her fate: to spend her days in the valley of her namesake.

By mid-morning we were ready to stop for ginger tea. A wide, flat yak pasture known as Djundje, at an altitude of 4540 metres, was the perfect picnic spot. As he poured our tea, Rinzin chatted animatedly with Norbu, pointing to a rocky overhang at the edge of the meadow. Norbu translated Rinzin's story for us. On a previous trek, Rinzin had been asked to wait here with a Japanese guest, who had been suffering from altitude sickness, while his friends continued their trek. A helicopter rescue had been arranged, but was unexpectedly delayed due to heavy snowfall, forcing Rinzin and his guest to sit out the storm with only basic shelter and limited supplies. When the weather finally cleared enough for the helicopter to land, the pilot was only able to take the guest, leaving Rinzin to make his own way out of the mountains. I couldn't imagine being abandoned here, alone, in a snowstorm, seven days' walk from civilisation. This quiet and unassuming guide just went up a notch in my estimation.

We were in a bowl, rimmed by unnamed peaks, thrown into sharp relief against a cloudless sky. Overhead, a flock of snow pigeons swooped above the ridge, easy to spot against the blue. We lay back on the grass in the warm sun. We'd been promised an easy walk for the rest of the day and being stuck in a blizzard was not something that had even crossed my mind.

The afternoon turned out to be a longer walk than expected. The trail wound around a series of rocky spurs until we finally spotted our tents in the distance, on a flat marshy plain next to a stream. Behind them, a line of saw-toothed snowy mountains formed the perfect Himalayan backdrop.

When we arrived into camp, somewhere beyond Djundje, Agye was already having a lie-down, ensconced in a pile of woven horse blankets that he'd stacked up between two tents. The idea of an afternoon nap was very appealing. This was one of our highest camps, at 4965 metres, and I was feeling tired and light-headed. It was a relief to be able to collapse in our tent.

By the time the light started to fade, a raw wind was blowing in icy gusts and oppressive clouds skimmed the surrounding summits. We missed Lunana mooching around outside our tent and wondered if she was now back in Thanza. But we weren't to be dogless for long. We were in the middle of nowhere, yet another black dog, who looked a bit like Lunana, appeared in camp to take her place. This one was bigger but with the same gentle temperament and perfect camp manners. We didn't manage to think of a name for him so he just became 'the Black Dog'.

Norbu joined us after dinner for a game of Hazaray. With my phone plugged into Krista's speaker, we managed to drown out the noise of the wind with an eclectic collection of music.

Half way through Beyoncé's 'Single Ladies (Put a Ring on It)' Norbu interrupted with a question that left us both stumped: 'Why she only has one leg?'

'What do you mean?' Krista asked.

After some back and forth, we discovered that Norbu thought Beyoncé was belting out 'I've a single leg, I've a single leg'.

'No, she says "single lady"!'

'Oh,' Norbu said, giggling, 'I thought it was strange, she is singing about having one leg.'

We'd all misheard song lyrics. The favourite in our family was Swedish House Mafia's 'Don't You Worry Child'. For months, Catherine, my younger daughter, was convinced they were singing 'See Heather's got a plan for you'. 'Heather' rather than 'heaven' made much greater sense.

Norbu won the game and disappeared to the kitchen tent, safe in the knowledge that Beyoncé's limbs were intact.

The wind rampaged from dusk until dawn. It tore at our tent, the demonic howl punctuated by the incessant barking of the Black Dog. Swaddled like a mummy in my sleeping bag and several layers of clothes, I could hardly move. It was a cold night of broken sleep.

FROM A FLURRY TO A BLIZZARD

In the morning, only the wind was awake. The crystal-clear light of the past few days had disappeared, replaced by an opaque greyness. Ominous banks of dark clouds had amassed overnight, suffocating the morning sun that we had come to take for granted. This unexpected weather was both unsettled and unsettling. But, despite the dreariness, today was a special day.

'Today we are crossing the highest pass – the Gophu La,' Norbu announced as we set off.

At 5345 metres it was just a few metres short of the altitude of Everest Base Camp.

It is traditional in the Himalayas to put up prayer flags and light butter lamps at mountain passes, as homage to the mountain. Where better to do so than at the highest pass of the trek?

'Ah, I have forgotten the prayer flags,' Norbu lamented, not far out of camp. 'They are in my tent. Sangay …'

Sangay knew before being told that he was being sent back for the roll of flags and took off at high speed, vaulting over the soft ground as he sprinted back the way we had come. I suddenly remembered the lamps.

'Do you have the butter lamps, Norbu?'

'I do have,' he replied.

'You don't really say "I do have" in English,' I said, correcting him. 'You could say "I do" or "I have some", but "I do have" sounds a bit odd.'

'Okay, thank you. I have some,' Norbu repeated.

'And matches?' Krista asked.

'I do not have.'

We yelled to Sangay to bring back matches, but our shouts were lost on the wind. There would be no butter lamps at the pass: another missed opportunity to improve our karma.

We trekked slowly upwards, heads bowed and shoulders hunched against the buffeting wind. The trail steepened. My legs felt leaden and heavy, like the grey sky that had closed in all around us. The trail was littered with rocks and boulders and, before long, a thin covering of patchy snow added to the challenges of the morning's walk. Most of the passes on the trek so far had involved a steady ascent, with a clear view of the pass itself. The Gophu La was different. False summit after false summit gave us hope, only to snatch it away again.

As we climbed higher the snow, which earlier in the day had settled here and there, blew across the ground in sudden swirls, picked up by the blustery wind. In a wide basin below the pass, a stretch of pearl-grey water, Tsorim Lake, spread out in front of us. I'd seen photographs of this vista in several guidebooks, an idyllic turquoise lake, watched over by snow-clad mountains. Looking across at the lake today was like looking at an image taken on black and white film. The snowy mountains of the Gongphula Range rose seamlessly from the silvery waters to meet a grey and brooding sky. There was no hint of contrast between water, snow and sky. It was a beguiling scene, yet dark and foreboding.

Norbu stopped for a moment to rummage in his daypack, producing both his water bottle and an unexpected box of matches. We would be lighting butter lamps at the pass after all. From his bottle, he sprinkled a few drops of water across the ground. This everyday offering was a sign of respect for the local deity and an acknowledgement of the sacredness of this place. Respect for the natural world in Bhutan reflects both Buddhist traditions and ancient mysticism and is an important feature of the rural way of life. To describe Bhutan as a Buddhist nation is accurate in one sense but also overly simplistic. In the years before Buddhism arrived in the seventh century, the early inhabitants of Bhutan's isolated valleys followed the Bon religion, an animist faith that treated the natural environment with great reverence. The overlaying of Buddhism on ancient Bon beliefs resulted in a fusion of the two faiths and a mind-boggling array of gods in different manifestations, local deities and other celestial beings, wrathful and benevolent. Many Bhutanese believe that spirits, both good and bad, inhabit the natural world, dwelling in lakes, rivers, forests, rocks and mountains. All must be treated with respect. The Bhutanese are just as likely to make an offering to the guardian deity of a lake or mountain as they are to pray to Buddha. These ancient beliefs, still held today by ordinary citizens, are born of a deep appreciation of the natural world and the complex inter-relationship between nature and human life. I love this about Bhutan. If Western nations followed the example of the Bhutanese in how we treat the environment, maybe the world would be a better place.

Having appeased the guardian deity of the lake with an offering of water, Norbu was content to approach the shore. We stumbled down the gentle slope, sinking into the soft, uneven ground that flattened with our every step. The water was perfectly still, shimmering metallic beneath an overcast sky, not a ripple disturbing the surface. I almost expected to see Excalibur held aloft by the Lady of the Lake, so otherworldly was this place.

A large flat stone beckoned. About a metre out into the lake, it was just far enough from the grassy bank to involve a slightly reckless leap. Ignoring the real possibility of skidding over the edge into knee-deep icy water, we took it in turns to vault onto this perfect meditative stone. There was a hint of snow in the air, imperceptible almost: tiny sparkling ice crystals, like delicate confetti that floated gently down and melted on contact.

We skirted around the lake to the other side and, from there, began a steady climb up towards the Gophu La. The ground was rocky again, dusted with snow.

Higher than 5300 metres, the rarefied air made every step an effort. Breathing was a conscious process, each gulp not quite giving me the oxygen fix my body craved. Despite the physical exertion, it was exhilarating, approaching the highest pass of the trek, one slow step at a time. Finally we were there, standing in a wide dip in the ridge, marked by cairns and strings of tangled prayer flags. I was 500 metres higher than Mont Blanc, Europe's highest mountain, higher than I had ever been anywhere on earth and quite possibly the highest I was ever likely to be. Out of breath but quietly elated, Krista and I gave thanks by shouting *Lha gyalo*, like seasoned locals. Norbu gave us both a hug: a celebration of our achievement and of our deepening friendship.

A light flurry of snowflakes swirled dreamily around us, blowing in the wind like a shower of tiny soft feathers. Snow at the highest pass on the Snowman Trek: it couldn't have been more fitting. Reaching the top of a high mountain pass was always special but the highest pass on a trek was that little bit extra. It wasn't just the physical achievement, although that was part of it. There was a spiritual aspect to it too. I could almost sense the deity of the Gophu La.

Looking out over this immense empty landscape, Krista and I each took a few moments alone, lost in our own thoughts. Although only metres from the others, I could have been a million miles away. There was something humbling about being among such mighty mountains: a reminder of how small and insignificant we were. I felt this acutely at the Gophu La.

My sense of calm was in direct contrast to the weather, which was gathering pace all around us. The wind was strengthening, blowing the snow harder, like it meant business. On the horizon the sky had darkened: a storm was brewing.

Sangay and Rinzin had been scouring the mounds of rocks at the pass, searching for a sheltered spot for our butter lamps. They called us over to a small ledge under an overhanging rock, where they carefully placed the lamps wrapped in a *khata*, the traditional Himalayan white silk scarf. Norbu said a prayer and explained that, by lighting these lamps, we were making an offering for ourselves, our friends and family, and all sentient beings. I felt close to tears.

My frozen fingers fumbled with the matches as I tried to light one of the lamps. The wind showed no mercy, snuffing out flame after flame. We were running out of matches and I was relieved when, finally, a match burned long enough for the wick of the lamp to catch. Krista and Norbu were much more efficient.

Norbu handed me a roll of prayer flags. I cursed the icy wind under my breath as it snatched at the flags. They flapped manically, as if they had a life of their own. Holding on tightly to one end of the unwilling string, I secured it under some loose rocks while Sangay anchored the other end. Our offerings to the deities of the pass were complete.

It didn't take long for the suggestion of snow to develop into something more serious: a foretaste of winter at these high altitudes. The Gophu La was no place to linger. A piercing wind cut through my jacket. I had donned extra layers while we milled around at the pass, but I was quickly starting to chill. The heavy clouds were ushering in some strong weather. I hoped this wasn't an omen from the mountain gods. It was time to get going.

We negotiated a steep descent across a boulder field, before scrambling up and over a rocky moraine. I glanced back to see our prayer flags flapping furiously in the wind, their prayers carried out across the frozen landscape. Below us, the black waters of another glacial lake were just visible through the thickening snow. The sky was menacing and the treeless plateau had taken on a sinister air, yet the land was imbued with a raw and savage beauty.

A freezing headwind lashed the snow against my face. My skin stung and my hands ached from the cold. I was hungry, but there was nowhere to stop and eat. We kept going, anxious to get down out of the intimidating weather. By two o'clock, there was still no shelter, so we hunkered down behind a large boulder for a quick and functional lunch stop. Krista and I insisted that the crew dispense with protocol today, and eat with, rather than after, us. Lunch didn't take long. In an instant, the falling snow had covered our lukewarm food, making it cold and unappetising. After just a few moments of sitting still, I was shivering. I blew air into my cupped hands to try to heat them a little. It made no difference. I was chilled to the bone.

We set off again across a snowy, windswept plain, following in Rinzin's footsteps. There were no signposts on the trails through Lunana. No official indication of either distance or direction. Without local guides, a maze of meandering yak tracks presented countless opportunities to get lost. And with so few locals and trekkers passing through Lunana, a wrong turn could easily end in disaster. I made sure I stayed close behind Rinzin.

Visibility was less than fifty metres. Until now, we had been on a well-defined trail. But no longer. We were on a high, frozen wasteland and the location of the path was anyone's guess. I was comforted by the occasional plastic wrapper, mounds of animal dung and even a discarded shoe: all signs of previous passers-by and proof that we were not yet completely removed from humanity. Still, this was an uncompromising landscape that would not suffer fools gladly. Even for those who knew the mountain trails like the back of their hand there was no room for complacency. I watched Rinzin carefully for any sign that he was less than sure of where he was taking us. So far so good.

I remembered feeling excited about a heavy snowfall as a child, anticipating the white world that it would bring. There was something magical about listening to the gentle tap of snowflakes on a window, watching the soft snow piling up outside, all from the comfort of a warm home. But my rose-tinted childhood memories of occasional snowstorms were a long way from trudging through a blizzard miles from anywhere. It was a miserable afternoon in the piercing cold. As we made our way across the featureless plateau, we should have been gazing at Gangkhar Puensum. Straddling the border with China, at 7541 metres, it is Bhutan's highest mountain and the highest unclimbed peak in the world. It will likely retain this accolade since, unlike other Himalayan countries, which generate large amounts of foreign revenue from mountaineering expeditions, Bhutan banned mountaineering in 2003, out of respect for the mountain deities. Sadly, as we descended from Gophu La, a veil of murky cloud cloaked the entire valley. Gangkhar Puensum remained shrouded in mist and entirely unseen.

Large flakes of snow fell in heavy sheets around us, burying the landscape. The scenery here was a bleak monotone, without obvious landmarks. The little flurry that had greeted our arrival at the pass was a distant memory. No one spoke. An empty silence smothered us, interrupted only by the noise of our boots on the rocky ground, partly cushioned by a coating of ever-deepening snow. We trudged on, into the wind and snow, following Rinzin, who confidently led the way.

All afternoon, it snowed. By the time we reached camp, at Zanam, the dull daylight had almost gone. The cold had permeated every bone in my body; my fingers were throbbing, my feet numb, the skin on my face red and stinging. The hood of my jacket was almost useless in the driving snow. My hair, sticking out on either side of the hood, had frozen solid. I tried to push it back inside my jacket but managed only to send crystals of ice down the back of my neck.

It had been a gruelling day. Krista and I were deeply tired and subdued by the weather. In the dining tent, we crouched around the gas heater, watching the steam rise into the cold night air from our soaking wet socks and boots, balanced dangerously close to the heater, to dry. I caught up on my journal, but no one was in the mood to play cards.

Norbu arrived with our hot water bottles.

'Agye thinks the weather will be clear in the morning,' he declared.

'I hope he's right,' Krista replied, not sounding very convinced.

Norbu returned to the kitchen tent and Krista and I headed off to bed, although it was only eight o'clock. There was no escape from the intense cold. Even wearing my down jacket in my sleeping bag seemed inadequate against the plummeting temperatures. The roof of our tent sagged under the weight of the snow that had fallen during dinner. We jabbed at it from the inside, sending blocks of snow whizzing down the nylon and thudding onto the ground. I wondered how many more times we'd need to do this during the night or risk our tent collapsing. A warm bed in a cosy home had never seemed so far away.

AVOIDING GASTRIC PROBLEMS

Waking to the pale light of dawn, I knew that a burning cold awaited. The top of my sleeping bag, encrusted with ice, lay wet against my face. Above my head, the tent roof struggled to support the overnight snowfall and droplets of condensation ran down the inside walls, adding to the dampness. I was apprehensive about what the day would hold. Still wrapped up inside my sleeping bag, I reached over and unzipped the door. A gust of wind blew little swirls of snowflakes inside, where they settled on every surface, like tiny falling leaves. In other circumstances, it would have been romantic.

It was a wintry scene outside, the ground covered in deep, velvety snow. The already desolate landscape had morphed into an empty whiteness, the grandeur of the mountains erased completely. The sky was solid and heavy, like a sheet of beaten tin. It was hard to believe that we were surrounded by towering summits. I wondered what this meant for the day ahead, apart from the fact that Agye's weather forecasting skills were a bit wide of the mark.

The flap of the dining tent door was pinned back at one end as we ate breakfast, and the Black Dog sat hopefully outside. He was rewarded with a handsome meal: neither of us was very hungry. The snow was falling thick and fast and I watched as if hypnotised by the silent flakes that tumbled down, down, down. Behind the tent, the horses stood mournfully side by side, ears back, snow forming little clumps on their thick coats. They seemed resigned to a dismal, cold day, with no grazing.

After breakfast Norbu, Krista and I debated whether we should keep going beyond the day's scheduled campsite and try to get some of tomorrow's walk under our belts. The following day we had to cross three passes. It would be the toughest day of the trek.

'The horsemen are worried,' Norbu said. 'The horses do not have enough food. We will try to get as far as the first pass today if we can.'

Earlier on the trek, we had watched the horsemen feed their animals every morning from nosebags. But they had run out of fodder and the horses were now dependent on grazing, when they were turned loose at the end of each day. A plan that would have worked well had the grass not been buried under snow.

'I am happy to push on,' Krista replied.

'And you Aum Heather?' Norbu asked.

'Yes, definitely. We don't want to be stuck in this storm,' I replied, letting the 'Aum' slip through unchecked.

From the campsite, our route took us across a flat snowy meadow. Rinzin led the way, with the Black Dog out in front. All sound was muffled by the deep blanket of snow. I listened to the silence.

After plodding for half an hour over rough grass softened by snow, we found ourselves on the banks of a fast-flowing river of glacial meltwater that pitched wildly over slippery boulders. A series of braided channels wound their way down the valley, leaving little islands of icy rocks between them. Rinzin pointed out our trail on the other side of the river. There was no obvious crossing point.

'Where's the bridge, Norbu?' I asked.

'We do not have.' It was the response I was half-expecting.

As we scoured the snowy bank, assessing the potential routes across, Sangay staggered over to the water's edge, heaving a heavy boulder. He launched it into the white water, only for it to disappear beneath the boisterous current. The water was too deep to build stepping stones.

Further upstream, I was amazed to see Rinzin, minus his socks and shoes, his trousers rolled up above his knees, gallantly making his way through the surging water. For a second, I considered doing the same, but thought better of it. This river coursed straight down from the glaciers and the temperature was barely above freezing. Rinzin was made of sterner stuff than me. As was the Black Dog, who miraculously appeared on the far side and was now waiting patiently while we weighed up our options. Finally, we agreed on what looked like our best route across, following a line of slippery boulders. Norbu and Sangay took up their positions in the bone-chilling water, ready to escort Krista and me to the other side.

I went first. Rinzin was just ahead of me, testing the unstable rocks and guiding me where to stand. The boulders that, from the bank, had looked to be close together, were at the limit of my stride. I was grateful for my walking poles for balance, although the current tugged at them viciously, threatening to pull them out from underneath. Norbu and Sangay stood solidly in the deepest water, clutching my hand tightly as I stepped, slowly and deliberately, from one slippery platform to another. I arrived, with a sigh of relief, on a thin strip of muddy ground in the middle of the flow. Halfway. The second section seemed easier but, as I took one last clumsy leap onto the slushy bank, I realised that I was shaking. It had taken less than ten minutes to cross the river, but it felt like an eternity. I was glad to have a chance to calm my breathing while Rinzin, Norbu and Sangay waded back into the water again, ready to guide Krista across.

With the perilous river crossing behind us, we scrambled over marshy mounds of grass, sinking into the soft, wet snow. The Black Dog had bounded ahead and now sat regally on a high, rocky outcrop, watching our approach.

Sangay and Rinzin had been leading the way before disappearing. I followed their tracks religiously, adjusting my steps to match their footprints. There they were again, up ahead. Sangay had put his daypack down and was rolling a ball of snow. By the time we caught up with them, the snowball was the size of a basketball and was balanced on the lopsided body of a snowman.

'He's definitely a Lunana snowman,' Krista laughed, pointing to his nose, which Sangay had fashioned from a lump of dried horse dung.

The snowfall eased a little and the sun made a feeble attempt to break through the heavy sky.

'Maybe Agye's forecast will be right after all,' I said hopefully.

Everyone's mood lightened and the boys slid around, throwing snowballs at each other. But the break in the weather was brief and it wasn't long before the hint of sun was obscured once more by cloud. Freezing sleet took over. It nipped my face and hands. I had long since lost all feeling in my feet.

Once again, there was no obvious place to stop for lunch. We ploughed on through the snow. My hood refused to tighten around my face. Snowflakes secreted themselves inside, melting on touch and dripping onto my neck. It was another hour before we saw some stone shelters in the distance, the abandoned carcass of a herders' camp, known as Minchugang. It was deserted in the winter, the remnants of a few crude stone huts with collapsed, tumbledown walls, their roofs long since gone. They were like dilapidated stone bothies in the Scottish moors. It was funny how perceptions could change. In this wild, brutal land, in atrocious weather, those ruined structures were a godsend.

Sangay arrived first and immediately set to work collecting a few bare branches that lay scattered around. By the time we stumbled, shivering and wet, over to the remains of the shelters, he was valiantly trying to light a fire behind a crumbling wall. Clouds of thick smoke billowed around us, as flames fought to take hold of unwilling branches. Sangay shook his head and muttered in frustration. It was too wet. Within a few minutes, the embers fizzled out.

The boys tried hard to make us comfortable. They built a makeshift shelter from a torn tarpaulin that someone had left wedged below a boulder, suspending it between our walking poles at either end and jamming one edge into a wall. Norbu carried two flat rocks over to our little refuge.

'You must sit on these rocks,' he insisted.

'Why?' I asked. They didn't look too comfortable.

'So you are not getting gastric.'

I didn't have the energy to question this any further. So Krista and I dutifully sat on our magic rocks, huddled under the awning, relieved to know we were warding off an unexpected bout of gastric.

It was mind-numbingly cold. The plastic sheeting sagged ever lower and struggled to provide any protection from the weather. Sleet fell in icy curtains all around us. My body seemed to shrink inside my down jacket, every muscle tensed in a concerted but futile effort to keep the cold at bay. I couldn't stop shivering.

Lunch, yet again, was a wretched affair, the food cold as soon as it was served. I made myself eat, although I didn't feel hungry.

'Can you imagine what everyone back home would think, if they could see us now' Krista asked, 'huddled under a piece of ripped plastic, in the middle of nowhere, in freezing sleet, on an anti-gastric rock?'

'Not forgetting that we are six days' walk from a small village at the end of a dirt road!' I reminded her.

No wonder no one had wanted to do this trek with us.

An hour passed as we waited for the horses, and I became more frustrated.

'I think we should get going,' I suggested to Krista. 'I am so cold.'

Sitting still in these conditions felt like utter madness.

'Yes, I agree,' she responded. 'We need to be walking to warm up. Norbu, can we head off? The horses can catch us up.'

But Norbu was apprehensive about us leaving before the horses arrived, concerned that, as the day wore on, they wouldn't make it over the first pass before nightfall. No horses meant no tents. If the horses couldn't make it to the pass, there was no point in us doing so. For now, there was nothing to do but wait.

'Hhhmmmm, pork bánh mì…' Krista said wistfully.

'Stop it!' I protested.

'Or chicken noodle salad,' she continued.

After our Wednesday training hikes at home, we often grabbed lunch at a local market, celebrating our exertions with our favourite sticky pork belly Vietnamese baguette or a chicken and glass noodle salad. Thinking about lunch spurred us on through the second half of our morning hike. On the trek, with our diet of rice and curry and, in my case mostly of vegetables, we tried to avoid drooling over unobtainable delicacies. But, with time on our hands waiting for the horses, we succumbed to indulgent food fantasies. Not surprisingly, it didn't make us feel any better about our predicament.

Eventually, the faint jangle of bells announced their arrival. Five minutes later the horses emerged, one by one, out of the gloom. They were a sorry sight. Soaking wet and bedraggled, they nuzzled the ground in search of grass but found only snow. I had never seen horses look so forlorn.

After a long discussion with the horsemen, Norbu declared that our day's walk was done.

'It is too risky to keep going,' he told us. 'The horsemen think it is too much for the horses to cross the pass before it gets dark and there is nowhere else to camp where there is water.'

So we would be camping here, at Minchugang. It wasn't what I wanted to hear. I would have preferred to use the afternoon to make some headway into the next day's route. But it was not to be and I reluctantly accepted the horsemen's decision.

Although it was still early in the afternoon, the light had almost gone. I felt flat, my mood a reflection of the dreariness around us.

The crew dragged the disconsolate horses another 50 metres across the meadow, where they began unloading gear and setting up camp.

'Please, stay here, while we are preparing your tent,' Norbu insisted.

So, with nowhere to go, we sat under the tarpaulin until our tent was ready. By the time Norbu called us over, my clothes were soaking wet and I was beyond freezing. I stumbled with Krista across to the campsite. With frozen skin and sodden clothes, we brought the cold and wet inside the tent, where it was no warmer than on the other side of the flimsy nylon.

'My hands and feet feel as if they are no longer attached to my body,' I said, through chattering teeth. 'I don't know if I'll ever warm up.'

'What are we doing here?' Krista muttered. 'We must be mad.'

'At least we don't have gastric,' I offered. She responded with a sardonic smile. I had to agree it was all beginning to seem a bit mad. The conversation made me think of the Cheshire Cat's response to Alice, when she asks, 'How do you know I'm mad?' 'You must be,' replies the Cat, 'or you wouldn't have come here.'

A few minutes later, there was a pile of soggy clothes on the floor of the tent and I was savouring the warmth of so many dry layers I could easily have passed for the Michelin Man. Slowly, very slowly, I was beginning to thaw. I could feel the blood throbbing in my fingers as my circulation cranked into gear.

The afternoon dragged on. In the dining tent, Sangay lit the gas heater, although its one little flame was fighting a losing battle against the intense cold. Krista and I huddled over it. Rotating our sopping wet socks, boots, rain jackets and trousers, dangling them from chairs so close to the heater they almost went up in smoke, provided some distraction. And then, after just a momentary lapse in concentration, one of Krista's socks did go up in smoke, adding the acrid smell of singed wool to the steamy odours already swirling in the tent.

Outside, the snow fell and the cold gloom of the afternoon merged into darkness. The roof of the dining tent bulged under 10 centimetres of snowfall. We took it in turns to prod at it, sending a whoosh of snow skidding to the ground. With such a build-up in just a few hours, I was nervous about how our sleeping tent would fare through the night.

Norbu appeared, to talk through the plan for the following day. Although not our longest day in terms of distance, it was one of the most challenging, with three passes to cross before we reached the next campsite, at Worithang, at an altitude of more than 4500 metres.

'Tomorrow we are supposed to camp at Worithang which is still a high camp,' Norbu explained. 'If it is still snowing, the horsemen want to keep going, to get below the snow. There is no grass for the horses for two days now so they are very hungry. The horsemen are quite worried.'

'So how far do they want to go?' I asked.

'To the guesthouse at Dhur,' Norbu replied.

Dhur was the following night's campsite so this would mean covering two days' distance in one.

'If you want to go to Dhur, that is fine and good,' Norbu said. 'But if not, it is okay. What do you think?'

I nodded to Krista.

'We are happy to go to Dhur,' Krista said, speaking for both of us.

It was a tall order but we would give it our best shot. We agreed to be up early, for a seven o'clock departure the next morning.

For the second evening in a row, Krista and I were sombre, anxious about the weather and what the next day might hold. Even Torchen's 'butter fry' didn't cheer us up. The world outside felt hostile. We were well beyond the point of no return on this trek but we still had a long way to go. Norbu didn't join us after dinner, as he normally did, perhaps preferring to share his worries with the crew, rather than his guests. By 8.30pm, Krista and I were ready for the day to be over. We tramped over to our sleeping tent, the fresh snow squeaking under our boots, snowflakes dancing across the beams of light from our head-torches. We stopped briefly to swipe the snow from the tent roof. After an evening beside the gas heater, our tent felt more like a butcher's deep freeze than somewhere to sleep. A thin ground sheet was all that separated us from the frozen earth. I took off my outdoor trousers but everything else stayed on: thermals, two fleeces, down jacket, two pairs of ski socks, beanie and neck gaiter. In a desperate attempt to feel warm, I tunnelled deeper into my sleeping bag until only the top of my head poked out. For once, Krista and I didn't chat before sleep. I prayed that the weather would improve by the morning. The last line in my journal entry for the day read: 'In a blizzard. Unbearably cold. I hope we make it through tomorrow.'

I turned off my head-torch and a cold darkness descended, bringing with it another wave of anxiety. I spent a freezing, uncomfortable night, sleeping only sporadically. The crew seemed noisier than usual, clattering around outside. I wondered if they were checking on the horses, although I didn't hear their bells. Lying awake, I was depleted of energy and emotional stamina, and conscious of being very far removed from my normality. I would be glad when morning came and we could get on with the day, rather than worry about it.

KRISTA IS NOT A HAPPY GUEST

I awoke, stiff from the cold. The wet roof of the tent, heavy with snow, drooped a couple of inches above my head and condensation ran down the walls.

With a sense of foreboding, I forced open the frozen zip of the tent door, just enough to peer outside.

'How does it look?' Krista asked nervously.

'You don't want to know' was a sanitised version of my response.

It was like a scene from *Fargo*. A thick blanket of snow covered the ground. Large flakes drifted down silently. Visibility was almost non-existent. This was not on the schedule.

The weather in early October in the mountains of Bhutan was typically sunny during the day and cold at night, with clear skies and minimal precipitation. We wondered what had gone wrong.

The camp was unusually quiet. No horse bells jangling, no pots and pans clattering in the kitchen tent, no Sangay leaping around, no crew shouting instructions to each other. All had been silenced by the snow.

The Black Dog was still asleep outside our tent door, covered in snow and curled up in a ball, his nose covered by his fluffy tail. He barely stirred when he saw me, burying his head deeper in the blanket of his tail. We waited for bed tea and washing water. When it didn't arrive, we got up to investigate.

The dining tent had all but collapsed on one side under the weight of the overnight snowfall. Krista and I set about clearing the build-up from the roof, refixing the poles that spiked at odd angles. Usually, when we tried to do anything around camp, one of the crew would appear from nowhere and take over. Not today. With the dining tent partially resurrected, we waited hopefully for someone to arrive. But no one came. No one stirred in the rest of the camp.

'Where is everyone?' Krista wondered.

'Maybe they panicked in the middle of the night and left us here,' I replied, only half-jokingly.

So much for setting off at seven o'clock.

Norbu finally turned up. He seemed agitated.

'The staff are all sick. Two of them have been vomiting,' he said, 'They have all been up through the night.'

That explained the noises during the night but it didn't bode well for our demanding day ahead.

Thinley came into the dining tent. He nodded to us, gathering up a pile of horse blankets.

'How are you?' I asked.

He clasped his head and mimed being dizzy. He seemed to tremble as he fumbled with the mound of blankets and saddles. Krista offered him some headache tablets, which he gratefully accepted.

Altitude sickness? Or a stomach bug? We couldn't tell, but we gave Norbu some medication to distribute to the rest of the crew. Krista and I set to work, packing up. For once, no one objected.

Breakfast finally arrived after eight o'clock and it was nine before we left camp. This was our latest departure to date and a very late start, given how far we were hoping to go in such abysmal weather. We had Sangay and Rinzin with us and, of course, Norbu and the Black Dog. I felt sorry for Sangay. He was not his usual dynamic self, stopping to hold his head in his hands and, on a couple of occasions, to be sick.

'Sangay looks really unwell,' Krista said, as Sangay stopped again, bent double.

'What's happened to our good karma?' I wondered.

'I know!' Krista replied. 'We brought gifts for the schools, lit butter lamps, strung up prayer flags … Now the crew are all sick and the weather just keeps getting worse.'

We should have insisted on the *sungkey* ceremony after all. Maybe then, the weather gods would have been appeased.

Rinzin led the way but progress was painfully slow. The trail, if there was a trail, was buried under a foot of snow. Rounded bumps and hollows hid sharp boulders and icy puddles, traps for the unwary. Every step had to be taken carefully, methodically. I jabbed my walking poles, like probes, into the snow, to check what lay beneath. But it was almost impossible to tell whether I was stepping on soft snow or slippery rocks, or down a hole.

We were following the Sasha Chu valley, teetering along a slippery ledge that curled above the river. The three guides and Krista were in front, just visible through the snow. I misjudged the edge of the trail and my right foot skidded over the side, almost sending me headfirst down the slope. I gathered myself up and brushed off the snow. No one had noticed my near tumble and I hurried to catch up with the others before they disappeared. How easy to be lost out here in this weather.

At some point, we had to turn away from the main valley, climbing through the mountains to our left, to reach the first pass of the day, the Phodrang La. Before we left camp, Rinzin had estimated two hours to the pass but, by eleven o'clock, we were scrambling about in a deep gully, running at right angles to the Sasha Chu, far below us. Gully after gully sliced the mountainside. This one was full of huge boulders and walking among them was tortuous. There was no sign of the pass, or of anything else. All around us, the mountains disappeared into blowing snow, the earth and the sky merging into the same gigantic whiteness. Ahead. Behind. Left. Right. It all looked the same. Any landmarks that Rinzin might have been searching for had simply disappeared, erased by the snow.

'Please tell me we're not doing something incredibly stupid,' Krista said dolefully.

I didn't think we had any choice at that point. 'The only alternative is to sit out the weather at Minchugang. But the risk is the snow gets worse before it gets better and we end up being stuck there.'

We imagined the headlines of our newspaper back home. 'Two local mums stranded in a blizzard in the Himalayas.' Everyone would think we were mad. Maybe we were.

We floundered on through the deepening snow. I told Krista the experience was good for her soul. I was sure she didn't believe me.

I wrestled with the struggle between reason and emotion. My voice of reason reminded me that we had a huge support crew, food and shelter, and there was no need to panic. My emotions, on the other hand, were running riot as I contemplated the possibility of becoming disorientated in the worsening weather and never finding the elusive pass. For now, reason was winning, but only just. Before we left, we had joked about being stuck in Lunana until March, if we got snowed in. It was no longer funny. We had lost the trail. We ought not have been in the gully but it was impossible to tell where we should have been. Perhaps the trail ran parallel to the river or maybe we were supposed to have been much higher up, above the gully. We had no way of knowing. I felt claustrophobic, despite the vastness of the landscape.

'Have you ever lost a guest, Norbu?' I asked.

'Never.'

'Let's hope this is not the first time. Imagine the paperwork involved.'

Norbu didn't like writing. We joked that if something happened to Krista I would complete the paperwork, and vice versa. It lightened the mood, though not for long. Krista was anxious.

'I think the trail is down there,' she said, pointing far below us. It was anyone's guess. The horses were nowhere to be seen, although with such poor visibility I doubted we would have seen them anyway. I could not imagine how they were going to make it through so much snow. If the horses got stuck, it would be a disaster: with no horses, we would have no shelter or supplies. It was still early in the day so I didn't feel too concerned. Yet.

Rinzin clenched his jaw in concentration. He stopped often to squint up at the mountains, searching for the mysterious pass. His hesitation was disconcerting. The horizon evaporated into infinite skies that enveloped everything around us. How could he possibly tell where we were or where we should be?

An important tenet of Bhutanese culture was saving face, coupled with a reluctance to say no, and this was causing Krista another level of anxiety. Turning to me, she whispered, 'What if Rinzin doesn't know where he's going and isn't telling us?'

'Yes, I know, he may not want to own up to that,' I replied.

'Where is the pass, Norbu?' Krista asked.

'Does Rinzin know where he's going?' I asked.

'How long to the pass?' Krista added.

Poor Norbu. He dutifully relayed the questions to Rinzin, who tried to reassure us that, despite appearances, he knew where he was going.

Still, Krista asked again and again, 'Does Rinzin know where he's going?'

Rinzin was becoming frustrated by the questions. Although I too had my doubts, I willed myself to have faith. He had done this trek eight times. He had delivered us through the blowing snow of the previous two days, crossing a desolate, empty plateau, where there had been no landmarks to show him the way. But it was a difficult situation. Krista was on the verge of tears. I was used to her strength of character and was unnerved to see her so concerned. I fell silent, not wanting to further undermine Rinzin but struggling to find anything positive to say. Jokes about losing guests were no longer funny.

Finally, we emerged from the gully to regain the main slope, still following the direction of the river but climbing now. It was exhausting, each step an effort through the deep snow. We heard a hint of bells and in the distance, through the haze of snow, I could just make out our horses, winding their way after us in a long crocodile. As they got closer I saw Agye in front, head down, pushing through the weather. Normally the horses led the way. Today, Agye was tugging a very reluctant lead horse, with a rope attached to his head collar. I was both staggered and relieved that they had made it this far. At least now we had access to food and gear, should we need to camp in an emergency. Although where we might pitch a tent, on this angled slope, was another matter. It was best not to dwell on that.

After what seemed like an eternity, Rinzin pointed out the pass high above us, a shallow dip in a barely discernible ridge. 'Where are the prayer flags?' Krista asked. Prayer flags had marked every pass we'd crossed. The fact that there were none on this one added to the uncertainty.

'Is that really the pass? Is it the right pass?'

'I am not a happy guest right now,' Krista announced.

'You will be the happy guest again,' Norbu said with conviction.

Norbu and Rinzin reassured us and we started the long, laborious ascent. Small talk petered out. We trudged on in silence, each of us fighting our own private battle against weather and terrain.

The pitch of the slope was deceptive. From afar, it had looked steep. From our position now, at the base of the climb up to the pass, it looked almost vertical. I was walking in slow motion, no more than twenty steps without a break. Breathing the cold, dry air left my mouth and throat parched. I needed a drink, but my water bottle was deep in my pack. And I was overheating, in too many clothes. I felt as if I was being cooked from the inside out. But there was nowhere to stop.

I lagged behind. *Don't look up.* The mantra of a friend in Australia, who came on a few training walks with me, stuck in my mind. She always maintained that looking up on a difficult slope made the upward slog so much harder. She might have been right. I focused, instead, on the next turn in the series of switchbacks, willing myself to keep going with the promise of a brief rest before the track abruptly changed direction and weaved its way back across the slope. I was completely sapped of energy, my limbs weary. If I had lain down in the snow, I might not have got up again. I took small, staccato steps, like the march of a clockwork soldier. Every single one was an effort.

The others were almost at the pass. At each turn, and sometimes in between, I stopped, leaning on my walking poles, to allow my body brief respite. The sheer physical exhaustion was overwhelming. When I finally sneaked a brief glance up towards the pass, the others were already there. I was only a couple of minutes behind them but those last few twists on the trail seemed interminable. This was now a test of determination as much as physical stamina. I needed one more rest. And then a willpower I didn't know I had propelled me to the pass.

There were no shouts of *lha gyalo* today: I didn't feel like celebrating. I was breathless in the thin air, too hot yet freezing, thinking I might faint.

I had a long history of fainting. From high school biology class, dissecting a bull's eye, to a busy platform at Clapham Junction Station in London, clutching a chicken and a bag of sausages; from a flight between New York and London when I was seven months pregnant, to a contact lens fitting when I split my head open on the eye-test machine as I fell. And at least a couple of times on the tops of mountains. But not yet in Bhutan. Krista had been warned about the possibility of a fainting fit and had been instructed not to panic. But thankfully the feeling passed. I lay down on my back in the snow, my heart thumping against the walls of my chest, enjoying the brief halt, which was just long enough for my breathing to soften. In other circumstances, I would have made a snow angel but I wasn't quite in the mood. It was already after one o'clock. Our optimism about taking two hours to reach the Phodrang La had been misguided. One down, two to go. We still had two passes and a long trek before tonight's camp. I felt daunted, but not defeated.

THE SAGA OF THE SAGA LA

The horses had slowly been gaining on me, as I inched my way upwards. They snorted and puffed as they crested the Phodrang La, expelling great clouds of steamy breath from their flared nostrils. Now, with the initial descent from the pass and the horses breaking trail as they kicked their way through the snow, our walking would be a little easier. Rinzin was up front, picking a path, followed by Agye dragging the hesitant lead horse by his short rope. Norbu explained that yaks could smell the trail through the snow, sniffing out the scent of other animals that had taken the same path. Horses, on the other hand, needed to see where they were going. Perhaps we should have changed to yaks in Thanza after all.

It was hard to get into a rhythm. The walk was a continual start–stop behind the horses as the crew tried to pick the best path for them. And still it snowed. We passed a deserted yak herder's hut, built on the side of a rocky outcrop. This was where we would have camped if we had pressed on to cross the Phodrang La the previous day.

As I looked across the white expanse, I thought I caught a glimpse of prayer flags through the murk, the tell-tale sign of a pass. Could that be the Saga La? I turned to Norbu, who confirmed my worst fears.

We followed a circuitous route to the slope below the Saga La. A sudden snap, then a roar, split the silence. A mass of snow and rock broke free, careering down the mountain, leaving a spray of ice crystals hanging in the air after the avalanche had settled. Although we were some distance away from this fall, there was no telling where the next one might be.

Norbu was convinced we were now on the trail, a slender ledge that wound its way up towards the pass. Although I was glad that we seemed to be back on track, I was concerned that the afternoon was wearing on. It was coming up to three o'clock and we still had a long climb to reach this pass. The snow was deep and the horses were struggling. Then a third pass and an unknown walk from there to the campsite. I didn't see how we'd make it before dark. My mind raced, wondering whether we would be bedding down for the night on a precipitous slope, in the shadow of the Saga La.

'I am not a happy guest,' Krista repeated. She could have been speaking for me too.

'We need a Plan B: in case we can't make it over the Saga La before it gets dark,' I suggested.

There weren't many options. We agreed we could go back to the yak herder's hut and spend the night there. We would have shelter without having to set up the tents and there was water in the lake behind us. Or, we could melt snow. Plan B, even if not ideal, was in place.

While we'd been talking, we'd come to another standstill behind the horses. It was a precarious place to stop. I slumped heavily over my poles, anchoring my weight into the slope, anxious to stop myself from slipping. As I glanced up, a drama was unfolding ahead. Where the ledge narrowed, at an outcrop of rock, one of the horses had lost its foothold in the snow, its hind legs desperately trying, and failing, to find solid ground. As the horse skidded down the slope through the deep snow, the crew sprinted to its aid, just managing to break its fall. Slowly, they succeeded in cajoling the terrified animal back up the slope to join the others. The knot in my stomach relaxed a little – the horse was safe – but would the climb to the Saga La defeat us? This was the steepest pass of the trek and we were standing in half a metre of snow. My optimism from earlier in the day was deserting me. For the first time I felt suddenly vulnerable, unsure of whether I would be able to keep going.

'I don't think we're going to get up there,' I said, half-fearful that someone might agree with me.

'We will.' Norbu was emphatic. I made myself believe him.

Endless possibilities as to how this day would pan out – most of them ending in drama, if not quite tragedy – flitted through my mind. I was well outside my comfort zone. I didn't believe we were in immediate danger but there was a lot of uncertainty about how far we could get before nightfall and even whether the horses could make it over this pass in the snow. It was hard to stay positive.

Up ahead, the crew were battling with rattled horses. With baskets, tents and all our other gear strapped to their backs, their loads were too wide for them to squeeze along the thin ledge without toppling over the edge. The solution: to relieve them of their loads, walk them around one by one and reload on the other side. My mouth was dry. I looked on anxiously as, one by one, the loads were unstrapped from the horses and the frightened animals were pushed, pulled and cajoled, one at a time, around the danger point, with a dizzying drop to one side. This was going to take a while.

Krista and I were both generally cheerful, happy to get on with whatever life threw at us, and keen to make the best of every situation. Over the course of this trek, we had been thankful for the soft drizzle that wasn't rain, for the rain that wasn't sleet, for the sleet that wasn't snow, and, throughout, for not having gastric. But standing on that slope in the blowing snow, shivering, exhausted and hungry, doubtful as to whether we would make it over the pass, I was struggling to see the silver lining.

'We will go ahead,' Norbu suggested. 'Let's go.'

We would make our way across the slope a few metres higher up where the pitch wasn't so steep. We just had to get up there first. I anchored myself with my walking poles. Taking one small step at a time, I gingerly edged up past the last few horses. So steep was the slope here that one slip and I would have skidded down unchecked. At that moment, more than anything else I wanted not to be there: not to be stuck on that snowy mountainside, in freezing weather, with no idea where I was going. But sometimes there weren't many options. There was nothing for it but to persevere. I inched carefully up to a higher ledge to join Norbu, with Krista following close behind. More than once, I put my hand down to regain my balance, only for it to sink, elbow deep, into the soft snow. It was a treacherous traverse and I was shaking, more from fear than cold. I breathed a huge sigh of relief when I slotted in behind Norbu on a gentler shelf.

Following Norbu, Sangay and Rinzin, we made our way hesitantly to the front of the string of horses. Sangay took charge, kicking snow down the side of the mountain, trying to carve a path for the horses to follow. Rinzin, Norbu, Krista and I followed his lead. With bare hands, red from the cold, Sangay scooped up armfuls of snow, launching it off the side of the ledge, while the rest of us, sticking to his tracks, kicked and stamped the snow. Gradually, the hidden dirt began to poke through and something resembling a path appeared. It was energy-sapping, at this altitude, but I tried to concentrate on the task in hand and not on how tired I was.

We stopped periodically, looking up towards the pass to plot the best route, zigzagging back and forth across the slope. Miraculously, we had reached a point where the pass looked attainable and, thankfully, the snowfall was easing a little. Behind us, the horses were slowly making their way along the track we'd cleared for them and, for the first time that day, I felt confident we were going to make it somewhere.

Finally, we stood at the pass. Hungry, drained but very relieved. And, as if by magic, the snow, which had fallen incessantly all day, suddenly stopped. Behind us, a few pale streaks of blue sky began to emerge from the clouds. Ahead was a whole new world.

I REFUSE TO GO ANY FURTHER

No one spoke. From the pass, we gazed across a sweeping basin blanketed in virgin snow and ringed by anonymous mountains. Beyond them, endless peaks concertinaed to the very edge of the world. Silence. That deep silence that went hand in hand with generous snowfall. It was achingly beautiful.

In an instant, the trials and tribulations of the day evaporated.

I would have given anything to stop here, to savour the relief of reaching this pass. But there wasn't enough time. We only had another hour and a half of daylight and still there was another pass to cross. We had to keep moving.

Buoyed by the break in the weather and the natural beauty of our surroundings, I plunged down from the pass with a new-found energy, through knee-deep powdery snow. Norbu and Krista were just ahead. Together we carved a trail that the horses would follow. With gravity on our side, we slipped and skidded, hurtling down through the snow with total abandon. I was grateful for my walking poles, which saved me, more than once, from tumbling headfirst down the slope. I felt elated to be over the Saga La and so grateful that it had finally stopped snowing.

'How far to the next pass, Rinzin?'

He estimated that another half-hour would bring us to the Worithang La, and assured us that this, the third pass of the day, would be a cinch, compared with the two that we had just overcome. We let the horses go ahead, with the Black Dog trotting along behind them. The sun suffused the mountains in a rosy pink glow and sent long shadows into the valley as it sank lower in the sky. Snow blew along the ground in low swirling eddies, wafted by a soft breeze. For a few seconds, one of the horses was silhouetted against the sun and behind it, stretching to the distant skyline, was an ethereal landscape of glacial lakes and soaring mountains, smothered in snow. I couldn't believe where I was. The sense of isolation, of transcendent, pristine beauty, was overwhelming. As the late afternoon sun faded to dusk I began to feel at one with the world, if a little hungry. It had been nine hours since breakfast.

'What happened to lunch? I am so hungry,' I said to Krista.

'Me too,' she said. But there had been nowhere to stop. 'How long to the camp after the pass, Norbu?' she asked.

Norbu walked back to consult with the horsemen. The discussion seemed quite animated, yet their voices were hushed as they glanced in our direction. Krista and I walked on. A few minutes later Norbu caught up to explain that the horsemen didn't want to stop at the scheduled camp at Worithang. They were planning instead to keep going to the following night's camp.

'This is what we discussed last night,' Norbu reminded us, as if by way of justification for this insane proposition.

'So how long will that take?'

'Four hours.'

'Four hours! There is no way we can do a full day's walk in four hours. In these conditions. And in the dark.'

Four hours was an improbably short time for a full day's walk and I didn't believe it possible for a minute. I looked at Krista. All my instincts told me this was bonkers. Yes, we had talked about it the previous evening, but that was when we had naively thought that today would be a typical day's walking. The hike to the first pass was supposed to have taken us two hours. It took over four. It was now almost five o'clock. We still had the third pass to cross and then however long it would take to get to tonight's original campsite.

Not to mention wading through snow, which slowed everyone to a snail's pace. We wouldn't reach the first campsite at Worithang much before 6.30pm. And the horsemen wanted us to walk for another four hours? It would be dark in just over an hour, and we wouldn't have even started this supposed four-hour walk by then. And no one had eaten since breakfast. It was the sublime to the ridiculous. I was flabbergasted this was even being proposed.

'How would they know where they're going in the dark?' I asked.

'Everyone has torches,' Norbu responded.

That didn't make it okay.

'The horsemen are worried the horses will die tonight,' he continued. 'The horses are weak. They haven't eaten for three days because of the snow. The horsemen are very worried.'

Although not a horse expert, I was fairly certain that a pack of healthy animals could make it through a few days without food, as long as they had water. And the alternative – getting lost in a blizzard – sounded far more dangerous to horse and human alike. 'I will talk to Krista,' I replied.

I walked on a little with Krista. 'This is bullshit,' I said. 'Horses don't just drop dead from starvation overnight. It's mad. I can't believe they're even thinking we should keep going.'

Krista looked uncertain.

'Okay,' I said, trying to think of alternatives. 'What if we stay at Worithang, with Norbu and Leki, and the horsemen carry on to below the snowline? They can camp wherever they like and come back for us in the morning. The horses get to graze tonight and we don't have to walk in the dark.'

It was not ideal but I hoped it would satisfy the horsemen.

'I'm not sure,' Krista mused. 'Maybe we should just keep going?'

'No, it's insane,' I replied. 'Who goes walking in the mountains in the snow and the dark? I am not going any further than tonight's camp.'

I would not back down on this. I stomped back to Norbu, who was standing with Torchen and Rinzin.

'It's crazy to keep walking tonight and we're not prepared to go further than Worithang,' I announced. 'We are all exhausted. We haven't eaten since eight o'clock this morning. If the horsemen wanted to go so far in one day, they should have got up earlier. Krista and I were ready at seven o'clock, but we didn't leave until nine. I know they were sick last night but the late start doesn't help us now.'

Norbu stood quietly while I ranted.

'The horses are not going to die tonight. I accept they are hungry – so am I – but the horsemen should have brought food for them. That's not my responsibility. It's going to be dark before we even start this extra walk. Yes, they may have torches, but torches won't help them find the trail when it's covered in snow. We could easily get lost. And apart from anything else, it's dangerous. Any one of us, or one of the horses, could fall over a rock or down a slope in the dark and break a leg.'

Not stopping to draw breath, I continued. 'It's well below zero and it's only going to get colder. What if it starts snowing again? How do they know it's an extra four hours? They haven't been here before. Today has taken twice as long as we thought it would. We could be flailing around all night in the snow.' I finished with my compromise proposal. 'Why don't we camp at Worithang and the horsemen can take the horses to wherever they can find grazing? They will have to walk back to Worithang in the morning. But I am not walking to another campsite tonight.'

I didn't wait for a response. I trudged back to Krista and the two of us set off up the slope towards the third pass. Krista was still uncertain, wanting to accommodate the horsemen. I felt like a truculent child, leaving Norbu to contemplate his second not-so-happy guest of the day. He would have to break the news to the horsemen. For the first time, there was a frisson of tension.

I looked over to see Norbu deep in discussion with the rest of the crew but he didn't come back to us. We stopped to wait for him.

'What's the plan, then?' Krista asked, when he'd caught up. 'Do the horsemen want to keep going?'

I began to mentally rehearse again why I would not be going any further than Worithang. But, thankfully, I didn't need to fall back on my Taurean obstinacy.

'We will camp at Worithang,' he replied. 'The chef will stay with us. The horsemen will go on to Dhur Tshachu.'

And that was that. Norbu didn't seem to want to elaborate. I couldn't work out if he was cross with us or with the horsemen or both.

I expected that we would be left with minimal supplies, enough to get us through the night. We might not have the luxury of a hot water bottle to warm our sleeping bags but that was a small price to pay for not having to wade through deep snow for most of the night.

'Do you think we should keep going with them?' Krista asked again.

'No, I don't,' I said, emphatically.

Stretching out in front of us was the solemn cortege of our horses and crew, struggling onwards while we followed a short distance behind. There was a palpable feeling of discontent and I felt that our group, which had until now been a harmonious unit, was newly divided. I muttered to Krista under my breath, annoyed that we had been put in the position of having to refuse to continue. I suspected the horsemen thought we were being feeble. I thought they were being reckless. I tried to forget my irritation and focus on the hour and a half's walk that still lay ahead of us. At least we were only going as far as Worithang.

Thankfully, the climb to the third pass was fairly short and the gradient gentle. In half an hour, we had scaled the pass and from there we wended our way down a gradual incline to an expansive, marshy plain. Flat, yes, but far from easy. A Gordian knot of partially frozen streams crisscrossed the meadow, and we tramped across snowy hummocks of spongy grass, unsure whether we would step on solid ground or sink ankle-deep into freezing water.

The last blush of the sun had disappeared slowly. In its place, an almost full moon reflected off the snow with a silvery glow. We marched on, grateful for the pool of cold light that alleviated the gathering darkness, painting the world in a metallic sheen. There was not a breath of wind. I listened to our footsteps breaking through the crust of snow. I felt as if this day would never end, that we would keep plodding on, as we had done for the last ten hours. And, to my surprise, I felt physically able to do so. Despite the cold and the lack of food, the rhythm of walking carried me along.

Another obstacle: an unexpected river, frozen along the banks but feisty further out. In the semi-darkness, shiny wet rocks and tumbling water became one. We searched for an obvious crossing place but found none, although, again, the Black Dog mysteriously appeared on the opposite bank. Norbu gallantly offered to give me a piggyback across. Perhaps it was a peace offering. Ordinarily I would have declined, too proud to accept help, but by now I didn't have the energy to refuse. I accepted his kind offer and was transported successfully, if not very elegantly, to the other side. Krista followed beside us, insistent that she could make it across herself.

In the moonlight, I could just see the dark silhouette of a herder's hut on top of a small rise. It was almost entombed under a cocoon of deep snow. We had arrived at Worithang.

NO ROOM AT THE INN

It was 7.30pm. We hadn't eaten for almost twelve hours and had walked through deep snow for ten hours straight. But we had arrived.

A steep, short climb brought us to the hut. It was built of rough grey rocks scavenged from the surrounding slopes. Drifting snow reached halfway up the walls, long slender icicles hung, like glassy daggers, from the eaves, and the roof was just visible under a thick covering of snow. In different circumstances, it would have made the perfect Santa's grotto. There was something comforting about this simple hut, evidence of others who had been here, though they were long since gone.

The crude door gave way stubbornly as Agye shouldered it open. I followed hesitantly, conscious that this was, for part of the year at least, someone's home. Yak herders lived here in summer, when the surroundings were alpine meadows, rich grazing for their animals. Now it was empty, abandoned until next year. There were no windows, and with only faint moonlight glinting through the doorway, we were immediately swallowed by the darkness. The air smelled stale and dank. Someone squeezed in behind me, torch beam bouncing off the bare stones. Inside was almost as barren as the world beyond the crumbling walls: a single room, a rough dirt floor, a stack of wood against the back wall, a pile of ash – the remains of a fire, lit by the rightful residents. I imagined colonies of tiny creatures lurking in the dark corners, with the hut closed up for months at a time. But not an insect stirred. The hut was empty – the yak herders had cleared out all their worldly possessions. Still, it was a welcome refuge and I was glad we had found it. Maybe, if the crew wanted to get away quickly and avoid putting up the tents, we could spend the night inside.

The horsemen tramped in and out, looking sullen. They stacked baskets and other gear in precarious piles against the walls until the hut was almost full. In a small space at the back Sangay was busy getting a fire going, making use of the stack of wood in the corner. I hoped whoever had left it there wouldn't mind too much that we had helped ourselves to some of it. Sangay crouched down and blew gently into the glowing sparks, coaxing the flames to take hold. As the branches sputtered and crackled, sooty smoke billowed all around us. My eyes stung sharply, driving me outside into the clean night air.

Krista was already outside. The temperature was well below zero, and I breathed deeply, clearing the choking smoke from my throat. All around us, the mountains stood like massive ghostly forms in the moonlight. Our weary horses stood untethered in a line, heads hanging. They were exhausted.

Norbu appeared.

'The horsemen are staying here tonight,' he announced. 'They are too tired.'

'What? What about their dying horses?'

'Everyone is exhausted. Today has been very tough. They would like to give the horses some rice.'

The standoff earlier had been unnecessary but I was relieved the horsemen would spend the night here in Worithang. We had all had a difficult day. Norbu explained that the horsemen were still very concerned about their weak and ravenous horses and had asked if they could cook some of our supplies for them. 'Of course!' I had already eaten more rice on this trek than I would normally consume in a year. If we could share some with the horses, I would be delighted.

'Are the horsemen angry with us for not continuing further tonight?' Krista asked.

'No, no, they are not,' Norbu assured her.

'What did you say to them earlier, when they wanted to continue?'

'I asked to them, "Why we are here? We are here because of the guest. The guest is frightened and does not want to walk in the dark." They understand.'

I bit my tongue. I could see no reason for the horsemen to be angry with us. If they were, at that moment, I didn't care. Staying at Worithang had nothing to do with being frightened. Had there been a compelling reason to walk through the night, I would have done so. But there was no point in inflaming the situation so I kept my thoughts to myself. Everyone had been pushed hard today and Norbu had been calm and encouraging, doing his best to hold the peace and to respect the horsemen's wishes to take care of their animals.

Ten metres across the snow, Rinzin and Torchen were setting up tents. So much for sleeping in the hut.

'What are they doing, Norbu?' I asked. 'Who is sleeping on the snow?'

'You are,' Norbu replied. 'There is not enough space in the hut for everyone to sleep.'

Another night on the snow. I was starting to shiver. From where we were standing outside, the orange light from the fire looked cosy and inviting. We followed Norbu back inside, stooping through the low doorway and finding a space next to the fire. The wood hissed and sparked but, now that the flames had taken hold, the smoke was bearable.

Sitting cross-legged on the floor, Norbu the horseman chopped up piles of vegetables. Using his *patang*, the knife the size of a small sword which he wore in a sheath hanging from his belt, he soon had a huge mound of diced carrots, potatoes and greens. The vegetables would be cooked up with rice for the horses. With luck, they wouldn't starve to death overnight. Outside, Leki was hard at work in the kitchen tent, preparing dinner.

When it was ready, we broke with protocol to eat together in the semi-darkness of the herders' shelter, huddled together around the fire. The horsemen's gigantic shadows, like the mythical stars of an Indonesian shadow-puppet show, played on the bare walls, bending across the low ceiling and dancing in tune to the flickering flames. The crew gulped down their soup in loud, contented slurps.

'Sorry, sorry,' Norbu said on behalf of our noisy dining companions. 'I know you do not eat your soup like this.'

Slurping soup was the least of my worries. I didn't care about slurping, burping or any other noises the horsemen chose to make. The main thing was that we were all safe, with shelter, a fire and hot food.

After walking through the snow all day, everyone's socks and boots were soaking wet. With dinner over, we wrung out our socks and draped them over a line of wet boots around the fire. The pungent smell of wet, sweaty wool, steaming next to the flames, was overpowering. Norbu felt obliged to apologise again: this time for the ignominy of his guests having to sit around a fire, competing with the horsemen's gnarled feet for sock-drying space. But I could not have been happier. The storm had passed and we were over the worst of the high passes. I relaxed for the first time in three days and the tiredness in my limbs began to melt away. Once again, I felt at one with this group of familiar strangers, of whom we knew so little but with whom we had experienced so much.

There was no need for conversation and we lapsed into companionable silence, watching the jumping flames. It was warm and almost comfortable in the hut and I was reluctant to leave when it was time for bed. Sleeping in a tent pitched on snow was not very appealing, but we had no choice. I paused for a moment in the doorway, savouring the relative warmth inside but awestruck by the scene outside. The light from a bright moon caught the ice crystals on the surface of the snow, making it sparkle like a vast sea of tiny jewels. A myriad of stars shone brightly in the blackness of the night sky and all around us colossal mountains loomed. I felt very small.

It was too cold to stand around for long. Krista and I tramped across the frozen ground to our tent. Our nightly ablutions would have to wait until tomorrow. A quick glance in my pocket mirror showed the skin on my cheeks had been reddened and scorched from this burst of Arctic weather. I slapped on some moisturiser, more thermal tops and leggings and climbed into my freezing sleeping bag. Even the hot water bottle made little impact on the cold nylon. 'We must be mad,' I said, not for the first time on this trek. I curled up tightly, trying to preserve what was left of my body heat.

The day had been a test of endurance, and full of dramatic contrasts: from the all-consuming white-out conditions in the morning to the intermittent sun and perfect calm of the late afternoon; from the anxiety and stress of getting to the summit of the Saga La to the relief of the gentle descent from the Worithang La; from the uncertain debate about where we would camp for the night to the relative security of the yak herders' hut. I felt drained, both physically and emotionally, but despite this, or perhaps because of it, sleep did not come easily. My mind raced, reliving the events of the day until exhaustion finally took over and I fell into a cold and restless sleep.

GOOD MORNING, SUNSHINE

The next morning, an ice-encrusted sleeping bag rested against my cheek once again. But unlike the last few mornings, when a pessimistic grey light had heralded the arrival of the new day, bright sunshine burst through the blue nylon of the tent. Still in that drowsy reverie between sleep and wakefulness, I wondered for an instant where I was.

'Good morning, Sunshine!' Krista, still buried in her sleeping bag, smiled across the tent.

'Good morning, Sunshine, indeed!'

Outside, our world had been transformed. The blizzard had vanished, taking with it the strain and pressures of the last few days. The sun, rising behind distant mountains, painted the sky with streaks of orange. The blanket of snow had gone from a depressing grey reflection of low, heavy clouds, to a dazzling, fluorescent brilliance. The previous day felt like a dream. I was elated. It didn't matter that inside the tent my water bottle was now a cylinder of ice and my snow boots were not only frozen solid but also frozen to the plastic sheeting on the floor. I peeled them off and put them outside to defrost. My camera was more of a problem. It was so cold that the battery had completely drained. I tried the old trick of putting the battery in an inside pocket of my jacket, hoping that the feeble heat from my body would be enough to bring it back to life. It wasn't.

The glare of the high Himalayan sun reflecting off the snow was intense, even at this early hour. Already the air was warming up. The snow, piled high on the roof of the hut, was beginning to melt, the drifts beneath the eaves catching the splash of the constant drips.

Our arrival in near darkness the previous evening had kept the setting of our campsite under wraps. Now all was revealed. It was like an image from *National Geographic* magazine. We were in a perfect amphitheatre, almost completely encircled by serried, unclimbed peaks etched against an empty sky. To one side, a precipice dropped away to a deep gorge below. Behind us, the summits of snowy mountains bobbed like the white caps of a churning ocean. And all around, the gods had thrown a mantle of ermine across the earth.

Norbu was organising the breakfast table outside the hut. 'Good morning. Did you sleep well?'

'Good morning, Norbu. Isn't this amazing? I'm so happy about the weather.' I looked around. 'But where are the horses?'

Usually, they stayed close to the camp but this morning they were nowhere to be seen. I fleetingly considered asking if the horsemen's worst fears had been realised and the horses had expired overnight, but thought better of it.

'They were so hungry,' Norbu said, 'they were eating everything, even the luggages, so the horsemen took them further away.'

The horses, though banished from camp, were safe, but there was a bigger problem: Rinzin and Thinley couldn't see. They had been snow-blinded and were in such pain they couldn't open their eyes.

'They have been crying during the night, they are so worried,' Norbu said.

How could this have happened?

'Wasn't Rinzin wearing sunglasses yesterday? I asked.

'Yes, but he gave them to Sangay in the afternoon,' Norbu explained. That was when the sun was at its brightest.

'But Thinley wore sunglasses all day yesterday,' Krista said.

'They are cheap, from India,' Norbu replied. 'The lenses are no good.'

As we were talking, Rinzin came stumbling out of the hut. He had pulled his beanie right down over his face and had wound a scarf over the top, around his eyes. Norbu rushed over to guide him away from the tent ropes. I wondered how we were going to find our way today when our trail guide couldn't see. Closely behind Rinzin, Thinley emerged from inside, tripping over a wicker basket in the doorway. Sangay took him gently by the arm and steered him away from the obstacles of the campsite. I felt terrible for these men who had looked after us so well.

'Tell them that snow blindness is usually temporary,' I told Norbu. 'It's like sunburn on their eyes. They must keep their eyes out the sun until they're better.'

Krista and I found our spare sunglasses and gave a pair each to Rinzin and Thinley, with strict instructions not to take them off. They put the glasses on under their beanies. I lathered high factor suncream over my face and insisted the crew did too. The last thing we needed now was a severe case of sunburn. The searing UV rays at these high altitudes were unforgiving.

Our plan for the day was for Krista and me to walk with Norbu, Rinzin and Sangay. Sangay would act as Rinzin's eyes and Thinley would be guided by Norbu the horseman and Agye.

The snow had obliterated all traces of the path but, without the accompanying blizzard, other landmarks were visible and the lack of an obvious trail was no longer a cause for concern. The Black Dog, who had joined us for breakfast, trotted along next to us as we set off.

Frozen streams cut across the hillside below the camp. Once babbling brooks, they were static now, silenced into glistening bands of grey-blue ice. Pretty to look at but potentially lethal to tread on, they fed into a wider stream that, predictably, barred our way. We walked up and down, scouring the channel for a crossing point. With potential stepping stones covered in slippery ice, there was no easy way across. Norbu came to the rescue again, wading across to offer Krista and me a piggyback, in turn, to the other side. Today, we both gratefully accepted.

Once on the far bank, we battled up a slope through fresh, knee-deep snow. With a frozen layer of ice on top, but soft powder underneath, it made for difficult and exhausting walking. Every step was an effort: breaking through the top crust then sinking down through soft snow, one slow step at a time. Still, the weather had turned, and I was at one with the world, spellbound by the undulating blanket of white.

A forty-minute climb brought us to the only pass of the day, the 4495-metre Nephu La. This was not a statement pass: there were no prayer flags to mark the top, just a modest cairn that was almost completely buried under a mound of snow. It was a relief to have reached the pass early in the day. The surrounding mountains were high but the snow had smoothed the sharp angles into softer curves. The landscape no longer seemed menacing, as it had over the past few days.

'Almost all downhill,' Norbu assured us, as we started down from the pass.

'It's never all downhill,' I replied.

But today, for a while at least, I was wrong. It was an abrupt descent, on a slippery surface, that dictated a careful pace. Below the snow covering, loose stones skidded under our feet. One careless step and a broken ankle was all but guaranteed. This was the path that the horsemen had wanted us to follow the previous night, assuming they'd been able to find it.

Krista and I discussed the treacherous trail.

'How crazy would it have been on this trail last night?' Krista remarked.

'Exactly!' I agreed.

'Can you imagine doing this in the dark, Norbu?' I asked. 'It would have been ridiculous.'

He might have agreed, but he didn't say so.

Poor Rinzin. He was shielding his eyes with his beanie and scarf and was being guided slowly by Sangay, who steered him gently by the arm. We were still relying on Rinzin to check that we hadn't lost the trail – not that we could see a trail under the snow. He stopped every now and then, peeled back his beanie and squinted at the mountains before issuing instructions to Norbu and Sangay.

Far below us, a sacred lake, Animo Tsho, dazzled in the sun. Norbu told us that some people claim to see a red scarf floating in the water, said to have been thrown in by a nun who jumped in after the scarf and drowned. Norbu warned us that speech is forbidden close to this holy lake. Today, no one was silent. After the tensions of the day before, it was good to chat.

An hour later, the snow cover was thinning and slushy. We were approaching the treeline. It was hard to believe that the previous night we had camped on a foot of snow. Now we were back in an alpine forest, with only a few pockets still frozen in sheltered dips and hollows.

Sangay stopped, pointing to the slopes high above us.

'Blue sheep!'

I squinted up at the towering cliff face but the blue sheep remained elusive, camouflaged against the grey crags. Finally, I saw one, then another and another. There were at least a dozen of them, flitting nimbly across precarious balconies on the near-vertical rock face. It wasn't clear how these mountain dwellers had come to be called blue sheep: they looked and moved more like mountain goats, and neither were they blue. Their grey coats blended seamlessly with their rocky domain and they were given away only by the vertical stripe of black and white on their legs and their extravagant backward-curled horns. I watched as they leapt gracefully from one rocky turret to another, sending showers of loose pebbles hurtling down the cliff. If only I were that agile on this challenging terrain. Despite the sheer drop and the lack of any obvious ledges, they seemed fearless, and almost invisible against the grey slabs of their mountain playground. They stopped every now and again to nibble the sparse grasses that managed to grow among the rocks and scree, looking around casually, confident they were safe from predators on such a precipice. It was a treat to watch them at home in their natural environment.

We continued our descent, Sangay taking care to guide Rinzin around unexpected obstacles on the trail. By late morning, we had dropped more than 1000 metres, to well below the snowline. Yet we were still a long way from Dhur Tshachu, our destination for the day. These natural hot springs, in a secluded valley, were just one of several locations across Bhutan where locals flocked to bathe in the therapeutic springs. For the Bhutanese, a dip in a hot spring was a popular pursuit, an excuse for a social get-together and an opportunity to benefit from the much-lauded healing properties of the mineral-infused water. And, in many cases, a rare chance to enjoy a hot bath. The springs at Dhur are some of the least visited in the country, requiring an energy-sapping, two-day hike from Bumthang to reach them. After fourteen days of walking, and despite my attempt at a shower in Thanza, the prospect of a soak in a hot tub was very appealing. I couldn't wait to get there.

By noon, we hadn't seen anywhere flat enough to camp. I thought again how dangerous it would have been to struggle with this descent late the previous night, in darkness and in a state of complete exhaustion, sliding through slush, tripping over tree branches and unstable rocks, in search of an elusive campsite. I was glad that I had been stubborn.

DESTINATION DHUR

Thickets of rhododendron bushes gave way to primordial forests of conifers and juniper. An energetic stream bubbled from fissures in the rock, next to our path. We were back to viscous mud and leaf litter underfoot, wet and soggy and almost as slippery as the snow higher up. We passed numerous landslides, the rotting trunks of fallen trees lying across the slope, snapped and broken as they'd been swept down the hillside. Another river to cross, deeper this time, gushing over muddled boulders and the carcasses of partly submerged trees, deposited by some previous landslide or flood. But at least there was an attempt at a bridge: a couple of wobbly tree trunks, wet and slippery, straddling the river. This was not the only time on the trek that I wondered how secure the bridge was and whether these decaying logs would hold out until we all made it to the other side. I needn't have worried. The boys, once again, guided us across without incident.

We stopped for a late lunch in a clearing high above the Mangde Chu, watched over attentively by the Black Dog. In front of us, a sheer vertical drop disappeared towards the valley floor. By leaning over the edge, I could just catch a glimpse of a foaming waterfall that plummeted over the cliff, into the river far below. The guides were alarmed that I might topple over.

'You're only bothered about all the forms you'd have to fill in if I fell over the edge, Norbu,' I teased. 'How would you explain setting off with two guests and coming back with just one?'

Norbu had it all worked out.

'This is how it is. We have already agreed,' he said, 'if I lose you, Krista will do the paperwork.'

'Okay la. Glad you have that all sorted.'

Overhead, a shiny blue-black raven swooped. This was the first time we had seen one, the national bird and representative of one of Bhutan's most powerful protective deities, Jarog Dongchen.

A biting wind began to blow, forcing us to wrap up our leisurely lunch stop and press on. Rinzin's eyes were a little better and he left them uncovered, but protected by sunglasses, for a few moments at a time. We'd gone less than 50 metres before the path disappeared, swallowed by another landslide of rubble and vegetation, trailing haphazardly across the path. Contorted trees, uprooted and dead now, their hollow, decaying trunks open to the sky, lay in a morass of saturated debris. We scrambled over the obstacles, trying not to sink through the rotting wood, confident we could tackle anything this trek could throw at us. The trail continued along the hillside. For the most part, it was just wide enough for one person, a pencil-thin ribbon threading along a ledge, high above the rushing river. On both sides of the valley, the folds of the mountains swept down to the river like a series of uneven pleats.

We were following the Mangde Chu valley, through coarse gorse bushes, low shrubs and rocks. And then we began to climb – there was always a climb – up to Dhur.

'See, I told you it wasn't all downhill,' I reminded Norbu.

The Black Dog led the way, trotting ahead as we toiled up a muddy trail. Suddenly, he veered off the path and barked loudly and incessantly, charging through the trees and then back to us. We couldn't see anything but felt sure that he could. Not long afterwards, Sangay spotted a bear print in the mud.

'There are many bears here,' Norbu told us.

'Do you know what to do if you meet a bear?' Krista asked.

Everyone stopped to listen.

'Do not look the bear in the eye,' she instructed. 'Hold your backpack above you head – which makes you look taller – and slowly walk backwards. Do not run!'

Norbu translated for the others who wasted no time in practising walking backwards through the trees, with their backpacks above their heads. I wondered if Krista might have been making it up.

Up ahead a 'No Camping' sign marked the approach to the hot springs. We had not seen another soul for four days by this point, not even a yak. We knew there was another trekking party somewhere behind us, but they might as well have been in Australia. Now, just that little sign was an indication that we were no longer in the wilderness. The path meandered alongside the river as it surged down a steep-sided valley. Nestled among the trees, seven or eight crude wooden huts were built around a series of hot springs. We left the path to investigate, dipping our hands into the water, sending clouds of steam billowing into the air. The springs ranged in temperature from warm to hot. Tubs about the size of a small bath were brimming full of hot water that flowed from a pipe in the ground and then drained away into the river. It was tempting to jump in there and then. But first we had to attend to the practicalities of setting up camp.

Just beyond the last bathing hut a large 'guesthouse' stood in a clearing. The front door was open but there was no one around. It was a bigger and cleaner version of the huts at Koina and Rodophu: not a guesthouse in the Western sense, but a big open main room, with smaller rooms off to the side. All were empty. When Norbu had told us, two days before, that the horsemen had been keen to reach the guesthouse at Dhur, I had imagined a bed and breakfast, or something resembling a basic family-run guesthouse. My Western brain still hadn't quite adapted to the Bhutanese way. But, although surprised, I was not disappointed. The contrast between this and the previous night's hut was vast.

'Would you like to sleep in the guesthouse?' Norbu asked.

'Yes please!' we both answered immediately. The idea of a level floor and a ceiling, tall enough to allow us to stand upright, was unadulterated luxury and we jumped at the chance. The last few days had been a baptism in trekking in extreme conditions. Tonight, we would have a hot bath and a roof over our heads. How could it get any better? Even the Black Dog seemed content to be here, flopping down in the yard for an afternoon snooze.

Back outside, we waited impatiently for the horses to arrive. I was distracted for a moment by a sculpture fixed above the front door of the guesthouse: a proud, carved wooden phallus, complete with black-painted balls. The whole ensemble was adorned with a white silk scarf, tied around the base. Norbu laughed as I toppled off a rock, trying to get the best camera angle.

'Penises are not a laughing matter,' I scolded.

'But they are,' Krista giggled, and proceeded to tell Norbu how we had traumatised the customs officer at Brisbane airport the previous year, when he asked to see the 'wooden souvenirs' declared on our customs forms, on our return from Bhutan. The poor man almost died of embarrassment when Susie, Krista and I each produced a wooden penis, about a foot long and painted scarlet or, in my case, fuchsia pink. He took one look at them and waved us quickly through.

Distracted by talk of phallic sculptures, we hadn't noticed a little boy who emerged, as if by magic, from the trees. Aged about four, he was blessed with smiling eyes, fringed with long dark eyelashes and an impish grin. Not far behind him a young man appeared, introducing himself in English as Tenzin. He told us he was standing in for his father-in-law, the caretaker of the guesthouse, who was receiving medical treatment. I gave the little boy, who it transpired was Tenzin's nephew, a striped fleece beanie in the style of a trapper hat, with two green pompoms hanging from the earflaps. He was tickled pink and spent the rest of the evening twirling the pompoms coquettishly.

Before long, the horses spilled down the narrow path into the yard. They were impatient to be free of their loads to graze, after their meagre rations in the snow. As soon as our bags were unloaded, Krista and I found our wash bags and towels and were ready for a dip in the hot springs.

Although the wooden bathing huts had both doorways and window frames, they had neither doors nor windows. A pair of boots outside the first hut indicated that it was already taken. We moved on to the next one. There was no obvious sign of anyone there so we went inside, hung our towels over the window frame, stripped off and jumped into the tub. There was no standing on ceremony. The water was deliciously hot, we were looking out onto a peaceful woodland scene, with a bubbling river running past, and I could finally scrub off the grime of the last two weeks. It was sublime. And I appreciated it so much more after those nights in the snow, when I'd thought I would never be warm again.

I told Krista about my previous outdoor bathing escapade in Bhutan, in 2011. At the end of a day exploring the village of Laya, Norbu had led us through narrow laneways between the farmhouses and part way down a hill. In the partial darkness, I could just make out the bath: a large wooden tub which bore more than a passing resemblance to a horse's drinking trough.

Next to the bathtub, a bow-legged old man, well wrapped against the evening chill, had stooped over a fire. The bath was already full of water when we'd arrived — a quick temperature test suggested it had come straight from the glacier above the village. The old man carefully picked up some smooth rocks with a pair of long metal tongs and placed them into the embers. Once the stones were hot, he collected them from the fire, one by one and dunked them into a bucket of water, to rinse off the soot and ash, before dropping them, hissing and spitting, into the water. A few minutes later, steam was rising in clouds from the tub. Satisfied that the bathwater was hot enough, he signalled for us to get in.

By this time, twilight had turned to darkness so, throwing modesty to the wind, we stripped off in turn and plunged into the hot bath. Norbu, determined to protect our modesty from any curious Layaps, had set up a tarpaulin in front of the bathtub. He stood guard on the other side, with arms folded, in case anyone should attempt to disturb his guests.

As the water had started to cool, our trusty spa attendant shuffled over to the bath with more hot stones balanced in his tongs, submerging them in the water. He had not been remotely interested in the giggling guests in his tub.

In Dhur, with the constant supply of flowing hot water, we were spared the excitement of scalding stones being dropped into one end of the bath. It made for a more relaxing soak. I could have sat in the hot tub for hours, the ache in my exhausted limbs gradually easing. The combination of being submerged in hot water and breathing through the sulphurous steam was soporific. I was beginning to feel light-headed, dizzy almost. Maybe it was the therapeutic effect of the natural minerals in the thermal spring or the billowing steam, rising from the hot water. Maybe it was just the sensation of being warm right through for the first time in two weeks. Whatever it was, I felt as if my mind had temporarily left my body and was floating somewhere above me. Bliss.

By the time we returned to the guesthouse, the crew had collected wood and soon had a blazing bonfire burning in the yard. The Black Dog sprawled next to it, enjoying the warmth.

Tenzin, the caretaker's son-in-law, joined us for ginger tea. I was fascinated by how his life had changed beyond recognition in the past year. A year before, he told us, he had been a senior student at a school in Bumthang. He had decided to leave school and seek his fortune in Lunana, searching for the elusive cordyceps. He didn't say whether he'd found many but his trip to the mountains had been successful on another front: he had found a wife. Although only nineteen years old, he was now married to a 31-year-old yak herder from Laya and was the proud co-owner of a herd of more than a hundred yaks. We asked about the value of a yak – anything from 35,000 to 70,000 ngultrums – about A$700 to A$1400. Life in the mountains may have been harsh but many yak herders had, by Bhutanese standards, vast amounts of wealth tied up in their livestock.

When Tenzin left for the evening, the Black Dog went with him. We never saw him again.

We ate dinner outside around the fire, feeling warm and relaxed, while the crew took it in turns to bathe in the springs. By the end of the evening we were all cleaner than we had been at any stage since leaving Gasa. Thankfully, too, by the end of the day, Rinzin's and Thinley's eyesight had almost returned to normal. And Krista was back to being a happy guest.

What a contrast to the day before. Retiring for the night to our little room, Krista and I edged past the sleeping horsemen, curled up on the floor in the main room of the guesthouse under their blankets. It was almost balmy now that we were at a mere 3100 metres. The air was replete with oxygen, making breathing easy after our nights at close to 5000 metres. Although I had only been in Dhur for a few hours, I already felt as though I had been transported to another world. I fell into a deep, peaceful sleep, the rushing river babbling just outside our window.

'LET'S HAVE SEX'

For the first time in many days we were camped among trees and were greeted with birdsong at dawn. We set off early, in bright sunshine. With just two days to go before the end of the trek, I was ready for an easy day's walking. But that was wishful thinking. Today would be one of the steepest and longest ascents of the trek.

Our first encounter of the day was with a knock-kneed old man who came hobbling along in the opposite direction. He seemed very excited to see us, talking animatedly and waving his arms wildly. We had no idea what he was trying to say. Summoning Norbu to translate, we discovered that he had just seen a bear and was warning us to be careful. Norbu thought he was probably drunk; still, remembering the bear print from the day before, we thought it was just possible that he wasn't making it up. We thanked him for his words of caution and pressed on. Keen to avoid adding a bear attack to our trekking experience, Norbu and Torchen didn't take any chances. They insisted on walking ahead of us, crashing along the path, wielding sticks and shouting loudly, just in case.

'I have my backpack ready to hold above my head,' Norbu said earnestly.

Krista laughed.

On a small flat ridge, we came upon a ramshackle yak herder's hut. A middle-aged man, with a grubby *gho* straining over his ample girth, waved to us from the doorway. About a dozen black yaks milled around, squelching up to their knees in the soft, churned earth. A young woman, wrapped up in a patterned headscarf, knelt in the mud, milking an enormous yak that looked as if it would rather be somewhere else. A few metres away, an elderly lady smiled as we approached. She was surrounded by a clutch of yak calves, feeding from her hand with noisy slurps as they nuzzled and pushed and shoved for prime position. I asked if I might take her photograph and she agreed readily, grinning for the camera. When I showed her the image on the digital display, she exploded with laughter. It turned out she was wearing her multicoloured hat – like a rainbow version of a Moroccan fez – back to front. She reversed the wardrobe malfunction so I could take another photo, with her hat duly adjusted.

Hanging from a tree near the hut was a collection of woven yak hair shoulder bags.

'Does the lady make these bags, Norbu?' I asked.

'Yes, she is selling them.'

'What do you think? Should I buy one?' Krista wondered aloud.

We debated the bag purchase but, in the end, she decided against it.

We left the herders behind, and the day's punishing ascent of more than 1000 metres continued without reprieve. It was a gruelling climb on a rocky trail of tight switchbacks. My heart was pounding.

'I wish I'd bought that yak hair bag,' Krista said ruefully, half an hour up the slope. 'It would have been nice to have one knowing it was made right there.'

'Next time!' I'd gone too far to contemplate going back.

We were under a tangle of trees that permitted little sunlight through to the forest floor. A monk accompanied by two young men appeared on the path, stopping to chat to Norbu. I stopped too, glad of the excuse for a rest. The monk was a *doma* aficionado, his lips and teeth stained the same maroon as his robes. He and his friends carried minimal bedding and, as far as I could see, no tent or other covering. They would have slept in a cave, or under whatever shelter they could find. They had travelled to Bumthang by bus, all the way from Eastern Bhutan, and were now on the final leg of their walk from Bumthang to the hot springs. The three of them were suffering from mild snow blindness, their eyes, unprotected by sunglasses, hurting from the bright glare of the snow during their walk the previous day. We gave them some of our remaining pairs of sunglasses and wished them well.

After I'd caught my breath I announced, *'Ju gey! Ju gey!'* Or so I thought. Norbu and the guides fell about laughing.

'What's so funny?' I asked, bemused.

'What you have said can mean 'Let's have sex''', Norbu explained, giggling.

'Oh dear.' At least the monk was out of earshot. But I needed to work on my Dzongkha. After two weeks in the company of our Bhutanese crew, my entire vocabulary comprised 'hello', 'thank you', 'yak cheese', 'let's go', 'mud', 'water', 'I'm doing fantastic', 'good luck' 'I've had enough' and 'let's have sex'. At least I had most essentials covered.

Eventually, we emerged from the trees into an open meadow, surrounded by slopes smothered in wall-to-wall rhododendrons. They would be stunning in spring, when the flowers were in bloom.

'What variety of rhododendron is this, Norbu?' Krista teased.

'I am no longer talking about rhododendrons,' he responded.

From our rest stop, there was another hour's climb to the Gongto La, at 4327 metres. We were once again above the treeline, the landscape becoming more dramatic. As we laboured breathlessly up the trail, the clouds closed in, mist wreathed around the ridges and we were back to a dusting of snow on the ground. Threadbare prayer flags, shredded by wind and weather, hung limply between upright poles, planted in clusters at the pass. It was noticeably colder and, with little in the way of a view, we kept going.

Beyond the Gongto La, our route took us along the shore of a malevolent dark green lake. Eddying mist settled over the water in low layers, as a cold wind sent ripples galloping across the surface. It was brought home to me yet again how quickly the weather in the mountains could change and I was glad I'd packed my fleece and Gore-Tex jacket in my daypack, despite feeling convinced, when we'd set off, that I wouldn't need either.

Our lunch stop for the day was a grassy pasture that swept down to the lake. The horses ambled past, stopping to graze urgently while they had the chance. As we made our way slowly up towards the next pass, the Djule La, the temperature fell as sharply as the gradient increased. Noble rhubarb stood tall across the hillside, still looking more like a series of trail markers than high-altitude plants. A wall of snow and rock reared up in front of us and I could just make out our horses, following a seemingly invisible path, before they disappeared. It was a slow, painful climb, on an uneven rocky trail hacked out of the mountainside, towards the final high pass of the trek. Spotting a cairn topped with a tall pole and bright red prayer flag, I was hopeful that we'd arrived. Frustratingly, and not for the first time, it turned out to be a false pass. But the actual pass wasn't too much further and, just as at the Saga La a few days earlier, the scene at the top opened out into a magnificent panorama, completely hidden until we stood, triumphantly, at the pass. Indigo lakes sparkled among jagged white peaks that stretched as far as we could see. With deep snow on the ground, it was a fitting scene for our last major pass of the trek. We stopped to enjoy the moment and take some photographs. We were at an elevation of 4550 metres, and I couldn't quite believe that with just one more day of walking, we would finish the trek almost 2000 metres lower. It was going to be a long, steep descent.

With heavy clouds massing behind the mountain ranges ahead, we hurried down. Snow wasn't far away. The trail scrolled around interlocking spurs, only a few pillows of snow lurking in the shadows as we descended, until we reached an area of wide open meadows. Although we had another hard day's walking to go, I felt that we were finally on the homeward stretch.

As Krista and I walked along on our own, I turned to her.

'I just wanted to say thank you for coming to Lunana with me,' I said, stopping to give her a hug.

'I'm so glad I came. It's been an amazing adventure – one I will never forget. Thank you for asking me,' she said

'Shall we do it all again next year?' I asked jokingly.

'Hmmm – I'm not so sure about that,' she replied.

A trek through Lunana wasn't everyone's cup of tea and I was grateful to have found a kindred spirit to join me. Krista and I walked at pretty much the same pace, despite my legs being considerably shorter than hers; we were content to chat for hours on end or not at all; we managed to share a tent without argument or mishap; and we both relished the opportunity to grab life by the horns and give it our best shot. We'd had a few unexpected challenges along the way but we had come through them together, in good spirits, at least for the most part. It had been good for the soul.

As we reached the valley bottom, we passed herds of yaks squelching contentedly through waterlogged ground, among a myriad of streams. There were several herders' settlements close to the trail. Only the bright blue of the tarpaulin roofs, stretched taut over the low stone walls, distinguished these basic homes from the stony ground.

The path wound up and down the valley like a roller-coaster track, as we climbed over gentle ridges and back down, all the time expecting to see the tell-tale blue of our tents in the distance. They should have been at a bend in the river known as Tshochenchen but the horsemen, out in front for once, had kept going. Finally, about an hour beyond where we had expected the camp to be, we spotted the tents on the opposite bank.

'Have you seen the angle of our tent?' Krista exclaimed, as we crossed the river. We were alarmed to see our sleeping tent pitched near the top of the steepest part of the slope. All the other tents were 20 metres below it, on a flat area of grass next to the river.

'That's ridiculous! What have we done to deserve that?'

We discussed asking the crew to move our tent but decided not to put them to further trouble. We never did discover why we had been banished to such an uncomfortable incline. It was our last night of the trek and we were going to spend it trying to defy gravity by remaining horizontal on our camp beds.

AGYE'S MUSINGS

Down by the river the boys had cajoled a fire into life and soon the flames were licking the low branches of an overhanging tree. Krista appeared from our tent, bearing gifts. She handed Norbu a bag of socks. Not just any old socks but black, knee-high Gold Toe socks: gifts for the crew. These highly sought-after American socks were proudly worn by Bhutanese men with their *gho*. They were a bit of a status symbol, the famous gold toe on display when shoes came off to enter a temple. The crew were delighted. For some, it was a long overdue upgrade of their hosiery.

Agye was exhausted. He lay on the ground next to the fire and, before long, was fast asleep, snoring gently. By the time we'd finished dinner and reconvened by the fire for our last night with the crew, he began to stir. Refreshed by his nap, he was keen to reminisce about the ups and downs of the last fifteen days.

Norbu translated for us as Agye relived the challenges of the second half of the trek, for both horses and horsemen. Although the horsemen had completed the Snowman Trek several times, they had always followed the Nikka Chu, to finish at Sephu. Our route over the Gophu La, ending a short drive from Jakar, was new territory for them and they hadn't known what to expect. They had been very anxious about the horses, Norbu said. Agye explained that, in Thanza, he had been confident about the weather. The sun had been shining, the sky a radiant blue and there had been no hint of the storm that was to come. Two days later, camped in a blizzard, he had looked up at the sky and said to himself, 'What a blunder I have made!' He had been very concerned that the horses would not make it over the Saga La, so weak were they from the long trek and lack of food when the snow set in. And he was astounded at how fast we had walked and how hard it had been for the horsemen to maintain our pace. He commented to Norbu that usually, when they went on a trek, the crew set up the tents mid-afternoon and then relaxed for a couple of hours before the guests strolled into camp late in the day. On our trek, the horsemen had had to rush all day to keep up with us, only to arrive at the campsite to find us already there, meaning they then had to rush to organise the camp. The crew were full of praise for our fitness and tenacity and told us that we might all still be stuck in the snow if we hadn't kept pushing on. Krista and I did not feel that we had been walking at breakneck pace but we returned their compliments, grateful to these hardy mountain men for getting us to where we were now, despite the atrocious and unexpected weather, which had tested them and their horses to their limits.

We were all looking forward to getting to Jakar the next day, although our motivations were very different. The horsemen were keen to get back to plentiful grazing for their weary horses and to the truck that would drive them all back to Gasa, for the short walk up to Laya. Krista and I, on the other hand, were eagerly anticipating an encounter with some naked, dancing monks.

The Treasure Dance was an ancient dance, traditionally performed by naked monks around a fire at Jambay Lhakhang temple in Bumthang, at some unearthly hour. I had read about it when we were planning the trip and it was no coincidence that we would finish the trek on the night the dance was scheduled to take place. Norbu explained that those who witnessed it were blessed with long life and, for those brave enough to sit close to the dancers, the blessing was even more significant. It was not to be missed.

On that note, and with the drizzle once again turning to rain, it was time for bed. I was awake for what seemed like an eternity, wrestling with the noise of the rain and the gravity issues posed by the angle of our tent. Not long after I'd finally managed to get to sleep, I awoke to find the cold wet nylon of the roof pressed against my cheek: the deluge had collapsed my side of the tent. It was too wet to go outside to try to fix it. Instead, I shuffled down the camp bed, and spent the rest of the night trying desperately not to fall off the bed at one end, or be slapped in the face by a wet tent roof at the other. So much for a restful sleep.

IN SEARCH OF NAKED MEN

The final day of the trek dawned wet and miserable. The heavy rain had subsided, to be replaced by a murky drizzle. The air was cool and tendrils of mist clung to the hillsides around the camp. It was not quite what I'd had in mind for our last day of walking.

There were always people wandering along the trails in Bhutan and it wasn't unusual for us to have visitors appear from nowhere at our campsite. So when two young Bhutanese men, with heavily laden backpacks, strolled up to the tents at daybreak on our last morning, I didn't pay any attention to them. But I was surprised, and rather bemused, when Norbu announced that these were our rescuers.

'Rescuers from what?' I asked.

It turned out that the owner of the trekking company had been unable to contact us and was worried that we were stranded in a snowstorm between two of the high passes, slowly wasting away, as we exhausted our nearly depleted food stocks. He had dispatched a rescue party with fresh supplies for us. Krista and I had been rescued once before on a hike – by two hunky firemen, when we'd unwittingly walked through a controlled burn in a local forest park. On that occasion, flames in the undergrowth and smouldering embers falling from the sky had fostered a sense of imminent danger and we'd been content to be driven out in a fire truck. By contrast, the need to be rescued this time seemed absurd. Still, it was comforting to know that we hadn't been completely forgotten and that if we had been stuck at least we wouldn't have starved.

Our rescuers, in turn, were amazed that we were where we were supposed to be, and on schedule, after the storm. Their rescue mission was aborted before it had truly begun.

Leki made the most of all the extra supplies to produce an enormous breakfast. And then it was back to wet weather gear yet again. I had consigned my jacket and waterproof over-trousers to the 'not to be worn until laundered' bag, hoping I wouldn't need them again on the trek. Now, as I extracted them from all the other mouldy clothes, they smelled as if they'd been resurrected from several months languishing in a peat bog.

We set off at a gallop, following Norbu and our 'rescuers', who seemed keen to get back to wherever they'd come from as quickly as possible.

Our last trekking day was our longest in terms of distance: we were combining two days into one, so we could squeeze this trek into sixteen days. A leisurely final stroll it was not. According to the guidebook, the total distance should have been about 27 kilometres, but, in the end, I measured it at 24 kilometres. It was still a long way and, as ever in Bhutan, not much of it was flat. The trail turned out to be as bad, if not worse, than any we had been on, overgrown and muddy with slippery rocks and snarled roots, waiting to trip us up. It had been raining all night and the ground was a mud bath. Yet another day of sluicing around on a waterlogged trail.

We soon left the wide river valley, trudging along through a dark tunnel of dripping foliage. The air was cold and musty. Adding to the trials of the wet weather and muddy path, several landslides had swept down the hill, with trees dislodged and flung indiscriminately down the slope. The aftermath of one landslide, about 20 metres across, had buried a whole section of the slope under a chaotic mess of mangled tree trunks and snapped branches. We picked our way carefully over the debris, wary of what lay underneath.

There were numerous streams to be crossed, on unsteady logs that served as makeshift bridges. In places, the path seemed to be more rushing stream than well-trodden trail. My feet were soaked.

By lunchtime, the rain slackened and we found ourselves out of the tree cover. The landscape was tamer now, the horizon filled with smooth curves, replacing the steely edges of the highlands. Rinzin estimated we would have another three hours to go after lunch, which would take us to about 4.30pm. It was an arduous day of walking, not least because of the lightning-fast pace we'd kept up.

'Almost all downhill,' Norbu announced again. Eventually, it was. From the top of a hill we could see the road in the far distance, a brown gash like a scar, running through the green carpet of the pine trees. We careered downhill, the path bounded by steep banks on either side. Around a corner, reclining on a tree stump, a dapper Bhutanese man, in a charcoal *gho* and mirrored aviator sunglasses, held court in his sylvan office, his feet stretched out, as he talked loudly into his mobile phone. His pose reminded me of *Wall Street*'s Gordon Gecko, lounging on his office chair, feet propped up on his desk, phone glued to his ear.

Soon after, we met another local: a trekking guide, powering up the hill. He stopped to gossip with Norbu. Walking in the mountains, Norbu often greeted the Bhutanese that we met like long-lost brothers. I was never sure whether he knew these people – he might well have known a fellow guide – or whether he was just relieved to chat to a compatriot, after days in the company of his guests. As he and the other guide swapped stories, behind me there was a thud, then giggling, and I looked around to see Krista flat on her back among the leaf litter: her first full fall of the trek. Then I too skidded on a patch of fallen leaves. Norbu rushed over to help us both up.

'Are you okay?' he asked anxiously.

Having survived knee-deep snow, icy river crossings and mud for sixteen days, we had been defeated by a halt on a leaf-covered slope. The other guide looked at us in astonishment. He must have wondered how we'd managed to trek all the way through Lunana when we couldn't stay upright while standing still.

As we continued, the first signs that we were nearing civilisation began to appear: a telephone mast, rustic fencing, woven from a lattice of bare branches and, in the distance, the roofs of a few isolated farmhouses. And then, without warning or fanfare, a final rickety suspension bridge across a churning river led to a small hamlet and the start of the road.

'We made it!' Krista whooped.

And that was it. We'd done it, sixteen days and approximately 240 kilometres. I felt slightly bewildered. And strangely deflated. We'd finished the trek. In less than an hour we would be sitting in the hotel restaurant, eating something other than rice and curry and wondering if it had all been a dream. Well, that was the plan.

A representative from the trekking company was there to meet us.

'Congratulations!' he said. 'How was the trek?'

Before we could respond and, in keeping with the previous year's tradition, he presented us with a selection of fizzy drinks and two enormous boxes of cakes from the legendary Swiss Bakery in Thimphu. Feeling slightly overwhelmed, we left Norbu to fill him in while we retreated to a stretch of grass where we sprawled on the ground to wait for the horses. We hadn't seen them all day but we weren't expecting them to be too far behind us.

There were enough cream cakes to feed a dozen trekkers and after a diet of rice and vegetables washed down with ginger tea, chocolate éclairs and cans of Coke and Fanta were delicacies from another world. We appreciated the gesture but I wasn't sure if my stomach could cope. Krista spotted some village children and wandered over to share some of our Swiss Bakery treats with them.

At 2800 metres, just over half the height of our highest elevation, the late afternoon still held on to the warmth of the day. For a while I enjoyed relaxing on the grass, overdosing on cakes and wondering how the last sixteen days had flown past so quickly. Despite the challenges, we had survived unscathed and, for the most part, still smiling. Perhaps naively, *not* making it had never been on the cards. I had had moments of anxiety, and the reluctant acceptance that, if the snow closed in, we might have had to spend an extra night on the trek, the major consequence of which would have been missing the Treasure Dance. I had briefly considered the drama of being stranded, but that outcome had seemed fanciful. Now that I thought about it, I hadn't contemplated the disappointment that would have come with having to turn back or, worse still, be rescued. Yet, on the Snowman route, neither eventuality was unusual.

By the time Krista came back, the horses still hadn't turned up.

'Still no horses?' Krista asked.

'No, not yet. I bet they're just taking it easy,' I replied.

'Where are the horses, Norbu?' Krista asked. 'Are they just being slow because it's the last day?'

'They will be here soon. As a general, they are not far behind us. I mean,' Norbu corrected himself, 'as a general rule.'

But, an hour later, Norbu's confidence proved misguided. When darkness fell, the temperature dropped like a stone. We had long since ditched the cold ground and taken refuge in the back of the car that had come to pick us up for the half-hour drive to our lodge. There was still no sign of either horses or horsemen. We were cold and hungry and a tiny bit grumpy. Norbu and Rinzin had made fruitless calls to Torchen on his mobile. They had shouted and whistled. They had walked back up the trail, all to no avail. The horses seemed to have disappeared into thin air. Instead of a hot shower and dinner we were sitting in the back of a cold car in our now steamy, damp clothes, watching our driver play a game on his phone.

By 6.30pm we resolved to leave without them if they hadn't arrived by seven. This would be less than ideal, with most of our clothes and toiletries still strapped to the back of a horse. Right on seven o'clock, just as we were about to give up all hope, we heard the horse bells. A full two and a half hours after us, the first of our horses stumbled into the village. There was lots of shouting in Dzongkha, as the horsemen appeared out of the darkness. One by one the horses trotted onto the green, and in a flurry of activity, all the bags and baskets were unloaded.

'What happened? Where have they been?' I asked.

Norbu explained. 'The horses walked into a wasps' nest. They got stung. The horsemen got stung. All the loads have come off.'

This was not a case of dawdling on the last day. The horses had disturbed the nest, sending the wasps into a frenzy, and had bolted in different directions, shedding their loads and disappearing off into the hills. Some had galloped some distance, desperate to escape the wasps. With twenty-three horses to locate and placate, the horsemen had had quite a job bringing them all under control again, before loading them up and continuing in the dark, all of them nursing painful stings.

No one was in the mood for extended farewells, and it was too dark for the usual end-of-trek photograph, so we thanked the horsemen and the crew, distributed their tips and finally set off for our lodge, along a potholed farm road. We were a dishevelled and grubby pair who staggered into the guest lounge at the lodge that evening. After sixteen days of walking, neither of us had any clean trekking clothes left. Collapsing onto the beds, Krista and I revelled in the clean sheets, the flush toilet and the bath: comforts that, just twenty-four hours earlier, had been unimaginable luxuries.

Three hours after saying goodbye to the horsemen, we were showered, fed and ready for action. We were in Bumthang on the night of the *Tercham*, the Treasure Dance, and, despite exhaustion bordering on delirium, we were not going to bed. We had arranged to meet Norbu at 10.30pm to drive to Jambay Lhakhang, the ancient temple dating back to the seventh century where the dance took place. But first, we had to take care of a very important housekeeping task.

Our beautifully clean and fragrant room made the fetid contents of our trekking bags look and smell even more unpleasant. Stuffed into plastic bags, the wet, filthy, mud-encrusted clothes, not to mention sodden footwear, had been festering for over two weeks. My boots smelled as if something had crawled inside them and died. The delicate laundry bag in the cupboard of the room, designed for no more than a couple of crumpled shirts, was woefully inadequate for the vast pile of post-trek kit. We decided that the best approach was just to leave it all in the trek bags, retrieve our toiletries and books, which were the only items not destined for a hot wash, and summon housekeeping to collect it all. The smell was so bad we placed our bags outside the room, thinking that the attendant would pick them up from there.

Ten minutes later, there was a knock at the door.

'I have come to collect your laundry, madam,' the unsuspecting young man explained politely.

'Ah, yes, it's in the two bags outside the door,' I replied.

There was no disguising the look of horror. 'All of that, madam?' he asked, incredulous. Just wait until you open the bag, I thought.

'We've just spent sixteen days on the Snowman Trek,' I offered by way of explanation. That seemed a worthy vindication and he smiled and nodded, hitching one bag over each shoulder and staggering down the stairs with more laundry than the rest of the guests together could generate in a week. I hoped Norbu had warned them that they might need reinforcements for the laundry shift.

With that taken care of, we set off to find Norbu. The hotel was blissfully warm and cosy after our sub-zero camping experience and it was tempting to forget about our long-anticipated encounter with dancing monks. But, despite the drizzle outside, I wouldn't have missed it for the world.

LORDS OF THE DANCE

The Treasure Dance was performed 'sometime after midnight' at the Jambay Lhakhang. No historical texts described the origins of this temple, but legends handed down through the generations told the story of its beginning. According to Buddhist mythology, this was one of 108 temples built in the Himalayan region in a single day in the seventh century, by the first Tibetan Buddhist King, Songtsen Gampo. His aim was to subdue a giant ogress, who sought to oppose the spread of Buddhism through the region, by placing temples over her body to pin her down.

It was strange, driving along narrow country roads at eleven o'clock at night, in the rain and darkness, to suddenly be confronted with traffic gridlock. With vehicles bumper to bumper, we weaved in and out of crowds of pedestrians, families with children, teenagers and young couples, dodging a crawling cavalcade of vans, cars and minibuses. Everyone was dressed in their finest traditional clothes, some carrying umbrellas, others just getting wet. And all were heading for the Treasure Dance.

Some drivers had squeezed their vehicles close to the verge. Others appeared to have just abandoned theirs in the middle of the road, leaving them parked at odd angles and further disrupting the traffic flow. It was a constant stop–start as our driver inched through the crowded thoroughfare. After our peaceful days in the wilds of Lunana, Bumthang felt like a teeming metropolis.

Outside the temple, a tent city had sprung up and a bustling market was in full swing. Tightly-packed temporary stalls sold an eclectic mix of clothes, handicrafts, jewellery, trinkets, Buddhist artefacts, household items and plastic tat. Food stalls offered *momos*, *ema datse*, *thukpa* (noodle soup) and unappetising cuts of meat, most of which I couldn't identify. Alongside the cafes, crowds flocked to the fun of the fair. Friends tried to outdo each other, throwing darts at a small target or shooting arrows from the traditional bamboo bow. For a few ngultrums, you could roll a couple of dice and win a plastic knick-knack. A large throng jostled around the edges of a makeshift room. Craning over the spectators, we watched half-a-dozen men leaning over a low table with a large wooden spinner in the centre, playing a gambling game. There was a lively vibe as the gamblers placed their bets, cheered on by the shrieking crowd of spectators. I couldn't tell who was winning or losing.

We found our way through the hordes at the stalls, stepping through a gateway into the grounds of the monastery. Over the heads of an excited audience, I could see the flames from a huge bonfire burning in the centre of the courtyard. They were mainly locals: families, groups of friends, even a few couples with young babies strapped to their mothers' backs with colourful shawls. Norbu told us that, in olden times, families from distant mountain communities might only travel into 'town' once or twice a year. Coming down for a *tsechu* (festival) was a special highlight, an excuse to dress up, socialise or maybe start a courtship, all the while receiving merit by watching the religious dances.

Norbu led the way, squeezing behind the crush of people to take up a place at the back. The air was thick with drizzle, smoke and expectation. The crowd stood five or six deep around the bonfire, shuffling back and forth to secure the best viewing position. The rain had eased a little, but it was cold and damp, and my hot shower earlier that evening was already a distant memory. Every fifteen or twenty minutes, an official emerged from one of the buildings to add more logs to the fire, sending a cloud of sparks high into the night sky. A frisson of excitement: was something happening at last? The crowd surged forward. We went with it, jammed against those on either side, all moving as one. There were several false alarms. Norbu had warned us that there was no fixed time for the dance to begin. It would start when the dancers were ready. Somehow, this added to the sense of anticipation. We waited eagerly, the mystique enhanced by the silhouette of the ancient monastery in the darkness, illuminated only by the orange flames of the bonfire. I should have been exhausted. Instead, I felt buoyed by an unexplained energy and the bodies, squashed against me on all sides, who were practically propping me up. Here, about to witness the Treasure Dance, I had a sense of quiet satisfaction. I looked around at the few other tourists in the crowd. I was confident none of them had walked 240 kilometres to be here tonight. The fact that we had, on schedule and at times in less than ideal conditions, made our attendance even more special.

I stamped my feet to bring life back to frozen toes. An unexpected clash of cymbals reverberated across the courtyard. At once, the murmurings of the crowd gave way to an excited hush. Emerging from the shadows, dark eyes just visible behind bands of white gauze, the dancers arrived. With heads bandaged like Egyptian mummies, their nakedness was all the more confronting. A troupe of sixteen dancers – all men – stumbled forward and congregated by the bonfire. Some stood. Others staggered.

More cymbals, rising to a crescendo: the dance was about to begin. The men paraded around the fire. First one direction, then the other. There was little rhythm or coordination to their movements. Some shuffled back and forth, while others broke off into pairs, swirling and twirling, their posturing at times overtly sexual. They began to move away from the fire, strutting close to the audience, thrusting themselves forward. I was as intrigued by the reaction of the onlookers as by the performance of the dancers. There were some gasps and suppressed giggles from the few tourists, but most spectators watched in silence. Others spoke in low voices. No one cheered, jeered or shouted. These were not voyeurs. They were here to witness a sacred dance.

Eagle-eyed community police officers patrolled the circle of spectators. They were on high alert, looking out for anyone bold enough to sneak a photographic souvenir of the dancers. We had been pre-warned. Our cameras and phones were safely back at the lodge. Away from temptation.

Legend has it that this dance originated hundreds of years ago, when some monks tried to build a monastery in a village near Trongsa. They worked hard all day but were thwarted by unruly demons who came every night to undo their good work. To distract the demons from their demolition efforts, a fifteenth-century saint, Terton Pema Lingpa, came up with a plan. He had the monks dance naked in the forest. It worked a treat. The demons had clearly never seen anything quite like it. Enthralled by the naked capers of the religious brothers, they forsook their sabotage of the construction of the monastery. The dance had been celebrated ever since, apart from a short period during which it was banned by the district administration. After the villagers reported that ill luck was befalling them, and an astrologer put it down to the ban, the dance was hastily reinstated.

The dance was no longer performed by monks. Instead, a group of local men chosen from four nearby villages had the dubious honour of keeping up the tradition. It was a bizarre scene, more like the antics of undergraduates celebrating their end-of-year exams than an ancient religious ritual in rural Bhutan. I wondered if the dancers had indulged in too much *ara,* the local moonshine, before coming out to entertain their audience. And who could blame them? Most of us would need a bit of Dutch courage before parading naked in front of a crowd of strangers.

As well as bringing good fortune to the locals, I was sure the Treasure Dance would continue to be a big draw for the many tourists who visited the Bumthang valley each autumn. For Krista and me, it was an extraordinary finale to an unforgettable trek.

BACK TO REALITY

Breakfast in the dining room of our lodge the next morning was such a civilised affair it was almost alien. Our chairs didn't wobble on an uneven surface. The temperature was at least twenty degrees above what it had been in the dining tent; I didn't need a beanie or down jacket. Our crockery was china rather than melamine, and the other guests were beautifully coiffured, in clean and neatly pressed clothes. There was a menu and a waiter and a newspaper.

We learned from the staff that, while we were in the mountains, Cyclone Phailin had crossed the Bay of Bengal, smashing into the east coast of India. It wreaked havoc on the weather patterns over the Eastern Himalayas and left a trail of destruction in its wake. Flights into and out of Paro had been cancelled and travellers had either been stuck in Bhutan or had been unable to get there. Guests had been confined to their hotels, no one was allowed into the mountains, and several trekkers who had already set off for Jhomolhari had been turned back. Meanwhile, in Lunana, we bore the brunt of the unseasonable snowstorms. No one had been able to contact us and the lodge manager was amazed that we'd made it to Bumthang at all.

Back in our room after breakfast, I was delighted to discover that our laundry had, by some miracle, been returned to its pre-trek state: the joys of being in the twenty-first century. We packed our bags and were soon ready for the short drive to the airport. We had decided to skip the long and tortuous two-day drive back to Paro, opting instead for the recently introduced Drukair domestic flight. We would be in Paro in less than an hour.

Norbu was waiting for us. He was on a high, proud to have completed the Lunana trek.

'None of my friends have done this trek. They are asking me so many questions. I think I am going to be famous,' he joked.

'We have one more stop to make before the airport,' he continued. 'We are going to Kurjey Lhakhang.'

Kurjey Lhakhang was one of Bhutan's most sacred temple complexes. There were three main temples, the oldest, dating back to 1652, was built around a place of meditation used by Guru Rinpoche, evidenced by the imprint of his body on a rock. As we walked across the courtyard, the only sound was the *clickety-clack* of prayer wheels being spun by a procession of devotees.

At the entrance to a temple, I stopped to admire a striking mandala, an intricate Buddhist painting, symbolising the wheel of life, that is often used as an aid to meditation. The previous year, I had decided to buy a beautifully painted dark blue mandala on canvas, inlaid with delicate gold and orange lettering. Mandalas are more than just art. They hold great religious significance and are the ultimate representation of the impermanence of life and the importance of letting go. The irony of this was not lost on me when, after I returned home, my dog decided to chew her way through the outer section of my mandala, leaving it frayed and torn.

In a chapel Norbu prayed quietly in front of the altar, before lighting a butter lamp. 'I am making an offering to give thanks for completing the trek,' he said. I wondered whether he'd ever thought this was in doubt.

We followed him down a series of stone staircases, over a high threshold, into a bare, dark room. The air was cold and the walls damp. At floor level, what looked like two small caves were just visible. Norbu explained that they were the entrance and exit to a short tunnel and that, by crawling through, we would be cleansed of our sins. And then he disappeared inside. Krista and I dutifully followed him, emerging at the other end. Now, purged of my sins, I was ready to return to the real world.

We had planned for Norbu to fly back to Paro with us, but it seemed that tourists were given priority over local guides and Norbu had been bumped off the flight. He would drive back, so we would say goodbye to him here.

But first, we each jumped onto the luggage scale. Krista and I had lost a couple of kilograms. Norbu had lost six. His bellies had well and truly gone.

I thanked Norbu for looking after us so well, gave him a hug goodbye, and promised that I would see him again, the next year. This time he believed me.

As we boarded the Drukair plane, already I could feel the serenity of our days in the mountains ebbing away. We were back in the world of air travel, a far cry from the usual mode of transport in the valleys of Lunana. Once airborne, I gazed down at the impenetrable forests far beneath us, searching, in vain, for a glimpse of the winding trails that we had followed a few days earlier. Moments from the trek flashed through my mind: the children at the schools, the characters we'd met along the way, evenings with Norbu and the crew, the challenges of the weather.

I was both elated and sad to have reached the end of this trip. Elated because we'd come through Lunana, without major incident, on an ambitious timetable and despite three days of atrocious weather. We had laughed and almost cried. We had made new friendships and strengthened existing ones. We had marvelled at awe-inspiring panoramas and been touched by the gratitude of the children and teachers we'd met at the two most remote schools in Bhutan. And, against the odds, we had been on time to watch an ancient dance, performed in the middle of the night by naked men, around a bonfire. And sad because soon we would be saying goodbye to Bhutan, to the pristine mountains and prehistoric forests, where my only responsibility was putting one foot in front of the other.

I was struck by how much I had enjoyed the peace and serenity of the mountains – being so close to nature, and so far removed, both literally and metaphorically, from the frenetic pace of life back home. I'd loved living in the moment, no rewriting of past mistakes, or planning of tomorrow's goals. I'd found a rhythm in my walking, enjoying the simplicity of days spent in a majestic landscape of breath-taking scenery. On those isolated mountain trails I'd felt beautifully detached from reality; now I was all too aware that it was rushing back to meet me.

And I realised, too, that I enjoyed adventures. That it was all too easy to stay within your comfort zone, but much more exciting to push yourself outside it. That when things didn't quite go according to plan, well, you could usually work something out. And that with planning and preparation, you could achieve goals you never thought possible. I thought back to my first trip with Molly when I'd been out of breath walking up the steps to Paro Dzong. Three years later, I had walked across Lunana. I had come a long way.

ACKNOWLEDGEMENTS

A very special thank you to the two people who got me through Lunana and who have been part of this amazing journey: Krista Waddell, who was the perfect trekking and tent buddy, both on the Lunana trek and many others; and Tshering Norbu, who has been my guide every year in Bhutan since 2010. A guide can make or break a trip and Norbu's enthusiasm, sense of humour and professionalism are partly why I have returned every year. And to the rest of the crew on the Lunana trek: Leki, Rinzin, Sangay, Torchen, Agye, Thinley and Norbu – thank you for all your hard work in often challenging conditions.

Before we set off for Bhutan, Sangay Tenzin devoted much time and effort to organising the trek for us and took care of the logistics of transporting books and stationery to Lunana: not a straightforward task.

A number of people read early versions of the manuscript, provided comments and/or responded to queries: my husband Graeme, Krista Waddell, Julie Gibbs, Carolyn Hamer-Smith, Susie Pitts, Lee Scott-Virtue and, in Bhutan, Tshering Uden Penjor, Tandin Wangmo and Tshering Norbu. Thank you for your time, feedback and answers to my many questions.

Thank you to my literary agent Fran Moore who convinced me that my manuscript would one day see the light of day and has been enthusiastic and encouraging throughout.

The team at my publisher, Affirm Press in Melbourne, in

particular, senior editor Ruby Ashby-Orr and editor Emma Schwarcz, did a fantastic job in helping to shape the manuscript. It would have been a much longer read without them. Thanks also to the publicity team, Grace Breen, Terri King and Dina Kluska.

Thanks to Joanna Lumley, Greg Mortimer, Bunty Avieson, Tahir Shah, Carolyn Hamer-Smith and Jono Lineen for taking the time to read and endorse my first book.

Thanks to Her Majesty Gyalyum Sangay Choden Wangchuck for providing the foreword, and for all the incredible work she does for RENEW.

To my husband Graeme, and children, Molly, Robbie and Catherine, for tolerating my annual forays into the mountains and the endless hours spent researching and writing this book. And a special thank you to Molly for coming with me on that first trip in 2010, even though she wasn't really in a position to say no. If we hadn't gone to the little school in Phobjikha, I may never have returned to Bhutan.

To my family and friends and especially the Noosa gang who have helped year after year with fundraising initiatives in Noosa and beyond, for the scholarship program: Krista Waddell, Susie Pitts, Karen Murray, Suzzanne Roughley and Nicola Heppell and all those people, too numerous to mention, who have made donations, come to events and supported us in so many ways. Our fundraising is entirely dependent on your generosity. Thank you.

Yak on Track is the story of just one of my treks in Bhutan. There have been many others, all as memorable, if not quite as dramatic, as the trek through Lunana. Thank you to everyone who has joined me on one or more of those trips and to the people of Bhutan who have made travelling in their Himalayan kingdom such a delight.

Kandinchey La and Tashi Delek!

AUTHOR'S NOTES

The transliteration into English of many Dzongkha words, and especially place names, often results in quite different spellings. I have tried to use the most common spellings or those that correspond with the pronunciation.

I have referred to the altitude of a number of peaks within Bhutan and of campsites and passes along our trek route. Many mountains in Bhutan have not been accurately surveyed and different publications record different heights. For the most part, I have taken the heights from Bart Jordans' guidebook, *Bhutan, A Trekker's Guide*. Campsite and pass measurements are my own, taken with a Garmin altimeter and may differ from others, depending on the exact location of where the measurement was taken and the accuracy of my device.

Names of the school students mentioned have been changed to protect their identity and some aspects of the pre- and post- trek days have been compressed or omitted.

Her Majesty Gyalyum Sangay Choden Wangchuck

Her Majesty Gyalyum Sangay Choden Wangchuck, one of the four wives of the Fourth King of Bhutan, founded RENEW in 2004 and is patron of the scholarship program that I have been supporting.

A year after our trek through Lunana, Her Majesty visited Australia at the invitation of the Australian Himalayan Foundation. At a dinner in Sydney, held in her honour, Krista and I were delighted to have the opportunity to meet her. She spoke passionately about the need to educate and empower women and children, to equip them for the crucial role they play in the social and economic development of Bhutan.

The following year, on our return to Bhutan, we were thrilled to be invited to meet privately with Her Majesty in Thimphu. She was the most gracious host, relaxed and engaging, sharing stories of her life, as well as explaining some of the challenges facing RENEW and the girls' education program.

Her Majesty works tirelessly to promote the culture, health and wellbeing of the people of Bhutan. In late 2017, she completed, for the second time, a high-level advocacy tour of all twenty *dzongkhags* (districts) of Bhutan, addressing priority public health and social issues. This extensive, two-year program took her to every corner of the country and is testament to her dedication to improving the lives of the most disadvantaged members of Bhutanese society.

RENEW Scholarship Program

Since my trek through Lunana, I have continued to organise trekking trips to Bhutan to raise money for the AHF/RENEW scholarship program. These annual trips have included visits to students at schools in Haa, Geynekha, Thinleygang, Jangothang, Lingshi, Laya, Choekhor Toe and Dhur. The trekking groups have raised money to buy books and stationery items for many of these schools and we have all been humbled and inspired by the commitment and dedication of the RENEW-sponsored students we've met.

We have visited the Gawailing Happy Home, a RENEW refuge facility between Paro and Thimphu, where women and children who are victims of domestic violence can rebuild their lives.

At home, fundraising for the program has gathered pace; an annual trivia night is one of the highlights of the local social calendar. With help from a small group of enthusiastic supporters, we have organised lunches, a ball, a cocktail party, a sausage sizzle, raffles and auctions, written articles, sent begging letters for donation requests, and spoken at schools and on local radio. At the time of writing, we have raised more than $230,000 for the RENEW scholarship program.

Thirty-five per cent of my royalties from this book will be donated to the Australian Himalayan Foundation for the benefit of RENEW's education program in Bhutan. If you would like to support this program, you can do so through the AHF website: www.australianhimalayanfoundation.org.au

For more information on the work of RENEW, visit their website: www.renew.org.bt

Travel to Bhutan

If you would like to travel to Bhutan with Norbu, you can contact him through his travel company, Bespoke Bhutan Tours: www.bespokebhutantours.com

Select Bibliography and Suggested Further Reading

Aris, Michael. *The Raven Crown: The Origins of Buddhist Monarchy in Bhutan*. London: Serindia Publications, 1994.

Ashi Dorji Wangmo Wangchuck, Queen of Bhutan. *Treasures of the Thunder Dragon, A Portrait of Bhutan*. New Delhi: Penguin Books India Pvt. Ltd., 2006.

Ashi Dorji Wangmo Wangchuck, Her Majesty The Queen of Bhutan. *of Rainbow and Clouds: The Life of Yab Ugyen Dorji as told to his Daughter*. London: Serindia Publications, 1999.

Avieson, Bunty. *A Baby in a Backpack to Bhutan: An Australian Family in the Land of the Thunder Dragon*. Sydney: Macmillan, 2004.

Avieson, Bunty. *The Dragon's Voice: How Modern Media Found Bhutan*. St, Lucia: University of Queensland Press, 2015.

Baker, Ian. *The Heart of the World: A Journey to Tibet's Lost Paradise*. New York: Penguin Press, 2004.

Bond, Rushkin. *The Sensualist*. New Delhi: Penguin Books India, 2009.

Bowman, W.E. *The Ascent of Rum Doodle*. London: Vintage Publishing, 2001.

Brown, Lindsay and Mayhew, Bradley. *Bhutan, 3rd edition*. Melbourne: Lonely Planet, 2007.

Choden, Karma. *Phallus: Crazy Wisdom from Bhutan*. Bhutan: Butter Lamp Publishers, 2014.

Choden, Kunzang. *Bhutanese Tales of the Yeti*. Bangkok: White Lotus, 1997.

Crossette, Barbara. *So Close to Heaven: The Vanishing Buddhist Kingdoms of the Himalayas*. New York: Alfred A. Knopf, 1995.

Grange, Kevin. *Beneath Blossom Rain: Discovering Bhutan on the Toughest Trek in the World*. Nebraska: University of Nebraska Press, 2011.

Haigh, Ken. *Under the Holy Lake: A Memoir of Eastern Bhutan*. Edmonton: The University of Alberta Press, 2008.

Jordans, Bart. *Bhutan: A Trekker's Guide*. Cumbria: Cicerone, 2012.

Klein, Wilhelm and Pfannmüller, Günter. *Bhutan*. New Delhi: Lustre/Roli Books, 2008.

Leaming, Linda. *Married to Bhutan: How One Woman Got Lost, Said "I Do" and Found Bliss* London: Hay House UK, 2011.

Lineen, Jono. *Into the Heart of the Himalayas*. Melbourne: Melbourne University Press, 2014.

Lowe, Peter (ed.). *Reflections*. Bhutan: RENEW, 2008.

Lumley, Joanna. *In the Kingdom of the Thunder Dragon*. London: BBC Books, 1997.

Napoli, Lisa. *Radio Shangri-La: What I Learned in Bhutan, the Happiest Kingdom on Earth*. New York: Crown Publishing Group, 2010.

Nicoholson, Trish. *Journey in Bhutan: Himalayan Trek in the Kingdom of the Thunder Dragon*. London: Troubador Publishing, 2012.

Palin, Michael. *Himalaya*. London: Weidenfeld & Nicolson, 2004.

Phuntsho, Karma. *The History of Bhutan*. Gurgaon: Random House India, 2013.

Pommaret, Francoise. *Bhutan: Himalayan Mountain Kingdom*. New York: Norton & Company, 1998.

Tshering, Gyonpo. *The Bhutanese Guide to Happiness*. New Delhi: Penguin Books India, 2013.

Turner, Captain Samuel. *An Account of an Embassy to the Court of the Teshoo Lama in Tibet: Containing a Narrative of a Journey through Bootan, and Part of Tibet*. London: W Bulmer & Co, 1800.

Twigger, Robert. *White Mountain: Real and Imagined Journeys in the Himalayas*. London: Weidenfield & Nicolson, 2016.

Utz, Martin. *Hidden Bhutan: Entering the Kingdom of the Thunder Dragon*. London: Haus Publishing, 2008.

Wood, Levison. *Walking the Himalayas*. London: Hodden and Stoughton, 2016.

Zeppa, Jamie. *Beyond the Sky and the Earth, A Journey into Bhutan*. New York: Penguin Putnam, 2000.

Research Papers

'Annual Report', Bhutan Tourism Monitor 2015, Tourism Council of Bhutan. https://www.tourism.gov.bt/resources/annual-reports

'Bhutan Disaster Management', Yeshey Lotay, Asian Disaster Research Center, February 2015. http://www.adrc.asia/countryreport/BTN/2014/BTN_CR2014B.pdf

'High Altitude Medicinal Plants of Bhutan: An Illustrated Guide for Practical Use', Phurpa Wangchuk, Samten, Ugyen, Pharmaceutical and Research Unit, Institute of Traditional Medicine Services, Ministry of Health, Thimphu, Bhutan 2009. https://researchonline.jcu.edu.au/34513/

'The Cost of Climate Change: The Story of Thorthormi Glacial Lake in Bhutan', Sameer M. Singh, 2009, World Wildlife Fund for Nature. https://wwf.fi/mediabank/1047.pdf

'Eleventh Five Year Plan (July 2013 – June 2018)', Local Government Plan Volume III, Gasa Dzongkhag, Gross National Happiness Commission (2013), Royal Government of Bhutan. https://www.gnhc.gov.bt/en/wp-content/uploads/2017/05/Eleventh-Five-Year-Plan-Gasa-Dzongkhag.pdf

'Gasa, Dzongkhag at a Glance', 2016, National Statistics Bureau, Thimphu, Bhutan. http://www.nsb.gov.bt/publication/files/pub3jb4959ej.pdf

'The Yak', Second Edition, Gerald Weiner, Han Jianlin, Long Ruijun, Food and Agriculture Organisation of the United Nations, Regional Office for Asia and the Pacific, RAP Publication 2003/06. http://www.fao.org/docrep/006/AD347E/ad347e00.htm

'Transhumant Grazing Systems in Temperate Asia', Suttie, J.M. and Reynolds, S.G., Food and Agriculture Organisation of the United Nations, 2003. http://www.fao.org/docrep/006/y4856e/y4856e00.HTM

Articles

'Two New Rhododendron Species Discovered', *Kuensel*, 26 April 2013 http://www.kuenselonline.com/two-new-rhododendron-species-discovered/#.WxI8U1JL2CQ

'Cordycep fetches highest price ever', *BBS*, 25 July 2012 http://www.bbs.bt/news/?p=15585

'Bhutan jails more smokers amid criticism', *The Age*, 27 May 2011 https://www.smh.com.au/world/bhutan-jails-more-smokers-amid-criticism-20110527-1f8an.html